THE
BLACK RAVEN

Murad Mathossentz

Policy Research Publications
1988

The Black Raven
© Murad Mathossentz 1988

This English text
© Irene Walton-Stiubey 1988

British Library Cataloguing in Publication Data

Mathossentz, Murad, *1897* -
The black raven
1. Soviet Union. Mathossentz, Murad, *1897* -
I. Title
947.08′092′4
ISBN 0-9511436-2-X

First published in the United Kingdom by
Policy Research Publications Ltd.
35 Westminster Bridge Road
London SE1 7JB

Typeset and printed by Pika Print Ltd.
Genotin Road, Enfield EN1 2AA

To the memory of my brother Sarkis,
to whom I owe my regained freedom.

ACKNOWLEDGMENTS

I am grateful to the following for their invaluable help and advice:

Mrs. Irene Walton-Stiubey, the daughter of my chief and great friend during the Second World War, Thomas Walton of SOE.

Mrs. Anahide Ter-Minassian, Lecturer in History at the Sorbonne University, Paris.

Mrs. Claire Muradian, Chair in History at the National Institute of Oriental Languages, Paris.

Prof. Frau Christine Hirszowics, at the University of Zurich, Switzerland.

Mrs. Victoria Krueger de Bichowsky, Buenos Aires, Argentina.

Prof. Richard G. Hovannisian, Chair in Modern Armenian History, University of California, Los Angeles, USA.

Mr. Jules Merleau-Ponty, novelist, Paris.

Mr. Arnauld Gay-Lussac, Paris.

Mr. Albert Gosset, Paris.

Mr. Laurent Gosset, Paris.

Mr. Pascal Maubert, Paris.

My nephew, Murad Mathossentz.

Mr. Peter Ford, editor of the English text.

M.M.

CONTENTS

PREFACE

In these pages you will find the true, simple and fantastic story of a brave man. He was born just before the beginning of this century, in the Christian community of Transcaucasia. Transcaucasia – the mere sound of its name is like music, and for those who have never been there, it evokes a beautiful, fabulous and mythical land. But the Armenian community living there, like so many ancient and rich cultures, was to be swept aside by 'the Black Tide of Modern Society' , as the historian A. Guchon calls it.

For the 19th century gave birth to the 20th in a series of violent jolts as the Ottoman and Russian empires clashed in the age-old dispute over their frontiers, and caught in the middle of the conflict, the Armenian nation was repeatedly massacred, and finally dispersed all over the world. The author witnessed these momentous events from a very young age. He too joined the Armenian diaspora and then, through a series of extraordinary events, was flung from Europe back into the wilds of Siberia, by a new and even more violent hurricane which swept the Western world in the first part of the 20th century.

Here, in a manner resounding with the language and historical memories of the peoples of both East and West, is an eye-witness account of the fifty years which fashioned the geo-political situation in Europe and the Soviet Union. It is an invaluable document, covering a wide stretch of the little-known tragic destiny of the Armenians of Transcaucasia. This is a tale of personal adventure, the tale of a man engulfed in events both terrible and droll, told with humour and wise benevolence, without malice or grudge. A tale which shows once again that evil can never completely vanquish the good, nor might defeat right, nor the all-powerful always defeat the little man.

So open the book quickly, and settle down to read this extraordinary tale.

J. Merleau-Ponty
Paris, 1988

7

INTRODUCTION

Richard G. Hovannisian
Holder, Chair in Modern Armenian History
University of California, Los Angeles

The Black Raven is a fascinating tale that links a world that once was with a world that is. It is the story of a single individual and of a single lifetime that spanned the twilight years of the Romanov dynasty, the revolutions and civil war in Russia, the years between the two world wars in Romania, the chilling episodes leading to the gulag labour camps of Siberia, and finally the restoration of freedom in Paris.

This is the story of an Armenian who became a citizen of the world and like others of his generation was imbued not only with Armenian traditions but also with Russian and European culture. These were the people who played prominent roles in the development of Armenian political and socioeconomic views, while at the same time becoming active participants in Russian and international movements. Although it may seem unusual, it was actually common, for example, that the organizers and leaders of the Republic of Armenia in 1918 were both nationalists and internationalists, both Armenian patriots and devotees of Russian culture. They were prepared to give their lives for the Armenian people, yet separated their personal and collective existences, often sharing their personal lives with non-Armenians who satisfied their internationalist dispositions.

The author's father was just such an individual. Playing an important role in Armenian national life in Transcaucasia, he was also a part of Russian intellectual and political movements and gave his children an international rather than a national education. Baku, the city of the author's birth, was itself a showplace of these seeming contradictions, as it was cosmopolitan but parochial, international but national, revolutionary but reactionary – and sometimes all of these opposites managed to coexist within a single individual.

Mathossentz is not the name by which the author's family was best known. His father, Abraham, was a prominent official and civic servant in Baku. After the Russian revolutions in 1917 and the partition of Transcaucasia into three separate republics in 1918, Abraham was made a member of the Azerbaidjani cabinet. This was done by the Azerbaidjani government to demonstrate to the British, who occupied Baku at the end of the world war, that Azerbaidjan intended to become a democratic republic in which the national minorities would play a significant role. Such a declaration was required because the Azerbaidjanis had used the Turkish armies to overthrow the Baku Soviet and capture the city from its Armenian and Russian defenders in September 1918, followed by a three-day blood bath in which thousands of Armenians lost their lives. After the sovietization of Azerbaidjan in April 1920, Abraham made his way to Tiflis and from there, at the behest of the Armenian government, departed on a mission to purchase oil in Romania for the needs of the struggling, landlocked Armenian republic. The Allied Powers had awarded Armenia a united state extending to Van, Bitlis, Erzerum, and including an outlet on the Black Sea, but this was a paper award and, in fact, the republic remained confined to the former Russian Armenian provinces of Erevan and Kars. The invasion of the Armenian republic by Mustafa Kemal's armies in September 1920, and the sovietization of what remained of the country in December stranded Abraham in Romania. He was subsequently joined there by his son, the author of *The Black Raven*, who had served as an officer in the Russian imperial army and was then caught up in the civil war in Russia and the chaos in Transcaucasia.

In Romania, the author enjoyed the relative peace and prosperity of the country during the interwar years. There, too, he made the acquaintance of prominent Armenian émigrés, including Drastamat Kanayan, a near legendary figure known everywhere as 'Dro'. It was undoubtedly because of the author's association with such individuals, although he was neither an Armenian activist nor community leader, that led to his eventual arrest and exile to Russia after the Red Army had liberated Romania from the Nazis. In Armenian history, the Soviet occupation of Romania brought about the eclipse of the centuries-old Romanian-Armenian community, as the nationalist leaders were arrested and exiled, a part of the community repatriated to Soviet Armenia, and subsequently many others emigrated, ending up for the most part in the United States of America.

Arrested on no other charge than his guilt by association, Mathossentz returned to Russia, now as a prisoner and ultimately as only a number in the great Siberian gulag so grippingly described in the latter part of the book. Yet he never lost his will to survive or his sense of humour. And surprisingly, he shows no hatred or deep antipathy toward his tormentors. Rather, it seems that he views them, too, as victims, having become the creatures of a terrible machine and system. He is a survivor, bringing with him the insights, wisdom, humanity, and perhaps even acceptance and resignation of the survivor. It is this universal aspect of *The Black Raven* that gives the story lasting value and appeal far beyond any specific ethnic bounds.

Mathossentz is not a historian, nor does he pretend to be. Rather, he describes the events as he remembers them over a span of nine decades. The events that I have come to know through documents are the personal life experiences of the author. That which I have recreated through reading and research, he knows first-hand, even though the angle from which he may have witnessed the events may have produced a different focus and colouration. That, too, is a part of the value of this autobiographical story. As a person deeply appreciative of the importance of oral history and the need of preserving the fragments of a shattered and lost Armenian past, I can only welcome this saga and salute the author of *The Black Raven*.

PROLOGUE

'I ask you, gentlemen, to note that I neither apportion blame, nor approve of what I am about to tell you. I just relate the events as they happened.'

- Talleyrand

It is the end of October 1956. I arrive in the capital of a Western European country from the USSR. My elder brother, his son and son-in-law are waiting to greet me at the airport. I am free at last after being kidnapped by the Soviet forces occupying Romania where I was living at the end of the war. I had spent eleven years and seven months as a political prisoner in the USSR (from March 1945 to October 1956) a declared enemy of the Soviet people, without having been tried or sentenced – the mere victim of an administrative resolution by the dreaded Soviet 'Troika' (Committee for State Security, the Ministry of Interior and the Ministry of Justice) similar to the orders of deportation issued by the Tsarist Governments in old Russia.

It was only thanks to the tireless efforts of my elder brother, to whose memory I dedicate this book, that I was at last pulled out of the abyss and regained my liberty. Although for over ten years the Soviet authorities refused to admit my existence, my brother did the impossible, appealing to anybody he thought might help to find a way to locate my whereabouts and save me. Nobody believed he would succeed, but in spite of all the obstacles placed in his path, he persisted with his inquiries undeterred. And so, at last, he had the happiness of seeing me arrive.

Everybody I met, all the members of my family and our friends, begged me to tell them the story of my captivity but there were already so many books on the burning issue of the Soviet enigma that I was discouraged. For a considerable number of years I could not envisage myself embarking on such a vast project. But the younger generation, who were born and grew up outside Russia, wanted to know more about the past history of our family. It was they who persuaded me to do it, and it was for them that I wrote this story about my father, a truly remarkable man, my childhood in Transcaucasia when Russia was still ruled by the Tsars, my military service in the First World War, the bloody events of the Russian Revolution in 1917, the first massacre of Armenians in Transcaucasia, which I witnessed as a child, and later, in 1918 the repeat performance when the Turkish armies marched into Baku to take possession of the Russian oil fields at the time of the formation of the independent Tartar, Armenian and Georgian Republics.

The first version I wrote was more a family chronicle, the story of an Armenian family which had emigrated to Russia from Persia in the nineteenth century, hoping to find there the protection of the Russian Christian government. But this hope was not fulfilled, and the family was exposed to many dangers, subjected to persecutions and massacres organized by the then weak Russian government for political reasons, to distract attention from the disturbances during the 1905 revolution; massacres which recommenced after the second Russian Revolution in 1917, when all that was left for the Armenian population was to anxiously await the arrival of the Soviet Red Army in 1920 to save their lives.

Subsequently, however, in the hope that this cautionary tale may prove a useful warning to others as well, I decided to rewrite it, leaving out all the very personal passages that were of no interest to anyone except my family. Similarly, I have taken care to omit all names (except for those already dead) to avoid any complications it might cause certain people. One never knows, even in these days of *Glasnost.*

1. SUBJECTS OF THE TSAR

The 1828 war between the Russia of Nicholas I and Persia (now Iran) ended with the Treaty of Turkmanchay, one of the conditions it imposed being the annexation by Russia of several provinces in northern Persia. The peace terms were hard on Persia, and the Teheran government set about provoking bloody street riots in revenge. The Russian Embassy was attacked and the entire staff massacred, including the small armed contingent guarding it. The Russian writer Griboyedov, who was Ambassador at the time, was killed, for the Persian government blamed him personally for the humiliating treaty and regarded him as one of its principal authors. Another condition imposed by the Turkmanchay Treaty was that the Christian minorities in Persia, including the Armenians, be allowed to emigrate to Christian Russia. This resulted in a massive exodus of the Christian population, convinced that, at last, they would find in Russia the longed-for peace and security they had lacked in Persia.

Several Persian-Armenian families took advantage of the rights offered them by the Treaty of Turkmanchay, our family among them, and when it arrived in the Caucasus it settled in Shusha, a small town in the province of Karabakh which was among those annexed by Russia. Shusha lay in the Karabakh mountains, close to the Russo-Iranian border, and there my father was born in December 1864. The town was inhabited by a mixture of Muslim Tartars and Christian Armenians each living in their own quarter. Racial conflict did not exist, and relations between the two communities were peaceful. The policy adopted by the Russian government in all provinces populated by ethnic minorities was to enforce a process of russification. All nationalist movements were forbidden and all the schools were Russian. Even ethnic family names were changed to make them sound more Russian, and so a Tartar named Mamed-Oglu became Mamedov and an Armenian named Akopian became Akopov. The official language was Russian, and everybody had to become used to being a loyal citizen of the Tsar. Children of Tartar and Armenian families went to the same school, and became friends.

My father attended the local school, and later was sent to live with relations in Georgia, where he attended the same Theological Seminary in Tiflis as Stalin. (As things turned out, neither the one nor the other would go into Holy Orders.) Then he was sent to study at the University of St Petersburg. Those were times of great revolutionary movements, and my father was drawn into the movement called 'The Will of the People' (Narodnaya Volya) while other students joined the Nechayev extremists who advocated acts of terrorism against the regime. My father was among the 19-year old students arrested and sentenced without trial, for the

Government had found that revolutionaries tried by juries would be acquitted in most cases. Instead they invoked sentencing by administrative edict by the notorious 'Okhranka' (State Security) a system of 'justice' inherited and perpetuated by the Soviet government after the Revolution.

To begin with, my father was detained in a modern prison for preliminary detention, but later he was transferred to the St Peter and Paul Fortress, where special cells were set aside for members of the 'Will of the People'.

There he spent eleven months, but happily, in those days, although one could not appeal against a decision of the Okhranka, one could make a personal intervention. Such an intervention was made by a highly placed cousin to save the young student who had not, in fact, represented any danger whatsoever to the State. This cousin was married to a relation of General Count Loris-Melikoff (also an Armenian) who had served as Prime Minister to Tsar Alexander II – the liberal Tsar who was assassinated on 1 March 1881, by revolutionary terrorists determined to have things their way. General Loris-Melikoff, like the Tsar, was a man of very liberal and far-seeing views. He worked hard to introduce the principal reforms decreed by Alexander II, such as the liberation of the Serfs, the reform of the Judiciary, and many other liberal measures greeted with enthusiasm by the Russian people. With the support and encouragement of the Tsar, he drafted a moderate Constitution which the Tsar should have signed on 1 March 1881, the very day he was assassinated. Alexander III then came to the throne, and horrified by his father's assassination, introduced a new and very severe Regime. Nevertheless, the new young Tsar retained the services of his father's trusted collaborator whom he held in great respect. He appointed Count Loris-Melikoff Minister of Internal Affairs, and the Count became known as the Tsar's Dictator with a Gallant Heart. And so my father was released and deported to the Caucasus, to the small town of Zakathaly, in the mountains inhabited by the Lezghin tribes. Zakathaly was not yet completely 'pacified', and the post would arrive once a week, escorted by a company of infantry, whose duty was to protect the mailcoach from attacks by mountain tribes. He remained in Zakathaly several years, with the family of another of our relatives and under police surveillance. He gave lessons to the children of Russian officials in the town and as the régime gradually became less strict, even received authorization to visit Tiflis, the capital of Georgia, where his cousin was chief editor of the local paper, the *Tiflis Sheet.*

While in exile at Zakathaly, my father met and married a Russian Cossack girl. Two children, a boy and a girl, were born there, myself and my younger brother being born later, after my father was allowed to take up residence in Tiflis, where he worked as editor on his cousin's paper until eventually being offered a job in Baku in the Statistics Department of the Association of Petroleum Producers. This offered immense possibilities for his energy and administrative talents. Little by little he was promoted until he became director general of the association. Father was widowed there in 1899, my mother dying when I was only two years old.

My father, by then almost forty years old, evolved a system of industrial and social security hitherto unheard of in Baku. The association built a network of roads throughout the oil fields surrounding the town, and my father personally supervised the construction of pipelines to link the oil fields with the refineries in the suburbs of Baku, known as 'Black Town'. Certificates were issued for pumping crude oil as a method of taxing each producer on the amount produced by his oil field. The system also facilitated sales of crude oil by the smaller oil companies, since these pumping certificates could be bought and sold.

One of the Annual General Meetings of the Petroleum Producers Association approved a budget proposed by my father for investing revenues from taxes in the construction of non-fee paying schools and libraries, as well as in free hospitals and public baths and several dispensaries and first aid posts to deal with accidents at work. Remembering his youthful revolutionary ideals, my father wanted to give the Baku oil workers the best possible facilities. Specialist consultants were enticed from St Petersburg and Moscow with magnificent salaries and the hospitals were equipped with the newest apparatus available in Russia and abroad – the best that medical science could offer. The reputation of the hospitals became so well-established that many people unconnected with the oil industry preferred the association's hospitals to the private clinics or hospitals in the town. Although hospital treatment was free for employees, others had to pay, but were only too happy to do so since the treatment they received was the best available. Father worked without taking any holidays, he was so absorbed by the administration of this vast organization.

Petroleum producers in other parts of Russia took the organization of the Association in Baku, as a model. The new oil fields in Northern Caucasus, at Grozny, formed their own Association. There were many large oil companies in Russia, formed with Russian or foreign capital – English, French, Belgian or others like the one founded by the Swedish Nobel family, the same one which also instituted the award of the Nobel Prize. The discovery of oil at the end of the nineteenth century had provoked something akin to a gold-rush in Baku and its environs. The town grew with lightning speed, and whereas in 1900 Baku had about 130,000 inhabitants, only ten years later this figure had increased to 200,000. The Armenians played a vital role in the development of industry and commerce, and it was only the terrible events of 1905, with the massacres in February and September, that broke the calm and steady growth of the city. It took several years for normal working conditions to return, and the seeds of bitter racial hatred sown at this time were ineradicable.

Baku is the capital of the province of Azerbaidjan, and as the province had originally belonged to Persia, most of the inhabitants were Shiite Moslems – the official religion in that country. For the Shiites, the only legal

Caliph and true descendant of the Great Prophet Mahomet is Ali – Mahomed's cousin and son-in-law who married his daughter Fatima and was assasinated by the Sunnites, another branch of Orthodox Moslems. These two religious movements – the Shiites and the Sunnites – represent the two main branches of the Moslem religion which have bitterly fought each other for more than 1,300 years. Each year, the Shiites organise religious processions to commemorate Ali's death. In Baku, these processions took place in September or October, depending on when the date fell in the Moslem calendar. Dozens of men would march in procession, dressed mostly in green (the colour of the Prophet) but leaving the torso naked. Some have daggers with which they cut their foreheads, so the blood runs down their face and chest as they march, chanting 'Shah Hussein ... Vah Hussein', and slashing themselves with the dagger to the rhythm of the chant. Others, marching behind, lash their backs with small chains knotted together on the same principle as the cat-o'-nine-tails, causing the back to bleed profusely. The marchers, heavily drugged, gradually sink into a trance as they move through the streets, frantically lashing their blood-spattered backs and cutting their foreheads. Covered in running blood, and all the time chanting the same rhythmic refrain, they march through the town, from one end to the other, roped off from the by-standers by a ring of chains carried by other participants in the procession. In the old days, they would march right through the centre of Baku, but nowadays they are only allowed to pass through the Tartar quarters as the danger to the public is considered too great. The procession lasts three days, and at night they marsh with lit torches. I myself witnessed, as a child, this truly terrifying spectacle. We were taken to see it, my brother and I, by our Lezghin cook Nassireh, who had followed my father to Baku from Zakhatali. We were very small at the time, my brother was six and I was seven years old, and were thoroughly frightened by it all, even though closely guarded and protected by the faithful Nassireh.

I well remember the happy summer holidays we spent in Shusha, long before the events of 1905. We used to take the Transcaucasian Railway up to Evlakh, where we all got into a waggon to continue our journey south, towards the Karabagh mountains. The waggon, which closely resembled the covered waggons one sees in Wild West films, was drawn by two pairs of horses along the sixty-mile road to Shusha, with only one halting stage half-way. How frightened I would be as we approached the mountains, the cart fording the river to the other side. The river current was strong, and the water rose to the top of the cart-wheels. The road then wound upwards between pretty slopes covered in vineyards, orchards and vegetable gardens.

In Shusha we used to stay with relatives who had a house in the higher part of the city, where the Armenian quarter was situated. Each morning we children would accompany our Aunt Almaz to the open market in the lower part of the town, where the Tartars lived. There we used to watch how they baked unleavened bread called *lavash*. The baker would stoke up a fire in a pit whose walls were lined with clay, and when the fire was really hot, large thin pieces of unleavened dough would be placed against the glazed wall. The bread stayed fresh for several days. All one needed to do was sprinkle it with a little water before warming it up and serving. It was the favourite bread of Armenians as well as of other people in the Orient.

The Shusha market stalls were loaded with vegetables, fruit and other country produce. I was always amazed by the strong aroma of fruit in the Caucasus. Nowhere in Europe would I ever come across such an aroma. The scent of peaches could be smelt at a great distance, also apricots and pears. On our return journey, we would see the vines in the vineyards weighed down with bunches of grapes, the leaves now a deep red with approaching autumn. Those grapes had very thick skins, which make their transportation possible over great distances, whereas the grapes grown in the area surrounding Baku could not travel. The strong sun and sandy soil around Baku produced a very sweet grape known as Sha-ani, but the skin of the Sha-ani was too fine and delicate to survive prolonged journeys.

Baku itself lay on the shores of a large bay, flanked by big sand dunes and hills devoid of vegetation. The winds blew hot and strong, especially the north wind, which brought a fine sandy dust that penetrated everywhere and everything, even though most houses had double glazing and windows were kept tightly shut. Nevertheless, everything in the house would be covered in the fine dust once the north wind started to blow.

The temperature in summer often rose towards 50° C (about 120° F), and there was hardly any rain, which meant there was a perennial shortage of water and a consequent lack of gardens. When the rains did come the whole town would be flooded as torrents of water rushed down from the mountains, transforming the streets into rivers. The only way to cross the street then was to be carried across on the back of a *hambal* – a Persian labourer willing to carry any weight, luggage or furniture, to earn a few kopecks. These *hambals* were always available, anxious for an opportunity to earn some money. Once I witnessed in amazement a giant *hambal* bearing on his back a grand piano, his two assistants merely carrying the piano legs.

The side-walks on streets in Baku were paved with a poor-quality asphalt called *kir*. At the height of summer, the fierce heat of the sun softened this into a jelly-like substance, so that pedestrians left their footprints behind them. The roads were surfaced with small, irregular stones, which made travelling bumpy. Public transport was by horse-drawn tram, called a *konka*, and run on concessionary rights by a Belgian company. Open on all sides, the tram had a running-board the length of the carriage along which the ticket-collector would move to collect the fares. The trams crossed the town from one end to the other, and a line also climbed right up to the Tartar quarters of the city. There were many hackney cabs, open horse-drawn carriages called Phaetons. They were beautifully polished, with silver harnesses. The horses were small and fast, and the drivers mostly Tartars.

Baku had two theatres: a rather mediocre opera house built by a rich Armenian family who owned the fishery and caviar concessions in the Caspian; and the drama theatre, built by a Tartar millionaire. The drama theatre had special trellis-fronted boxes to screen the wives of the rich and more emancipated Tartars, for few Tartar women would appear in public with uncovered faces. Baku being a town of big business, both theatres were well-endowed. Thus the opera management could afford to invite artists from St Petersburg and Moscow, such as Shaliapin or Sobino. The price of seats was high, yet every seat was sold, the rich vying for seats in the front row. The drama theatre often staged plays by Tartar authors, as well as folk operas, Azerbaidjani folk music being far more advanced than the Persian or Turkish. Even so, attending these performances could be a risky business. One evening my elder brother Sarkis went to the famous folk opera, *Arshin Mal Alan*, only to telephone home in the first interval and ask that a bath be run for him as he urgently needed to get rid of fleas. As for the cinemas, there were plenty in Baku, the biggest being called the Phenomenon.

The hot climate could make life in Baku quite intolerable in the summer. Father's working day began at nine when he went into the Petroleum Association's offices located in the same building where we had our apartment. He continued to work without a break until three in the afternoon, when the temperature became too hot for comfort. Then he would return home for lunch, and after lunch lie down for maybe an hour and a half to rest. He always insisted that he never actually slept, he merely 'rested with his eyes closed'. But we children did not believe him, and protested that one could not do this if one snored.

A story my father told me illustrated the good relations he enjoyed with the various racial groups inhabiting Baku. Because of the intense heat in the summer months, the chief rabbi liked to have a respite in one of the spas in the Northern Caucasus, so would ask father to stand in for him in his civic duties, undertaking to carry out the rabbi's official functions of registrar of births, marriages and deaths in the Jewish colony. Thus, in summer, father took charge of registers, seals and forms to be filled in, signing all necessary documents in the name of the rabbi and collecting the registration taxes. Naturally, he could not conduct the religious ceremonies, but he carried out all the other duties. Father would laugh heartily as he related to us his role of assistant rabbi. Perhaps the rabbi chose him because he knew the money collected would be in safe hands. Besides, the arrangement cost him nothing since he did not have to pay wages to the 'honorary rabbi'.

But this peaceful, tranquil life-style lasted only until the turn of the century, when events showed clearly that the then Tsarist Government was prepared to sacrifice the whole Armenian people in the pursuit of imperialist policies. In 1896, after the massacre of Armenians in Turkey, the Tsarist Minister for Foreign Affairs, Prince Lobanov-Rostovsky, in collusion with Bismark's Government in Germany, refused to support the proposal of the Gladstone Government in Britain that a strong Note of Protest be handed to the Turkish Government, urging them to take action to stop these massacres. Furthermore several years later, in 1905, the Tsarist Government allowed the massacre of Armenians in Baku, for the sole purpose of deflecting the attention of the people from the revolutionary incidents that followed on the ill-fated war with Japan. Extreme nationalist politicians had dragged Russia into a war first with China, then with Japan, on whom war was declared despite the expressed wish of the Japanese to reach a compromise. Russia lost the war, and widespread political disturbances followed. The internal situation became uncontrollable. To facilitate the task of Government, the ultra-nationalist clique advised the provoking of racial conflict between the various nationalities. Pogroms were organised against the Jews, and in Transcaucasia, the Governor-General in Baku, Prince Nakashidze encouraged the Tartars to embark on large-scale massacres of Christian Armenians. The Tartars were promised total immunity from punishment. They could kill, rape, pillage, burn, but neither the Police nor the Cossack units which replaced the constabulary would do anything to stop them. My family personally witnessed these terrible events.

The building that housed our apartment was on an island formed by four streets on a slope beyond and above the Russian Cathedral of Alexander Nevsky. From our windows we could see the cathedral and its large square, on which military parades took place on the imperial holidays. I was just seven years old one February morning in 1905 when I looked out of the window and saw the body of a man lying in the square. I called to my brother, a year younger than myself, to come and have a look. We were too young to understand what was happening, and ran in great excitement to call father. Fortunately, he had not yet gone down to the office of the Association of Petroleum Producers on the ground floor, and he realized at once what had happened and went to telephone the authorities. He was told that the Tartars had begun to attack the Armenian population in Baku.

There was not a moment to lose. Everybody in the building, including the employees of the association, met and decided to organize a Defence HQ, to be located in the apartment of the association's director, Mr Delyanov. All arms available were collected and distributed, and armed pickets organized to protect and defend the entrances to the building. Only the main entrance was to be left open, and all other entrances guarded to watch out for attacks or attempted arson.

Father also telephoned the Governor-General, Prince Nakashidze, and asked for his protection for the building. The Petroleum Association was far too important to be abandoned to the Tartar hordes, for the industry brought millions of roubles each year to the Russian Exchequer. Before long we saw a small detachment of Cossacks taking up their positions on the street corners. But, in other quarters of the town, police and Cossack detachments had been given orders not to intervene. They walked along the streets without paying any attention to the fires, the killing and raping. As far as they were concerned, everything was permitted. Several thousand Armenians were massacred, and their wives and daughters were kidnapped and taken into the surrounding Tartar villages, together with the spoils, which were considerable, for they had looted and plundered the richest quarters of the town, setting fire to pillaged houses before retreating.

It was only at the end of the third day that the massacres were suddenly halted by the arrival of a group of so-called revolutionary commandoes of the Armenian Dashnak Party, a small group of twenty-five led by Niko Tuman. They had left their post on the Russo-Turkish borders and hastened with all speed through Georgia to Baku as soon as the news reached them. They were armed only with Mauser automatic pistols – the favourite weapon of the Dashnaks, since it could be easily transformed into a rifle by fixing it to a wooden butt with a twenty-cartridge loader.

The news of the commando group's arrival spread like wildfire through Baku, and the bands of Tartar assassins began to disperse. Within hours they had vanished completely. Thus had a town of 150,000 inhabitants been liberated by a commando group of twenty-five. Only after they had gone into action did the police and Cossacks make a show of having re-established order. Taken by surprise, the Tartar bands fled as fast as they could, even leaving some of their booty behind. Of course, I knew little of all this at the age of seven, but this was how my father described it to me several years later. He decided to take advantage of the lull in the fighting to send my sister, my younger brother and myself to the house of a friend, a doctor attached to the naval base at Bailov, south of Baku, where we would be safe for the time being.

After order was restored, Niko asked to address a gathering of the entire Armenian colony in Baku. He especially wanted to speak to the richer classes, represented by the leaders of industry and commerce. He wanted to organize a system of defence, to cover not only the Armenians in Baku but all the Armenians in Transcaucasia and Turkey, and this would require money for the purchase of arms and so forth. As soon as they were gathered together, he addressed them thus: 'You have summoned me from the Turkish border to come to your aid. This I have done. But I want you to know that there are in Turkey hundreds of thousands of Armenians who are always in need of our help, even more so than you. The massacres organized by the Sultan Abdul-Hamid continue all the time, perpetrated by detachments of Kurdish troops commanded by Turkish officers. Every day our brothers in Turkey are killed, and our party is doing all it can to parry these massacres. Armenians in Turkey are threatened with extermination, but have no means to defend themselves. They are poor. Peasants and workers give what they can to help, they join with us in the struggle to save our people. You, here, are rich, and you must help us. You, too, must contribute to the defence of our people. The danger of their extermination is ever-present in Turkey, and it may rebound on you here later. There is no time to lose. You must prepare a list of all Armenians and Armenian companies in Baku, indicating how much each can contribute to our national cause. And I want the completed list within a week.'

Years later my father told me what happened when the list of voluntary contributions from the Armenians in Baku was submitted to Niko on the date specified. He took it, looked at the sum total at the bottom of the list and then tore it up slowly into little pieces. And then this is what he said: 'This miserable sum you offer us is simply not enough. It shows that you have already forgotten what we have done for you. I will now make out a revised list of the contributions I expect from you, and those who refuse to pay will be killed.'

Everybody hastened to pay the amounts indicated by Niko. Some tried to bargain, but Niko would not admit any reduction in the sums he had indicated. The Dashnak Revolutionary Party was not prepared to play games. One of our relatives, a very rich man, tried to bargain to be allowed to make smaller contributions. He appealed to a nephew, a member of the Dashnak committee, to intervene with Niko on his behalf. The nephew just said he was in a hurry, and if his uncle wished to walk with him part of the way, they could talk it over as they went. The uncle agreed, and as they were walking along one of the main streets in Baku, the nephew pointed to the photographic studio they were passing, that of the best photographer in town, and suggested they go in. 'What on earth for?' asked the uncle in astonishment. 'So that I have your photograph to remember you by when you're dead,' replied the nephew grimly. There were no further arguments from the rich uncle.

Another rich Armenian called Djanoumoff, was not so lucky. Member of a very rich banking family in St Petersburg, he fled there from Baku, hoping thus to avoid having to pay the required contribution. But one Sunday morning, as he was leaving the Armenian church on the famous Nevski Avenue in St Petersburg, a young man came up to him and asked if his name was Djanoumoff. 'Yes, I am Djanoumoff,' he replied, whereupon the young man cried 'You have refused to pay, but your family will pay for you,' and stabbed the banker who fell down dead. The young Dashnak did not flee at once, he turned to the other members of the congregation who were coming out from the church into the square and announced the reason for Djanoumoff's execution, shouting: 'All those who refuse to pay will be killed!' There was no longer any doubt that the Dashnaks were determined to get what they wanted.

The massive purchase and distribution of arms among the Armenian population in Baku was to save many lives in the second wave of massacres in September 1905. After these events, the Central Committee of the Dashnak Party (in Armenian, *Dashnakzutyun* actually means 'confederation of parties') sent a message to the Governor-General, Prince Nakashidze, informing him that the Armenian National Party had condemned him to death for his part in organizing the masscres. The prince approached the Armenian bourgeoisie to ask them to intervene and get the death sentence annulled. But the Dashnaks were determined to go ahead, and they chose a young man of eighteen, a party member, to carry out the execution. His name was Drastamat Kanayan but his party nickname was Dro, and he was considered a good choice despite his youth.

The Governor-General's palace was situated on the Embankment Boulevard that ran along the sea-shore from the town centre to the Naval Base of the Caspian Fleet at Bailov, and the Governor-General was due to attend an important function in town. His route took him along the boulevard, entering town through Olga Street and continuing along the Avenue of the Grand Duke. Several years later Dro himself was to tell me what happened on that fateful day. The Avenue of the Grand Duke was not very wide, and Dro stood on the pavement a few yards from the spot where the landau must pass, a bomb, already primed, concealed in a brown paper bag topped up with grapes. He stood eating the grapes as he calmly awaited the arrival of the landau, but when he saw that the Prince's wife sat beside him, he did not throw the bomb then, but waited for the return journey. And indeed, when the landau came back, the Prince was alone except for his grand escort of Cossacks. As the landau drew level, Dro threw the paper bag and crouched behind a Tartar street-trader on the pavement to protect himself from the flying fragments. The explosion was terrible. The Governor-General was killed instantly, as were several cossacks and their horses. Other members of the Dashnak Party, who had taken up positions nearby, then began to fire from all directions. General panic broke out as injured bystanders and Cossacks tried to take cover, while the Dashnaks made their getaway and disappeared into the milling crowds. The Dashnaks had their plans ready. Dro was smuggled across the border into Turkey, and he hid there in a village where he had many friends, both Armenians and Kurds, remaining there right up to the outbreak of the hostilities between Russia and Turkey in 1914.

After the first Armenian massacre in February 1905, father thought it prudent to send us, the children, to the safety of Russia itself. And so we left Baku, my elder brother and sister going to St Petersburg to continue their education in a public school, while my younger brother and I were sent to the famous spas of Zheleznovodsk and Kislovodsk in the Northern Caucasus, where we spent the whole summer in the care of our Aunt Almaz. We were far enough from Baku to be safe from any recurring massacres, but father stayed on there to continue fulfilling his duties as managing director of the Petroleum Association.

When the second wave of massacres began in September, they were even more terrible than those in February and claimed thousands of innocent victims. This time they began on the initiative of the Tartars, who hoped to benefit from the same immunity from prosecution they had enjoyed in February. But this time the fighting was fierce as the Armenians were better equipped to defend themselves. The Tsarist authorities were caught totally unprepared, and paid dearly for their earlier perfidy. The widespread destruction of the oil fields, set on fire by looting mobs, led to a catastrophic drop in oil production and revenue. The government was suddenly faced with thousands massacred, immense material damage to the oil fields, and the loss of tens of millions of roubles from lost oil taxes.

In the autumn of 1905 father realized that our return to Baku was out of the question. He made arrangements for Aunt Almaz to take my younger brother and I to Yalta in the Crimea, where we were to remain for two or three months before a decision could be taken as to what should be done with us. In Yalta, in October 1905, I saw my first political demonstration. The crowd carried red banners to celebrate the Manifesto of 17 October, by which Tsar Nicholas II – faced with the pressure of revolutionary events and a general strike throughout Russia–promised the people all possible and impossible freedoms, including the creation of a Parliament, the Duma.

Early in 1906, we had a surprise visit from father, who suddenly arrived with Mrs Kantzel, the wife of the former chief surgeon at the Balakhany Hospital. To us, she was 'Aunt Olya' (a diminutive of Olga). The Kantzels had left Baku in 1904, soon after the troubles and strikes began, to return to St Petersburg, and it was they who had taken in my elder brother Sarkis and my sister Lenotchka while they completed their studies. Now father had come to say that we, too, must go to St Petersburg, to live with Uncle Fima and Aunt Olya, and that we would not be returning to Baku.

Both Uncle Fima and Aunt Olya were Jewish, and both were doctors of medicine. He had become a Christian convert so as to be allowed to study at the Military Academy of Medicine in St Petersburg, but Aunt Olya, on the other hand, had become a Christian out of conviction. It had meant a complete break with her family. Her father, a rich Moscow banker and a devout Jew, disowned her, and they were never reconciled. Aunt Olya became a second mother to us. A highly cultured woman, she had completed her medical studies at the University of Bordeaux in France. On returning to Russia she had opened a medical practice in Balakhany.

Before we left Yalta, father took us, together with Aunts Olya and Almaz, for a drive in an open carriage to see the palaces at Livadia and Alupka. We visited the beautiful Livadia Palace grounds, though in those days one could not visit the palace, even though the Imperial family were no longer in residence. Following the troubles and demonstrations in St Petersburg, they had gone to live in Tsarskoe Selo (literally the 'Tsar's Village'). Close by was the lovely Alupka Palace, residence of Count Vorontsov-Dashtov, and once the sight-seeing was over, father took us all to a restaurant in Alupka where we had a wonderful meal. It was a great event – the first time we had eaten out in a restaurant. The only sad thing about the excursion was the distress of dear Aunt Almaz – 'Azia' as we called her. She had been with us from our earliest childhood, ever since mother died, and now would soon be parted from us.

We left Yalta on a sunny warm day in January 1906, travelling by horse-drawn carriage along the coast road to Sebastopol, passing along the picturesque Crimean coastline with its magnificent views of the Black Sea.

It closely resembled the Cote d'Azur in the South of France, the only difference being that the Crimean coastline was still in its natural state, unspoilt by commercial development. We arrived in Sebastopol in the evening, just in time to catch the direct express train to St Petersburg. Father accompanied us for the first part of the journey, until the train reached the main junction in southern Russia, where he left us to take the train for Rostov and back to Baku, while we continued to St Petersburg. It had still been very warm in southern Russia, but as we crossed into the northern part of the country we saw, for the first time in our lives, everything covered in thick snow. The beauty of the landscape between Moscow and St Petersburg was breathtaking with mile upon mile of birch forests. All the beauty of a Russian winter was spread before our eyes.

We arrived in St Petersburg at the enormous Tsar Nicholas the First railway station, exactly on time, punctuality being the proud tradition of the Nicholas railway system. The plan of the line had been traced on the map, with a ruler, by the Tsar himself. The strange thing is that, although the expert engineers in charge of the railway's construction had raised many objections, suggesting alternative routes which would allow them to economise on the costs of construction and the Tsar had refused to change anything, as it turned out, the Tsar's idea was proved to be the right one since, because of its straight line, the cost of maintenance of rolling stock and running the railway had, in the final analysis, resulted in far greater economies than would have been achieved had the engineers succeeded in pushing through their plans for the alternative route.

On approaching the station, the engine driver would either slow down or increase speed so as to arrive exactly on the minute indicated in the timetable. Uncle Fima was waiting on the platform to greet us, and two horse-drawn sleighs were standing by to take us to his apartment. It was our first ride in a sleigh, and although the St Petersburg sleighs were only one-horse sleighs, moving along at a slow pace, we were delighted. Uncle Fima asked the driver to make a detour, so that we might see the city in all its splendour, and in due course we arrived at 34 Poldskaya Street where Uncle Fima and Aunt Olya lived in the royal borough of Moskovskaya. All mansion blocks in the street were five or six storeys high, with a wide frontage along the street and the high-ceilinged rooms that no longer exist in modern buildings. There were no lifts, and you just had to climb the stairs to whichever floor you wanted. The Kantzels occupied a large flat on the fourth floor. It had four bedrooms, a large sitting room, dining room and all usual facilities. There was no central heating, but each room was kept beautifully warm by a big tiled stove. Every block had a spacious courtyard where tenants could store firewood, and every morning a *dvornik* (maintenance man) would climb the back-stairs, carrying up firewood for tenants. Each mansion block on the street had twelve large apartments facing the street, like ours, and another twelve smaller apartments with windows overlooking the inner courtyard. This meant a lot of work for the chief *dvornik* and his assistants. In the larger mansion blocks, like ours, there was also a porter, known as the *schweitzar* (which in Russian means 'Swiss guard'). Their duties included filling in all the forms required by the police, concerning residents. Because of the strict regime which came into force after the spread of revolutionary movements and terrorist outrages in Russia, all local inhabitants, as well as visitors to the capital had to register with the police, visitors within twenty-four hours of their arrival. They also acted as auxiliary police constables at the same time.

As soon as we had settled down in the Kantzels' apartment, Aunt Olya took the education of my brother and myself seriously in hand. She engaged a young German governess from Revel (now Tallin) in the Baltic States where there was a large German colony. Her name was Fraülein Emma, and as she spoke practically no Russian, we had plenty of opportunities to practise our German with her every day. But we also had to have a Russian teacher because in the family at home, in Baku, we spoke Armenian. She was an old family friend, Evgenya Mikhajlovna Vedenskaya. Her father was a colleague and close collaborator of my father in the Petroleum Association in Baku, and her younger sister had been to school with my elder sister Lenochka. To begin with, Evgenya Mikhajlovna came to us five days a week, but later, as we got to know our way round the city, we used to go for Russian lessons to the Vedenskys' flat in the very centre of St Petersburg.

The Kantzels had no children of their own. They adored dogs. When they had lived in Balakhany, in the Caucasus, they had two Great Danes. When we visited them Uncle Fima would put us on the backs of these two huge monsters and we would ride them round and round the big drawing room. But their rooms in St Petersburg were smaller, and so were their dogs. There was a basset-hound called Topka (after the *top-top* sound of his paws as he padded round the flat). Topka's coat was black with brown patches on his paws. He was a great favourite and we used to quarrel over who would have him on his bed at night. Bassets are very intelligent dogs, and Topka used to become very angry and bark loudly whenever I teased him by imitating the funny walk of our young cook Matreshka, saying, 'Is this the way Matreshka walks?' Even though he could not understand the exact meaning he got the gist of it, and he was not going to have anybody making fun of the woman who gave him his food.

Our beloved Aunt Olya, whom we all adored, did her best to create for us a happy family atmosphere, but we were never spoiled. Discipline was strict, but not harsh. We had to eat everything that was served on our plate, and we had to wait to be offered a second helping. No drinking was allowed until after the second course, when half a glass of water was allowed. The only thing we could refuse was the pudding. For instance, I hate chestnut mousse with whipped cream, and was allowed to ask not to eat it since it was too sweet for me. The main dishes, essential for our health were, however, served in the prescribed quantities, and everything must be eaten to the last mouthful.

Fraülein Emma took care of my brother and I, and later of the three of us when the Kantzels adopted a third boy, an orphan called Boris. Boris was the son of a political detainee, deported to the Arctic Circle in Eastern Siberia, who died in Yakutia. Poor Fraülein Emma had her hands full with three lively boys always devising all sorts of eccentric exploits. When the situation became impossible, she would appeal to higher authority – Aunt Olya. The guilty ones would then be summoned for a personal interview, sometimes a very prolonged one. The confrontation with Aunt Olya was morally exhausting and depressing, and after undergoing it we would try to avoid another at all costs. Fraülein Emma would then enjoy a period of respite, the truce lasting until the next explosion of energy on the part of my little brother or Boris. I was the least enterprising of the three, and of a quieter disposition, which led to the two younger boys branding me a traitor.

Aunt Olya also took care of our health. My brother and I, having been born in the hot climate of the Caucasus, needed to be protected from the dangers of the cold northern climate. The strong winds blowing from the Gulf of Finland, and the humidity in the atmosphere of St Petersburg made the northern cold even more difficult to bear, and when the temperature fell below -25°C (-13°F) all the schools closed. To make us fit and healthy, we had to take a cold bath each morning. Neither hot-water systems nor shower installations had yet been introduced in Russia, and it was Fraülein Emma who filled two large buckets with cold water from the tap. Half a bucketful was used to rub us all over with soap, the other bucket and a half to wash it off. We emerged from the tub with our teeth chattering with cold, but a quick rub with bath sheets helped to restore the circulation and warmed us up a bit.

However harsh the regime may have seemed, it did prevent us from catching colds, flu or other diseases. Every Saturday, however, we were allowed a moderately hot bath, the water being heated by a wood fire in a tall cylindrical geyser. Uncle Fima, on the other hand, always ordered his bath to be run very hot. He was a great advocate of the Finnish sauna, and our hot bath, too, usually ended with a bucket of cold water being poured over us.

Every afternoon, Fraülein Emma took us to the ice-skating rink next to the barracks of the famous Simionovsky Regiment founded by Peter the Great. The ice rink was very big, and there was also a special roller-coaster for sleigh rides. We never missed a day's skating throughout the winter, and when we started going to school in the autumn, we still went skating each evening so as to have some exercise and fresh air after sitting still in class all day. When we came out of school, Fraülein Emma would be waiting for us with our skating boots. We would skate till six o'clock, and then walk all the way home, a distance of about a mile. This was another of Aunt Olya's ploys for ensuring that we were always fit and healthy and had plenty of fresh air.

Aunt Olya also instilled in us a strict discipline of manners, to prepare us for life in general and for how to behave in society. She emphasized the need for courteous behaviour always, especially towards the elderly. She would explain at length the rules of politeness and why they were necessary. These rules became so deeply imprinted in me that I followed them automatically all my life, without any effort or sacrifice. How different was our upbringing from the way children are brought up now. Today's parents do not realize how they themselves destroy the natural equilibrium in their children, by giving them too much freedom and all the material things they desire, spoiling them with costly toys and gifts that they come to take for granted. They then come to expect this sort of treatment from everybody, and expect it all their lives. As a result, when they grow up and find themselves faced with the harsh realities of life and its problems, they are lost.

During the years we lived with the Kantzels, I came to appreciate and admire Uncle Fima, not only for his hard work and expertise as a doctor but also for his warm-hearted personality. An eminent and busy surgeon, he did not just forget his patients after an operation, but continued to take an interest in their well-being, an attitude rare indeed among medical men. His working day started at eight o'clock in the morning when he went to the Obukhovskaya Hospital where he gave his services free in exchange for the opportunities it offered him to extend his surgical experience. He then returned home at 2 p.m. for a quick lunch, and spent the afternoon seeing patients at his private practice. At six o'clock he went to a private clinic, of which he was a partner, to operate on private patients. He would return home late for dinner, usually at ten o'clock, and after dinner would often retire to his study to research in preparation for a difficult operation next day, for despite his vast experience he was always anxious to refresh his memory. Finally, satisfied he had all the information he needed, he would retire to bed with a book.

That was the most pleasant hour of the day for Uncle Fima. He loved Russian literature, the classics and contemporary writers, and subscribed to all the best magazines and monthly reviews. Uncle Fima sought to awaken my taste for literature and history without making his intentions too obvious. As the monthlies were thickly bound, he would ask me to cut them up into separate loose-leafed articles and stories to make them easier to read in bed. I loved doing this, and while cutting them up would automatically start to read the stories. Thus, I became more and more interested in reading and discussing what I had read with Uncle Fima. His political views inclined towards the moderate centre, and he regularly used to read *The Word*, the daily newspaper of the Constitutional Democratic Party (KD).

The Kantzels, however, also used to receive at their home many who held more radical views, including revolutionaries and Social Democrats who had spent periods of 'administrative deportation' in Siberia. For these, the political programme of the centrist KD was too archaic. They were members of the two streams of the Social Democratic Party – the

Bolsheviks (the 'majority') and the Mensheviks (the 'minority'). Among them I remember in particular a group of Jews who had fought against the Tsarist Regime for many years and who later attained positions of power in the wake of the Bolshevik Revolution in October 1917. The group included Nahamkis, or Steklov as he was known in the Communist Party, who became the editor of *Izvestia*, the official organ of the Soviet Government in Moscow.

We remained for ten years in St Petersburg, living in the Kantzels' apartment. It was a pleasant life in the Russian style of the 'Old Regime', and we were happy. The school we went to was co-educational, with children of many nationalities – Russians, Germans, Jews, and even some English pupils. I had almost completely forgotten my native Armenian, having had little chance to speak it – only on the few occasions when we met with our cousins, who were also studying in St Petersburg. School was followed by two years studies at the famous Civil Engineering Academy founded by the Emperor Alexander I, who brought over eminent French professors to organize it.

I only visited the Caucasus twice in those ten years, the first time when we went back to spend Christmas with father in Baku, in 1912. It was a magnificent journey, by train, and we travelled third class, as Aunt Olya decreed. There were four of us: my elder sister, a cousin who was studying law at the University of St Petersburg, my younger brother and myself, in one compartment. My elder brother Sarkis was on the same train, but had a sleeping berth in the more expensive Wagon-Lits compartment. Nevertheless he spent the day with us in our third-class carriage, where each of us had our own couchette, as was customary on long-distance trains in Russia. In the evening, the car attendant would bring us each a small mattress, pillow and blanket. You had to pay an extra charge for this luxury. Aunt Olya had supplied us with a wicker basket filled with enough food to last us the three-day journey, as she thought. But we tucked in with such healthy appetites that all the food was gone by the end of the first day.

Our journey began at the main railway station in St Petersburg, and ten hours and three stops later we arrived in Moscow early the next morning. As the train left Moscow station on its onward journey south, my cousin suggested we celebrate and have something to eat. My elder brother produced a small bottle of *pertzovka* (vodka spiced with pepper), and the feasting began. My younger brother and I were also given a small glass, and so for the first time in our lives tasted vodka!

My elder brother would join us each morning on waking, preferring our company to sitting alone in his luxurious Wagon-Lits compartment with the morning tea brought round by the conductor. A restaurant car was attached to the train, but Aunt Olya had given strict instructions that we, the children, should not eat there. Instead, we could have a proper meal once a day in one of the main station restaurants *en route*. All the big stations had a hot buffet with cooked meals awaiting the arrival of each train. The steaming hot 'borsh' soup would be ready, poured out into soup bowls, and there was enough time to order a second course and to eat it in the twenty-five minutes or so that the train remained in the station.

After breakfast, my sister tidied up the compartment, and we would all settle down to a game of cards, my cousin and elder brother having decided it was time to teach us *preferance*, a card game popular at the time. We, the younger ones, were absolutely delighted, especially as we had already learned how to play, though we didn't let on we had. When Uncle Fima invited friends in to play cards on a Saturday we were allowed to watch for half an hour or so before being sent off to bed. In this way, we had even learnt how to play the infinitely more complicated game of *wint*, which is played rather like bridge.

What struck me most in Baku, in contrast with St Petersburg, was the prevalence of police patrols. Police were stationed along all the principal streets in pairs, armed with Mauser pistols attached to a shoulder strap, and with a wooden butt that could transform them instantly into a small rifle. Father told me that the Martial Law declared in 1905 was still in force, and that the authorities were no longer prepared to banter with either the Tartar or the revolutionary elements. That apart, daily life went on and the weather was perfect.

We took full advantage of it. Although it was Christmas time, we could walk along the sea front without an overcoat in the company of our cousins and their friends. Every day we were invited out by relations or friends of the family, and were terribly spoilt. My widowed father had moved into a hotel in the centre of the town – the Europa, managed by a Frenchwoman called Mme Charpentier. A room was reserved for us next to his. During the day he would be busy at the offices of the Petroleum Association, and so we used to meet in the evenings, sometimes going out to dinner together, sometimes separately. Dinners in Baku were lavish affairs: first came a dish of fish, sturgeon or salmon, both plentiful in the Caspian Sea; then the meat dish – the famous *shashlik* of meat grilled on a skewer, usually lamb from the Karatchai steppes in Northern Caucasus, or from the Volga salt marshes – the lands of the Nogaj and Kalmuk Tartars. Then there was pilaff of rice served with chicken, or the salted fish from the Kura river (the Georgian *shamaika*), turkey, and so on, followed by ice cream or fruit. Everybody drank wine, and we, the children, were also allowed some – an unheard of thing at the Kantzels' apartment. All our friends and acquaintances were either Russian or Armenian. Tartars were never invited. The 1905 massacres had left a deep scar on the relationship between the Christian and Tartar communities.

Our next visit to Baku was for Christmas 1915, when my younger brother and I were already students at the Civil Engineering Academy in St Petersburg. Russia was already at war with both Germany and Turkey, and like most students throughout Russia we were anxious to fight against the aggressors. We were both completely russified, having grown up and been educated in the totally Russian environment of St Petersburg. We had been too young at the time of the 1905 Baku massacres to understand what was happening, and throughout our years in St Petersburg we never heard a word said on the Armenian question or of how the perfidious policy of the Tsarist Government of the time had manipulated and precipitated the terror. We both enlisted as volunteers.

Back in Baku, we heard many terrible tales of events in the first year of the Russo-Turkish war, adding yet another chapter to the tragic history of the Armenians in Turkey. My elder brother, who had left St Petersburg at the outbreak of the war to join our father in Baku, told us how, when Turkey declared war on Russia in October 1914, the Turkish armies had advanced deep into Sarakamysh Province, on the Russo-Turkish frontier, pushing back the Russian forces without much difficulty. There had been a growing danger that the Turkish penetration might go deep into Georgia itself, and the Russian High Command quickly called in reserves to strengthen their positions, and soon the Turks were being pushed back beyond their own frontiers.

The moment war was declared, the Armenians in Russia forgot all the injustices inflicted upon them by the Tsarist Government and flocked to join the Russian Army to fight against the main enemy, the Turks, in the hope of thus also rescuing the Armenians living on the other side of the frontier. Five legions of Armenian volunteers were formed under the command of Dashnak resistance chiefs, including Andronik (later promoted general), Dro, Hapasasp, Keri and Khetcho. They were familiar with the mountainous areas on either side of the frontier, and served as advance reconnaissance units for the Russian armies. It was a bitter campaign, fought in difficult conditions, not only because of the barbarism of the Turkish armies, but also because of the savage landscape. Dro had returned from Turkey, where he had been in hiding, since the 'execution' of Prince Nakashidze, to command one of the legions.

In April 1915, the Ottoman Government of Enver Pasha decreed the total annihilation of all Armenians living in Turkey. The Minister of the Interior, Tallaat Pasha, gave the order for the arrest of 600 Armenians living in Constantinople – those considered to be the leaders of the Armenian community there: lawyers, doctors, journalists and so on. They were put on a special train and taken to a distant province where they were shot. Simultaneously the Government enforced a general plan, conceived and executed with the aid of the head of the German Military Mission in Turkey, General von der Goltz, who advised the Turkish Government to take advantage of the war situation to enforce 'a final solution' for the Armenian problem, everyone else, he argued, being too busy with other things to protest or intervene.

And so Tallaat Pasha issued with the Minister of War Enver Pasha an edict ordering the deportation to Syria of the entire Armenian population of Eastern Anatolia. There are no exact statistics of the numbers involved, but the most conservative estimates indicate that, of the two and a half million Armenians living in Turkey at the outbreak of the 1914 war, at least a million died as a result of the massacres and deportations enforced during 1915-16, when the big Armenian cities of Van, Erzeroum, Trebizond, Erzindjan and others were attacked and ravaged by the Turks. Only the prompt arrival of the Legion of Armenian Volunteers, commanded by Dro, saved from certain death those Armenians still alive in Van. They were at the end of their tether after weeks of resistance to the Turkish siege of the city when the news of the arrival of Dro's legion as a spearhead of the full force of the Russian armies spread fear among the Turks and persuaded them to lift the siege at once. As a result, the 300,000 Armenian inhabitants of the region were given the chance of being evacuated to Transcaucasia under the protection of the Russian armed forces.

Dro himself was seriously wounded in the fighting. A bullet entered his chest so close to his heart that the doctors were afraid to operate to remove it, and he was evacuated to a military hospital in the Georgian capital of Tiflis. It so happened that the Tsar was making an inspection tour of the Caucasian front at the time. Hearing that Dro was one of the wounded officers in the hospital, he asked to be taken to his bedside. Having congratulated him on his bravery, the Tsar asked Dro where he had learnt to fight so well. Dro calmly replied: 'Your Imperial Majesty, I learnt it all as Revolutionary Commando!' At least, that was the version Dro himself told many years later. Admittedly, Dro had good reason for telling the Tsar that he had done his commando training at the time of the 1905 revolution. For the Dashnaks too, had taken part in the terrorist outrages organised by Stalin himself at the time of the strikes of the workers in the Baku oil fields. It was there that Dro met Stalin, who was busy at the time organizing the so-called 'expropriations', as the revolutionaries described their successful raids against the armoured trains carrying money to various banks, including the State Bank, in Baku – in order to raise the necessary funds to pay for arms, often bought from soldiers or even from the police themselves! But fate plays strange tricks – when Dro's son Luther was serving in the French Foreign Legion, he was parachuted with the relief forces at the siege of Dien Bin Phu in Vietnam, and landed on a mine which exploded, a splinter entering his chest so near his heart that the French doctors were afraid to remove it! So both father and son went through the same experience in two different parts of the world in two different wars!

2. WAR AND REVOLUTION

The 1915 Christmas holidays over, we returned to St Petersburg which had, in the meantime, been renamed Petrograd, the Russian version of 'the city of Peter the Great', in place of the old Dutch one, Petersburg, which Peter himself chose to commemorate his first venture to study the craft of shipbuilding in Western Europe, but which was now considered to have German connotations. In May 1916, I began my military training at the famous Mikhajlovskoe School of Artillery in St Petersburg. Having completed a crash course for artillery officers and experienced several months fighting on the Austrian front in the Carpathian mountains, I was sent – a nineteen-year-old second-lieutenant – to serve in a battery in Bukovina on the Austro-Romanian frontier.

By this time it was March 1917. The débâcle of the Russian Army, precipitated by the outbreak of revolution in February 1917, was now further aggravated by the total inability of the new Provisional Government to take decisions. The situation at the front deteriorated daily. We received orders to leave our positions in the mountains and retreat towards the Romanian frontier. The 8th Army, of which our division formed part, was in an isolated position and therefore had not yet become contaminated by revolutionary propaganda. We had not yet lost our fighting spirit, but continued to counter the combined Austro-German attacks while making an orderly withdrawal.

A few brief reports filtered through to our part of the front, saying that there had been some troubles in Petrograd in July – a revolt against the Provisional Government – but that order had been re-established. All the soldiers in my unit were regulars, having served throughout the war under the command of the same regular officers. They were unaware of the revolutionary fever spreading through other infantry regiments that had suffered terrible losses and had needed to have their units re-staffed several times with new intakes. But as our retreat from our mountain position continued, we came more and more into contact with neighbouring units whose discipline was being steadily undermined by the unceasing activities of Communist agitators, advocating a cease-fire, immediate peace and fraternizing with the enemy – a theme readily acceptable to the German High Command.

Once on Romanian soil we were ordered to stand fast and defend our new positions. Twice I had a miraculous escape from certain death, the first time when I was standing with my battery commander in an exposed observation post, and we were suddenly fired at, by a sniper, at short range. It was my luck that he was not aiming at me, for the young soldier next to me was fatally hit, a bullet in his forehead. The second time was when our battery was under fire from heavy German artillery. One gun in my section was put out of action, the dead and wounded fell all around me, yet again I emerged from battle without even a scratch, which only went to prove the truth of the modified Russian proverb: 'He who is destined for a spell in a Soviet labour and re-education camp will never drown'. At that age, I believed I was invulnerable, and I wanted to set an example of courage to the soldiers under my command.

We were overjoyed when news arrived from Brigade HQ that officers would be allowed home leave, taking turns from the beginning of October. According to the list, I was scheduled for December, but again luck was on my side. A fellow officer who had lost a lot of money at cards suggested we swap places, to give him more time to accumulate some spending money. Thus I left the front late in the evening of 3 October 1917, arriving at the railway station of Nova Sulita in Northern Romania just in time to catch the train leaving at midnight. The trains only travelled at night, and only stopped for several minutes before resuming their journey, as stations were subject to frequent shelling.

The train was quite empty, and made up of several third-class carriages and some goods waggons that had brought supplies for the front. I climbed into an upper bunk in the last carriage, and fell asleep almost at once, only to be woken several hours later by a loud crash as the train was hit by an engine coming in the opposite direction. The impact sent me tumbling on to the lower bunk, which had in the meantime been occupied by a Red Cross nurse, who proved to be a convenient cushion to break my fall. Fortunately, neither of us was hurt, although there were dead and wounded in the carriages at the front that took the main shock and had been derailed. As dawn broke, we could see the first carriage and the goods-waggon next to it completely wrecked with the unfortunate engine driver crushed between the two. They had to remove his body piece by piece.

It took hours for another engine to arrive with a team of workers to disentangle the carriages and clear the line, and meanwhile all the pleasant nurse and I could do was to walk up and down the embankment, waiting for help to get there. She told me she had been visiting her husband at the front and was now returning to work at the military hospital in Moghilev. We discussed various nationalities, and she told me she did not like Armenians. I fully agreed, at the same time confessing that, as it happened, I was Armenian. She thought I was joking and refused to believe it, saying I did not look the Armenian type. And when she asked me which nationality I disliked, I mentioned the Poles, whose arrogance and pride I found intolerable. Now it was her turn to burst out laughing and confess to being a Pole.

Eventually some ambulances appeared, and seeing their Red Cross markings the nurse ran to the first one and spoke to the soldier-driver whom she had recognized as one of the drivers attached to her hospital. The driver promised to take us there, and this piece of luck enabled me to continue on my onward journey south. It was evening by the time we arrived at Moghilev railway station, where I bade farewell to the nurse and hurried to catch my train. The scene in the station was indescribable. As the October Revolution gathered momentum, it was permeating even to the front lines. Total chaos reigned: vast crowds, mostly undisciplined soldiers deserting from the front, shouted, swore and pushed, trying to get to the edge of the platform before the train arrived. There was no ticket control or any order whatsoever. I tried to find a porter to take my suitcase and direct me to the right platform. Finally, I found an old man willing to show me the way, and after I had given him a generous tip, he himself undertook to carry my case. The train arrived already crammed but he helped me to climb in at the window of a second-class carriage which seemed slightly less full. Once I was inside the compartment, he handed me my heavy suitcase in which I had stupidly packed, as a souvenir, a fragment of eight-inch shell which had landed near me during the last bombardment to which my battery had been subjected. Everybody was pushing, trying to squeeze through corridors already full of bad-tempered soldiers deserting from the front.

After a long delay, the train finally started. I was lucky indeed to have found a seat. There were two soldiers, however, who sat staring at me in a manner both aggressive and distrustful, for I still wore the shoulder tabs of a second-lieutenant in the 32nd Artillery Brigade. Now that the Revolution had broken out, nearly all the officers one saw had removed their epaulettes, and their uniforms were in disarray and deliberately crumpled. After a while, one of the soldiers turned to me and, addressing me defiantly as 'comrade', demanded to know why I still wore badges of rank. I replied calmly that I came direct from the front line where all officers and soldiers still wore them since no orders had been received to the contrary. Unable to think of an adequate retort, the soldier remained silent for the rest of the journey. We were, after all, still in a war zone, so nobody else dared to challenge me in any way; or perhaps the clearly visible Colt 42 revolver that I wore had an influence.

Next evening we arrived at Tsvetkovo, a main rail junction in southern Ukraine, where I had to change to catch the train for Rostov at 6 a.m. Here, at last, I could have something to eat and rest, after forty-eight hours without food or sleep. I was lucky enough to find a chair for the night in a waiting room already crammed with people sitting or lying on the floor – a typical scene throughout the country at the time. The whole atmosphere was both shocking and sickening.

Once again, I was lucky enough to contact a porter willing to show me the way, and an hour before my train was due to leave he came to guide me to the depot where it was being made up – the only way of ensuring a seat. We arrived the following evening at Rostov-on-Don, and I hurried across the platforms to get on to the express train from Moscow to Baku. The scene at Rostov station was the same: a vast milling crowd of soldiers – mostly deserters – and civilians pushing and shoving across the platforms. This time I succeeded in getting into the train through the door, just managing to squeeze into a corridor jammed full of people. I asked to put my suitcase on the luggage racks in one of the compartments, whose occupants readily agreed. They were Caucasians leaving for their homelands, anxious to escape the increasingly strained political atmosphere in Moscow and Petrograd. This was, in fact, the train due in Rostov the previous day, and its departure southwards was again further delayed before we finally moved off. I stood in the corridor for a day and night, dozing fitfully, but on the second day, one of the passengers, speaking with a strong Georgian accent, offered me his top bunk while he sat with his friends. 'Mr Officer, sir, please come and rest a while with us, we can see how tired you are,' he said full of compassion. I accepted with gratitude and fell asleep at once, for how long I do not know. When I awoke, another Georgian offered me half a glass of what looked like tea. I gulped it down avidly, only to discover, to the merriment of the other passengers, that I had been given pure brandy. I was then given a piece of lemon dipped in sugar to soften the effect of the alcohol as a *zakuska*.

On hearing that I came from the front, my obliging fellow passengers started to bombard me with questions, anxious to hear what was happening there in comparison with the general rout and confusion speading through the rest of the country. In return, they told me things of which we, at the front, were totally unaware: how the authority wielded by the soldiers' and workers' Soviets in Petrograd was far more important than that of the Provisional Government of Kerensky, who was terrified of them! The army, headed by General Kornilov, had offered Kerensky full support, and with his approval the Cossack units of General Krasnov had arrived at a surburban station ready to march into Petrograd itself. At the last minute Kerensky panicked and rescinded the order, afraid of a confrontation with the Soviet (the Russian word for 'council') of Soldiers and Workers. According to the Georgians, everybody in Petrograd was certain that the Soviets would soon take over the reins of power as a result of their oft-repeated promises of 'immediate peace, land for the peasants and freedom for everybody'. That is why they were now fleeing all the big Russian cities as quickly as possible, in order to return to the Caucasus where the situation in the newly established National Republics seemed more stable.

The train pulled into the station of Mineralnye Vody ('Mineral Waters') spa in the Northern Caucasus on the afternoon of 8 October. The atmosphere here was completely different. War and revolution seemed far away. Food was plentiful and the big station restaurant still served steaming platefuls of the famous Russian 'borsh' (cabbage soup with tomatoes and other vegetables) as it always had. For the first time since leaving my battery at the front, I was able to eat in comfort, without being pushed or hurried.

There was another train standing in front of ours, also bound for Baku, and ten minutes after its departure we, too, were invited to take our seats with all the old traditional ceremonial. The old station-master in his uniform, heavily adorned with gold braid, sounded the first stroke of the bell ten minutes before departure calling out the principal stations *en route* –Petrovsk, Baku, Tiflis, and finally Batum on the Black Sea. Then, a minute before the train left, there were two strokes of the bell, and three as the train stood ready to go. The head guard, wearing wide plus-four trousers halfway down his boots, then blew his whistle, the engine-driver responding with a whistle from the steam valve, and the train slowly drew out of the station, waiting for the signalman in the signal-box to blow his bugle to confirm that the line ahead was clear before gathering speed.

I soon found a seat and settled down to enjoy the rest of the journey in comfort. We arrived in Baku in the evening of 9 October, six days after I had left the Austrian front. Here, everything was as I remembered it. It was as if war had never broken out. A porter took my case to a horse-drawn phaeton and soon I was home again! As I entered, I noticed some suitcases in the hall, and suddenly my younger brother appeared. Amid shouts of joy and embraces, I discovered that, by an extraordinary coincidence, he had arrived only ten minutes before, having travelled in the train standing just in front of mine on the same platform at Mineralnye Vody.

I had last seen my brother in Kamenetz-Podolsk, in the spring of 1917, when he was attached to GHQ of the South-Western Front, commanded by General Brusilov. Since then he had been transferred to Kiev where special heavy artillery units were being formed. The Allies had started to supply the Russian army with pieces of heavy artillery, and heavy guns and ammunition, armoured cars and so on had been steadily arriving in considerable quantities. The Russian army was thus well-prepared to counter the German offensive in the spring of 1917, but the February Revolution in Petrograd completely upset the Allies' plans. They had completely failed to understand the gravity of the situation and what a revolution in war-time really means! They rejoiced in the down-fall of the Tsarist Regime, and were happy to see the desired 'Victory of Democracy in Russia!' The Germans alone had understood at once what benefits the Russian Revolution could bring them.

The Kiev barracks allocated to the special units of heavy artillery were situated on the banks of the river Dnieper, on the other side of the river itself. Having only recently been formed, the units had no experienced officer-cadres and the officers were not well known to the men. All forms of discipline therefore rapidly disintegrated with the spread of the Revolution. A mutual hostility between officers and men created an unhealthy atmosphere of instability and gave rise to all sorts of unpleasant incidents. My brother himself had been involved in one such incident when he tried to intervene in a dispute which suddenly erupted between an old woman and a soldier travelling on a tram he had taken into town. His attempts to smooth ruffled tempers, however, only served to inflame a group of soldiers who started to hurl insults and to molest my brother, threatening to throw him into the river, which the tram was just then crossing. They even tried to make the conductor stop the tram and put their threats into action. Fortunately, the old woman succeeded in calming down the inflamed soldiers and so saved my brother's life.

Salaries were no longer being paid in the unit either to officers or men, and initially the officers formed themselves into groups and offered their services to load and unload goods trains arriving at the freight train terminus so as to earn enough money to survive. As soon as the soldiers found out, they attacked the officers and chased them away so they could take their place. Faced with a state of anarchy they couldn't control, officers began to leave their posts and my brother decided to follow suit. The commanding officer himself having fled, there was no one to sign the movement order allowing him a free travel permit to go home on leave. So he forged the necessary papers, affixed the regimental seal and left.

The atmosphere in Baku was more or less calm, the Communists not yet having made any serious impact there. Although one might occasionally see soldiers with untidy uniforms in the streets, the vast majority of the armed forces continued to maintain correct dress and deportment. Soldiers still saluted officers in the street, and this was why, as I walked with my elder brother on the main street one day and we encountered a soldier who neglected to salute, I stopped him and reminded him that the order to salute officers was still in force. He did not reply, nor did he show any hostility. It was an obvious case of absent-mindedness, and so I explained to him that failure to salute an officer showed lack of discipline and that he should always do so in future. I considered the incident closed, but the whole thing greatly alarmed my brother, who was fearful that such confrontations might lead to serious consequences, whereas I, having just returned from the front, had no qualms whatsoever about the correctness of my reprimand.

Gradually, however, the situation deteriorated and several weeks later, when the Soviets took over the reins of power in Baku, the military commandant, in an effort to avoid such incidents, published an order that 'all officers are invited to remove their shoulder tabs and all other insignia of rank'. The order that soldiers must always salute an officer was also cancelled. This was followed later by another order, inviting all military personnel to present themselves for demobilization. My brother and I hastened to do so, obtaining the necessary demob papers as a first step to becoming ordinary civilians. The next step was to obtain identity cards and passports.

I took the initiative and went to the local *pristav* (police superintendent) to ask him to issue me with a passport. A pleasant, obliging man who knew my father well, the *pristav* explained that there was a small difficulty – he had no passports left in stock, and the total break in communications with Petrograd over the past months made it impossible for him to get any new supplies. However, he did have a solution, which he proceeded to outline with a twinkle in his eye. There was a stock of unused 'yellow passports' which the police issued to prostitutes. They were the same as ordinary passports, except that the papers were yellow. This marvellous offer I accepted with alacrity, especially since I was very fond of yellow. Back at home, the whole family were highly entertained by the ploy, and my younger brother hastened off to get himself a similar passport.

It was necessary to act quickly. All communications between Transcaucasia and Russia itself had become impossible. The railway had been cut, the mountain tribes of Daghestan having declared themselves an independent republic. By the beginning of 1918, the situation in Baku had become increasingly unstable. All local power lay in the hands of the Soviet of Workers and Soldiers, but the Tartar mobs were determined to seize their share of it. They organized themselves into armed bands, set on recommencing the massacres of the city's Armenian inhabitants along the same lines as in 1905. This time, however, they had chosen the wrong moment. Many Armenian soldiers and officers had returned home from the front, and the Armenians now had the experience, training and arms necessary to fight off any attack. The well-organised Dashnak Commando units were still around, whereas the Tartar bands had no experienced soldiers, Moslems having been exempted from compulsory service.

In March 1918, when the Tartars launched their attack against the Armenians they found the defences well prepared. A protective cordon had been set up between the old Tartar quarter and the centre of the city which was inhabited by Armenians, Russians and other nationalities. There were some Armenian families who lived within the Tartar quarter, and they, alas, could not be saved. We knew one entire family, the Ayvazians, who perished. The parents, the son, a young student at the university, and their charming daughter Assya were all killed and their house was burned down.

My younger brother took active part in the street fighting, having joined a commando of volunteers led by our cousin Ossip, a lieutenant in the Russian army who had been decorated with the Cross of St George for exceptional bravery in the 1914-15 campaign on the Galician and Carpathian fronts. Armed with several machine-guns, Ossip's commandos stood firm and kept their positions along Nikolaevskaya Street, which descended from the Tartar quarter in the hills to the centre of the city itself. They succeeded in stopping the Tartar hordes in their tracks and finally dispersed them after three days of fighting.

Meanwhile, I, too, had been entrusted with a mission by my father, himself an active member of the Armenian National Defence Committee. Fully aware that the city's Armenian inhabitants were in the minority, the committee devised a plan to give them a trump card, that trump card being a VIP hostage. I was therefore instructed to go to the house of the Tartar leader, a millionaire called Hadji Zeinal Taghiev, of whom it was said he had once cruelly tortured to death his wife's lover before her eyes. The house lay in the Armenian quarter, and I was to remain there, guarding him as a hostage, until such time as all fighting ceased. The committee had already detained several other important Tartar personages under house arrest, not only because of their importance as hostages but also because the committee was determined to protect them and their families from roaming groups of inflamed Armenians, set on avenging the massacre of their own people. This would have only further aggravated the situation, and Taghiev's death in particular would have serious consequences. My instructions were that, in the event of trouble, I must phone my father immediately and ask for reinforcements.

Taghiev had been forewarned that a young man wearing Russian uniform would come to his house for his protection, so when I rang the imposing front-door bell at the appointed hour I was expected. The door was opened by Taghiev's son-in-law, a heavily built Tartar of about twenty-five. All other doors had been barricaded and covered with iron grills, so turning the house into a fortress. The young Tartar offered to show me the house, which was like a small palace, the furnishing have been entrusted to Svirsky, a famous St Petersburg firm of interior designers. He took me first to an immense, beautifully furnished drawing room, then to the library with its shelf upon shelf of beautifully bound books that nobody touched since the old man could not read. All this was done to impress visitors and prove that, with his riches, he could afford to indulge any whim. Shortly afterwards the old man himself came in. He was by then ninety-six though he only admitted to eighty-five, and was almost blind. He was accompanied by his wife, their sixteen-year-old son and the married daughter whose husband had greeted me on arrival. The wife was subdued and her appearance seemed normal. It was generally known the the shock of her lover's death had completely unbalanced her, but it was a passive, non-violent form of madness. I explained my mission and assured them that they were in no immediate danger.

The first day did indeed pass uneventfully, but on the afternoon of the second day there was a loud ringing and banging on the front door. I went downstairs to be faced by a group of armed but disciplined Armenians who were out to kidnap Taghiev and take him to a hiding-place. I turned to the one who seemed to be their leader and explained my mission. He knew my father and accepted what I said, agreeing to come into the house to phone the National Committee while the others remained outside. I introduced him to the Taghievs and obtained their permission for him to use the phone. The National Committee having confirmed that the Taghiev family were not to be touched, the group of Armenians left and the rest of the day passed calmly. Next morning, the committee decided to transfer the Taghiev family to the house of a notable Armenian, the move to be kept secret. Thus my brief mission came to an end.

After three days of bitter fighting in the streets, an armistice was signed between the Tartars and Armenians, and so my younger brother also returned home from fighting with the volunteer commandos. Peace had been restored in Baku, but now alarming news came to us from the Turkish frontier with the newly created republics of Georgia and Armenia. The republic of Azerbaidjan, of which Baku is the capital, came under the control of Communist Soviets, but Georgia had a Socialist government composed of Mensheviks, opposed to the Bolsheviks, who had their own national and moderate programme. Meanwhile, in the Armenian Republic, the National Government included representatives of both the National Movement and the Dashnak Confederation of Armenian Revolutionary Parties, whose principal aim was the defence of Armenians in Turkey.

After the February Revolution, the Dashnaks played an active role in the Armenian National Government and the defence of the country. Now the Turkish front was in collapse and the Russian army retreating in disarray, its soldiers' only concern being to return to their villages in Russia as soon as possible. The Soviets signed an armistice with the Turks in December 1917, which was followed by a separate Peace Treaty with Germany on 3 March 1918. The Turks took advantage of the Soviets' weakness, and on 31 May reoccupied Batum in Georgia as well as the old provinces of Kars and Ardaghan. The Turks were now advancing right up to Alexandropol – an important rail junction on the Tiflis line to Erevan, the capital of Armenia.

Abandoned first by the retreating Russian armies and then by the Soviets, the Armenians had to defend themselves as best they could, but their military capability was now no match for the massed force of the Turkish armies. At the outset, units under the command of General Nazarbekov combined with the Dashnak commando groups led by Andranik and Dro succeeded in pushing back the Turkish advance. But after four days their ammunition ran out and they had to retreat to Sardarabad, in the direction of the capital, Erevan.

As soon as the Georgians realized that the Turks had opened the road to Tiflis, and that there was nothing to stop their advance on the Georgian capital, they hastened to seek the protection of the Germans. A German military mission, supported by a contingent of German troops, landed at Poti, the Georgian Black Sea port north of Batum. Soon after their arrival, a Turco-German-Georgian armistice was signed, stipulating the return of Batum to Georgia. The Turks agreed, but only on condition that their army be allowed free passage through Georgia in the direction of Baku. The Germans supported this: their aim was to reach Baku and take possession of the oil fields before the arrival of British armies from Mesopotamia. As for the Armenian Republic, her new frontiers were defined by the Peace Treaty of 4 June 1918, which reduced her territory to a much smaller area than that fixed by the Tsarist Government.

As the disintegration of the Russian armies intensified, more and more soldiers from the Turkish front hurried to board trains on the Batum-Tiflis-Baku line to get home as soon as possible. They carried with them their arms, which would be needed to fight to achieve the goals of the Revolution and to obtain the land promised to the peasants by the Soviets. The Azerbaidjani Tartars, meanwhile, watched with increasing greed and envy all this stock of arms and amunition disappearing before their eyes.

They organized themselves to ambush the Russian echelons, to disarm the soldiers and take their arms for the needs of the new Tartar Republic of Azerbaidjan. Several trains were successfully waylaid and the Russian soldiers forced to disembark and disarm. But when the soldiers still at the front realized what was happening, they arranged for the next convoy to stop some distance back up the line and proceeded to encircle the Tartar position, killing them all. After that, the trains got through to Baku without further hitches.

In Baku, however, another unpleasant surprise awaited the returning soldiers. There was no way they could get back home, the railway link with Russia having been cut off by the newly established Republic of Daghestan. Furthermore, the rapid developments on the Turkish front, following the signing of the Georgian-Turkish Treaty, prompted the Baku Soviet to declare a general mobilization, to prepare for the defence of the city against the advancing Turkish Armies. And so it was in June 1918 that my younger brother and I found ourselves back in our uniforms and presenting ourselves at the old Salyanny Regimental Barracks, on one of the hills that surrounded the city. I was immediately given the rank of instructor, a rank automatically given to former officers, and, as an artillery officer, attached to Armoured Train No.3 of the Red Army in the Caucasus. This patrolled the sector of the Transcaucasian railway in the direction of the Georgian frontier where it was expected that the Turkish forces would launch an attempt to breach the lines of defence.

The Tartar population in Baku received the news of the advancing Turkish armies with great rejoicing, whereas the Armenians became increasingly alarmed. Those rich enough bought themselves a passage on the boats leaving Baku, *en route* for the port of Astrakhan, where the Volga flows into the Caspian Sea. Several Armenian families managed to escape this way, among them my elder brother's wife with their eight-month-old daughter and her aged mother. Meanwhile I travelled to my new assignment by hitching a lift on a goods train heading for the Georgian frontier.

The railway stations of Hadji Kabul and Kurda Mir were close to a large lake, infested with mosquitoes. As soon as night fell, thick clouds of mosquitoes descended. By just lifting one's hand and quickly closing the fist, one could squash several insects at one go. Armoured Train No.3 was composed of two units, one consisting of two passenger carriages for the military personnel, plus several goods waggons carrying spare ammunition and explosives as well as food, the other forming the armoured train itself. This was constructed from a carriage, the engine and a covered goods-waggon to carry ammunition in addition to a simple open platform on which was mounted a 75-mm. mountain gun, shielded on either side by a wall of sandbags. The armour-plated carriage had been manufactured in Baku and was, in fact, an ordinary open goods platform on which were superimposed walls of armour-plating. But the calculations had been so badly done, that the train was not properly balanced and could not exceed a speed of 12 m.p.h. The superstructure was too heavy for the simple platform base, and any attempts to exceed the maximum speed inevitably resulted in derailment. The soldiers on board were quite used to this eventuality and knew exactly what to do to right the carriage and put it back on the rails with the aid of large jacks.

The train had ten Maxim machine guns fitted into the small apertures at the sides of the carriage, while in the front a sliding door could be moved to left or right to reveal another small 75-mm. mountain gun, also mounted on wheels, which allowed a limited range of firing. To protect itself, the train pushed two empty platforms in front of it to cause any mine to explode and take the full impact, leaving the armoured part undamaged.

When I presented myself to the commanding officer of this extraordinary contraption, I discovered him to be a commissar whose party nickname was 'Comrade Mudryj' (which in Russian means 'The Wise One'). He was in fact a chemist and an amiable, highly educated Jew. I didn't know what his fighting abilities were, but his musical talents soon became obvious as he settled down in the evening to sing, accompanying himself on a guitar. I was allowed a compartment to myself, which my new commander advised me to fumigate each day to avoid a massive invasion of mosquitoes. But the best way to get a good night's sleep, he said, was to lie on the platform fitted on top of the wooden tower near the railway station. It meant climbing up a narrow ladder some forty feet tall, but at least one was safe from the mosquitoes which never rose that high. These towers had been specially built by the management of the Transcaucasian Railway for the station staff to enable them to get some sleep. Otherwise rest was impossible.

The heat in the compartment was suffocating, and it was difficult to say which was worse: the mosquitoes or the smell of sulphur; and so I took Commissar Mudryj's advice and spent a comfortable night on the platform. The following morning he showed me over the train, explaining the control system. The commissar sat in the armour-plated carriage, giving orders to the engine driver to start or stop by blowing a bugle. It was a primitive system, but it worked. When I asked to meet the artillery personnel on the train, I was told there was only one – a Russian NCO found among the deserters stranded in Baku through lack of transport. Fortunately, he was a genuine artillery-man, who had served in the campaign on the Caucasian front. Stranded penniless in Baku he had earned his living by working in a circus as a wrestler. A well-built fellow, he was a great asset since his strength enabled him to alter the position of the small mountain gun by simply grabbing the two wheels and lifting the gun-carriage.

The task of finding gunners proved to be far from simple. The matter was urgent and there was not much to choose from, so we had no option but to face a well-trained army of Turkish regulars with a bunch of untrained men. While the train was busy patrolling the designated sector, we set out to teach our recruits how to operate the gun – all the elementary manoeuvres, fixing the fuse, opening the breech, loading, closing the breech, changing the gradient and direction in accordance with the command, how to fire the gun on order, then unload and so on. Fortunately, they were quick learners, for they had already been in action. Fortunately, the atmosphere was quiet during the first weeks after my arrival, and this made it possible for the training to be completed. The swarms of mosquitoes from the neighbouring lakes and marshes remained our main worry.

But soon another problem arose. Near Kurdamir Station stood the cellar-warehouses in which were stored the barrels of wine and brandy produced by the famous house of Agriev, who owned all the vineyards in the neighbouring villages. The soldiers soon found out and would often return to the train with buckets filled to the brim with wine and brandy. The trouble was that, in their haste to fill as many containers as possible, they could never be bothered to close the barrel taps. And since using a tap took too long anyway, some of them decided to speed things up Russian way, by shooting holes in the barrels, many drinking their fill there and then. Soon, the inevitable happened. A wine lake formed on the cellar floor and several soldiers fell into it, dead drunk, and were drowned. Nobody bothered to remove the bodies, and soon the decomposing corpses began to poison the wine in the cellar.

As soon as Commissar Mudryj heard about it, the warehouse cellars were put out of bounds, but this did not stop some soldiers from going there and filling their flasks with poisoned wine. And before long many became very ill indeed, with agonizing pains and constant vomiting. Fortunately none died, but at least it discouraged the others. Nevertheless the fact remained that the soldiers did not want to fight any more, their only concern being to return to their villages in Russia. So far as they were concerned, the war was over. Mobilized forcibly by the Baku Soviet and sent to the Turkish front, all they could think about was how to desert again. They had already fled from the Caucasian front in the general retreat and were not prepared to risk their lives further.

One day we received an order to take the armoured train beyond the lines of the estimated Russian postion. We were looking for our practically non-existent troops and their so-called defence position when, a little over a mile away, we saw a troop of Turkish cavalry. I was ordered to fire, and with the help of several among my few gunners, managed to send off several rounds, watching with satisfaction as the Turkish detachment dispersed hastily and took flight. But to achieve this amazing result I had to do all the necessary manoeuvres myself, then open fire and observe the effect on the enemy through my binoculars. The company commander and the gunners declared the operation a great success. We had put the enemy to flight! Yet despite this famous victory we were obliged to join the general retreat of the Russian troops now in full flight and no longer offering any opposition. Our orders from Baku came over the Transcaucasian Railway telegraph system, and it was obvious to me that the enemy was interrupting the messages and therefore knew their contents before we did. Nevertheless, we carried on!

One evening, Commissar Mudryj ordered me to go to the ordnance depot next to the Alyati railway station, not far from Baku, to take on new supplies of explosives and ammunition. During the last few days of retreat our sappers had blown up several railway bridges and pumping stations along the pipe-line that carried oil from Baku to Batum on the Black Sea, besides blowing up parts of the pipe-line itself. All along the line of retreat, high columns of smoke rose from these explosions, ordered by Baku in a last-ditch effort to delay the advance of the Turkish armies and deprive them of the oil they and their German allies were coming in search of.

At Alyati, the soldiers loaded on to the platform at the rear of the train several cases of explosives, shells and all sorts of ammunition, and that done we set off on our return journey, with me riding in the engine. Half an hour later, just as we were approaching a small station, I looked back along the train and saw, to my horror, smoke rising from the rear platform. I told the engine driver to stop, got down and ran along the embankment to the rear, where my worst fears were confirmed. The rear platform, on which the supplies of explosives and ammunition had been loaded was now blazing merrily. I ran back to the front of the train, and the engine driver at once started to manoeuvre the train into a siding near the station water-tower, where the Russian NCO and I, together with several soldiers, managed to unload the few crates of explosives which were not yet burning. The blazing platform was then uncoupled and manoeuvred right under the water-tower so that the NCO could turn the hose on to the remaining crates. But just as we thought everything was under control, the shells began to explode from the heat. The sappers, who had jumped off the platform when the fire started, now came running back. The fire had started through their negligence – a badly stubbed-out cigarette had set fire to the surrounding straw. There was nothing to do except watch the burning platform from a safe distance for about half an hour until the explosions ceased.

Meanwhile, the retreat was continuing unabated. At Alyati station I had unexpectedly run into my younger brother who was now also attached to the armoured train, and heard from him how the situation in Baku was becoming increasingly grim. People were being forcibly mobilized on the streets and sent to man the city's defences in hastily prepared trenches. Workers and civilians had been sent to dig trenches in the chalk and sandy hills surrounding the western and northern approaches to the city as a last line of defence, but not even the declaration of a general mobilization by the Baku Soviet succeeded in raising the forces to provide a serious resistance to the Turkish advances. The army was disorganized, and there was no control. Defence arrangements within the city itself were non-existent, although the civilian population had been given arms.

An order was issued that our Armoured Train No.3 should now be joined by Armoured Train No.1, the task being to patrol the sector of the line running beyond the hills on the outskirts of the city. But no sooner was the order issued that it was rescinded, it being realized that the train would merely make an easy target for the enemy without presenting any advantage

to the defence. It was at this moment, at the end of July 1918, that our commissar suddenly disappeared, having just supervised the destruction of a
railway bridge. He vanished without warning and we never saw him again,
though we subsequently heard that his disappearance was prompted by the
fact that the Baku Soviet had been ousted by a group of Social
Revolutionaries who had the support of the sailors manning the Caspian
Fleet. The new administration called itself the Central Caspian Committee.
It was they who were now issuing orders, and promising great reforms.
Rumours were rife that a British contingent was about to arrive to reinforce
the city's defences, and all these stories did much to raise the morale of the
defenders. We received instructions to withdraw to Baladjari, near the main
junction north-east of Baku, where the Transcaucasian Railway joined the
line going north into Russia. In the absence of Commissar Mudryj, I was
appointed commander in charge of Train No.3, and I, in turn, appointed my
younger brother as my second-in-command.

It soon became obvious that the great reforms promised by the new
administration restricted themselved to names and titles. Instead of 'commissar' and 'comrade' we were able to use our old military ranks again:
colonels became colonels again, generals were called generals again. An
Armenian, Colonel Avetissyan, was responsible for operations on the front,
and on the morning of 6 August 1918 he summoned me to his office at
Baladjari Station and told me curtly: 'Our infantry is advancing northwards.
We have already occupied the first stop on the line – at Hurdalan. You must
go there at once, to support our infantry against the Turks.' I left his office,
little realizing how badly informed the colonel was, and returned to the train
to give the order to leave at once.

After about two and a half miles I noticed some detachments of
soldiers advancing, in dispersed formation, northwards, as we were. I
assumed they were reinforcements. They waved joyfully as we passed,
travelling slowly as usual for fear of derailing the badly balanced carriages.
Further along the line, the railway made a large curve as it entered a cutting
between two hills. Beyond the curve was Hurdalan, and just as we reached
the curve I noticed that the empty platforms at the front were wobbling so
badly that the whole train was on the verge of derailment. I shouted to the
bugler next to me to sound the signal to stop the train, but he was so shaken
by what was happening that he dropped his bugle. The several seconds it
took him to pick it up again proved to be a fatal delay. The armoured carriage, already swaying badly, derailed as the train came to a halt. The Turks
had unscrewed the rails, leaving them in place to conceal the fact, and the
weight of the platform had displaced them. The armoured car was completely derailed, and the front wheels of the engine were also off the rails. I
ordered the engine driver to reverse slowly, and fortunately all the engine's
wheels came back on the rails, but there was nothing to be done with the
armoured car. We uncoupled it from the engine and I ordered my brother to
take the engine back to Baladjari to arrange for a party of workmen to be
sent out with jacks to try and put the armoured carriage back on the rails,

believing that Hurdalan was still in Russian hands. In fact it was already in the hands of the Turks and we had driven straight into the trap laid for us. The scattered detachments we passed on our way were in fact our front line troops.

We were soon made aware of our true situation as the Turks opened intensive fire against our armoured train, now immobile after the departure of the engine. We were being fired on simultaneously from both sides, and although my machine-gunners started firing back, I ordered them to stop. It was a waste of ammunition. Far better to save it for the moment when the Turkish infantry closed in for a direct attack. At the moment, they were firing from a great distance, hidden in the trenches high up in the hillside. Even so their bullets registered direct hits again and again, penetrating even the small slits in the carriage wall and wounding several soldiers, fortunately none seriously.

After two hours of heavy fire, my Russian NCO asked me to come to the sliding door at the front of our armoured carriage. Drawing it slightly ajar, he pointed to the increased activity on the distant hillside directly opposite. The Turks were installing a cannon, aimed directly at the train, to blow us to bits. With the aid of several well-aimed shrapnel shots, we succeeded in dislodging them, together with their cannon, but the danger was not yet over. True, the engine had gone to fetch help, but since the maintenance men would come under fire, it would be impossible for them to get the armoured carriage back on the rails. There was also the possibility of the Turks installing their cannon in a new position. I therefore gave the order to abandon the train. The soldiers took advantage of the brief respite between the Turkish firing to jump down and take cover. Thus my brave machine-gunners managed to get away, and I was left alone with my Russian NCO. My honour as an Artillery Officer was at stake. I could not possibly leave to the enemy the breech of the gun to be used against us, so we removed the mechanism from the closing hatch, as well as the optical view-finder, before climbing down to follow the others.

We were half-hidden in the ditch, so were not visible to the enemy as we ran a short distance, then flung ourselves to the ground. But as we emerged round the curve into the enemy's field of vision, the firing became more intense, and rifle and machine-gun bullets whistled all around us. I brought up the rear, carrying the breech, close behind the NCO, carrying the view-finder. Suddenly I felt a sharp blow on my left shoulder as though someone had thrown a stone at me. Convinced it was the NCO playing one of his pranks, I shouted that now was not the time for silly games. As he loudly protested his innocence, I noticed blood beginning to ooze from my shoulder. But there was no time to lose, and we hurried on to catch up with the rest of the unit and get out of the line of Turkish fire. Soon we came across the machine-gunners, carrying a comrade who had been wounded in the chest. Finally we reached our infantry's front line, and the unit we passed earlier had not advanced very far! As I had no first-aid kit, I asked one of the infantrymen to lend me his, but he refused. He might need it himself later.

We saw from afar our engine returning, with a platform carrying the maintenance men, but there was nothing to be done about it, and so we returned with the maintenance team. At Baladjari I went straight to the colonel to report and he gave orders for a unit to go out at dusk to blow up the armoured carriage. Several days later I heard that our famous Armoured Carriage No.3 had indeed been destroyed and therefore made useless for the enemy. Only after I had delivered my report did I go to the Red Cross post to have my shoulder bandaged. Fortunately, the bullet had passed through the joint without damaging the nerve.

That done, my brother and I returned to base – a carriage standing outside the station. We ate, then settled down to a game of cards, but soon physical exhaustion following such an eventful day began to tell, and I started having dizzy spells. Early next morning I caught a local train for Baku and fifteen minutes later arrived at the main railway station. There were no cabs, all the Tartar coachmen having disappeared to their villages to await the arrival of their Turkish friends and protectors. A Persian porter took my suitcase, and we set off on foot to walk the mile and a half to my father's house, I still carrying my rifle.

As we entered Record Square I saw father standing at the street corner, reading a newspaper. 'Good morning, father,' I said cheerfully. 'What are you doing here?' he asked, looking at me over his spectacles. 'I've been wounded in the shoulder, so have been sent home for medical treatment. It's all right, only a light wound,' I replied just as calmly. Father gave me a searching look, then continued reading the news item that had caught his attention. Only when he had finished did he fold the paper and say, 'Right, let's go home then!' He was never one to become over-excited.

On the way, I told him about the skirmish at Hurdalan and as soon as we arrived father telephoned Dr Okinchevich, a well-known surgeon who lived nearby. The surgeon examined me, changed the dressing and confirmed the diagnosis made by the Red Cross doctor. There was nothing serious, he reassured my father. All I needed was a two-day rest, he said. And indeed, I was completely recovered several days later, with my arm in an elegant silk scarf sling. Shortly afterwards, my brother also arrived home in search of supplies. Our mutilated armoured train was no longer, but our soldiers who had been with us throughout the summer campaign were still there, and he had to get uniforms and boots to clothe them before winter set in, as they were lacking in everything. We went to see the Quartermaster - General, Michael (Mishik) Ter-Pogossyan, an Armenian lawyer who was a member of the Social Revolutionary Party now in power, whom we had already met shortly after his arrival in Baku, at the end of 1917, with General Bagratouni. He received us very cordially and on hearing what my brother had to say, he at once gave orders that we be issued with everything we needed. Our poor soldiers deserved at least that.

Meanwhile the Turks were rapidly closing on Baku and the siege of the city had begun. They had cut the water mains supplying the city, and the municipal authorities tried to keep the water supply going by cleaning and reactivating old boilers that had been used for the desalination and purification of sea water. From now on water consumption was rationed, but despite all efforts to purify it, the water still had a faint taste of petrol. We tried to dissimulate it with lemon or other fruit juice, but the taste persisted. The fact that there was a war invalid in the house (myself) meant that our water ration was slightly larger than usual, and this allowed my poor father to have his daily bath which meant so much to him.

There was also a food shortage. The bread ration was very small, and to make up for it everybody was issued with enormous quantities of caviar. Hard as this may be to believe, we soon became heartily sick of it and the sight of another plateful of caviar was intolerable.

The siege continued throughout August and the first weeks of September 1918, the city's defenders fighting fiercely. But they were poorly armed and badly organised, consisting of a mobilized civilian militia and a few units of Dashnak guerillas. The Central Caspian Committee had appealed to the British forces in Mesopotamia, under the command of General Dunsterville, to send out a British relief force to help defeat the Turks, in exchange for 2000 tons of petrol which the Committee undertook to deliver to meet the British transport requirements. The situation was becoming intolerable, and faced with desperate appeals from the Committee for more reinforcements, Colonel Stokes (the Commanding Officer at British HQ in Kazvin in Northern Persia) agreed on the need to do something to improve the morale of the Christian population, living in constant terror of further massacres. Forty jeeps with eighty British officers arrived in Baku and drove throughout the city's main streets, to the great rejoicing of the population, who all rushed out to greet them. More troops arrived later, and although they took part in the bitter fighting, several British battalions could not fill the gap left by the desertion of large units of the Red Army, under the command of a certain comrade Petrov, who refused to take part in the defence of Baku, after the coup d'etat ousting the Communist Soviet and its replacement by the Central Caspian Committee. It was their desertion which sealed the city's fate.

It so happened that I knew two Armenian ladies who worked as secretaries at the British HQ located in the Hotel Europa in the centre of town. I used to go there to see them from time to time, to find out the latest developments. The situation at the front was very serious, and fighting now raged at the gates to the north-west of the city, where the Tartar quarters were situated. The Armenians knew only too well what fate awaited them once the city fell to the hands of the Turks, and they feared even more the savagery of the Tartar inhabitants of the surrounding villages.

On the afternoon of 14 September I went as usual to the Hotel Europa and to my amazement found the place deserted, the offices empty, pieces of paper scattered over the floor. The Hotel Manager told me that the entire staff of the British HQ had left, having embarked the previous evening on several ships that were just about to leave port. I couldn't believe it. I telephoned the ladies' homes, to be told that they, too, were on board ship and leaving for an undisclosed destination.

I telephoned my father at once to tell him the grievous news, and was ordered to return home at once while he contacted the Armenian National Committee. And as I walked in through the front door fifteen minutes later, my father confirmed that the city had been abandoned to the enemy and there was no option but to try to reach an understanding with the Turkish army commanders. The British had withdrawn their units, having given ample warning of their intention to the Central Caspian Committee, to allow them to arrange a cease-fire and agree on the terms of surrender.

My elder brother was ill with typhoid, and alone in his small flat. Father had already arranged that a bed be prepared for him in the 'Black City' hospital, where a cousin was resident surgeon and our step-mother (father having re-married in 1916) worked as a doctor. My younger brother and I hastened round to help him dress and pack a small bag. He was totally exhausted by the high fever. We took him to the hospital, and having made sure he was in good hands, made our way home again. In the meantime, father had consulted the Armenian National Committee who advised that, as serving officers, it was dangerous for us to remain in Baku. There were several ships reserved for the evacuation of the wounded, women and children, and we should embark as soon as possible, to be on board before the ships left, which could be at any moment. Father gave us the little money he had on him, and we left the house in company with him and our step-mother, who planned to stay in the 'Black City' hospital, for there was hope that the Turkish Army would at least protect the hospitals from the ravaging Tartar hordes. At the hospital we bade them a quick farewell and hurried to the quayside. It was already late evening and a mass of desperate people were pushing and jostling, hoping to be the lucky ones chosen for evacuation. A military cordon blocked the entry to the gangway, but luck was still with me, and when a soldier on guard saw my arm in a sling, he at once made way and helped us to embark.

The deck was crammed full with people, squashed against each other like sardines in a tin. It was impossible to sit anywhere. There were innumerable women and children sitting on suitcases, but very few men. Seconds after we embarked, the captain gave orders to raise anchor and the ship moved slowly out into the channel between the port itself and the island of Narguene which lay across the bay of Baku. This was no easy task as the channel was already full of other ships crowded with refugees. As dawn broke the next morning, there was smoke rising above the town where fires had been started by Tartar mobs on the rampage. Later we heard that the commander of the Turkish forces had allowed them three days and nights to do as they wished, massacring, raping, burning, pillaging and looting at will as they set about destroying the Christian quarters of Baku. And it was only after the carnage got completely out of hand that an official order was given to try and bring the situation under control. 'All those caught in the act of burning and looting will be hanged,' it said. Gallows were erected all over the city, and anxious to give the impression that he really meant business, the Turkish commander gave orders to hang some corpses from the gibbets, but these were corpses of Armenians killed in the three days of carnage during which some 25,000 – 30,000 Christians lost their lives. Nor was that the end of the story, for having killed the men, the Tartars then took the women and young girls back with them to their villages, to replenish their harems. But, by a miracle, the hospital in the 'Black City' escaped untouched.

The ship we were on sailed southwards, in the direction of Persia, while other ships went to Krasnovodsk, or Astrakhan on the Volga. Twenty-four hours later we docked at Enzeli, the Persian port on the southern shores of the Caspian Sea. It was occupied by the British, who gave permission for the ship to dock and the passengers to disembark. We at once made contact with Mrs Pertchui Tumanyan, an attractive widow we had met in Baku. The Tumanyans were one of the richest families in Persia, similar to the Rothschilds in France. They owned much property, a lot of land, and big companies exporting dried fruit to Russia, as well as banks. It was their bank which negotiated loans on behalf of the old Shahs of Persia before the enthronement of Reza-Khan Pahlavi. She received us with open arms, but regretted she could only offer us a couple of mattresses on the big veranda as the house was already full of refugees, among them another family friend, Dr Nersessian, who had treated my younger brother for a deep abscess on his thigh during the siege. Now both patient and doctor were refugees in the same house.

We left our small suitcase there and went into town to change some money and to try to find other accommodation. In the narrow streets of the bazaar could be found an array of colourful money-changers, known as *sharafs*. They sat on the pavements, cross-legged in Oriental fashion, in front of each a small table with a glass top, under which were gold or silver coins and banknotes from many countries. The first *sharaf* we approached offered a price for our banknotes which seemed much too low, so we approached another but he offered even less. It soon became obvious that the exchange rates were falling lower and lower as more refugees arrived, and it was therefore advisable to accept whatever was offered.

Three days later we met a Russian officer who suggested that we move into one of the cabins on board the empty ship docked in Enzeli port, where he had already taken up residence. There were several empty cabins, and the captain would be willing to allow us, as Russian officers, to live there until we found something better. We accepted with alacrity, and returned to the Tumanyan house to collect our few belongings and thank Pertchui for her hospitality. Just then, Dr Nersessian appeared with the news that the chief of the British Military Police at Enzeli, Colonel Cockerell, had appointed him sanitary inspector in charge of Armenian refugees, who were now flooding into Enzeli in such large numbers that there was a growing risk of epidemics because of the miserable conditions they lived in, in tents, with no sanitary facilities, or whole families crammed into one room. The colonel urgently needed a detailed map of the city, and Dr Nersessian had suggested that my brother and I, as former students of the Civil Engineering Academy in St Petersburg, were just the people to help him solve the problem.

Colonel Cockerell received us in a friendly way, noting our ranks from the insignia we still wore on our tunics. A highly educated and delightful man in his early fifties, the colonel spoke fluent French, German and Greek, as well as several Indian dialects and we soon became great friends. He explained that he needed a detailed plan of the city streets, and he gave us three days to complete the task. To assist us, he seconded to us two Persian policemen to help with reading the street names, which were written in Persian. We soon discovered, however, that only the main streets and the centre of the town were signposted, the majority of streets bearing no indication whatsoever of names or numbers, and so we went to the Town Hall to see if we could borrow a town map, however incomplete. There was none to be had, but the pleasant official who received us did not like the British, considering that they treated the Persians as an inferior race. He had far more sympathy with the Russians, on the other hand, who had treated the inhabitants of northern Persia well after the last Russo-Turkish war, and referred us to the Enzeli Port Authority, which was still run by the Russians who actually built the port.

The director in charge was a Russian engineer called Smelov, who turned out to be a relative of a former classmate of mine in St Petersburg. More than that, he was himself a graduate of the Civil Engineering Academy where my brother and I studied until we enlisted. As soon as these facts were established, nothing was too much trouble. On his wall was a diagram-map of Enzeli port, though the street names were not marked. It was only a general map, and it did not include the recently built quarters of the town, but he offered us a copy to serve as a basis for our own map and gave us all the material necessary to carry out the task: Indian ink, tracing paper, pens and pencils, even a drawing board.

We divided the city into two sectors and set off on foot in opposite directions, each carrying a copy of the old map, to be filled in street by street, and each accompanied by a Persian policeman. We worked throughout the day, and in the evening filled in the master map. The task was completed ahead of time, at the end of the second day, and we proudly presented ourselves to the colonel. He was so satisfied with the map that he offered us a permanent job on his staff. There were no vacancies for officers, but he suggested we stay on as sergeants in the Military Police at a salary of 60 Tumans a month with free lodging. Once again we accepted, and were duly lodged in a room in the barracks of the British Military Police – just a bed, a locker and facilities for making tea in the mornings and evenings. We took our meals in a small restaurant in the bazaar which served the same sort of Oriental dishes we had so enjoyed on our school holidays in Baku.

We now proudly wore MP armbands, and this gave us great authority among the Persians.

There was not much for us to do. Our main task was to visit and keep a watchful eye on the refugees and the precarious sanitary conditions they lived in. For a while I was detailed to take a patrol of a dozen Persian soldiers and an Indian NCO of the British Army, to guard the oil and petrol storage depots in the bay of Enzeli. They had to be protected from any potential acts of sabotage, the petrol being essential for the motorized units of the British Dunsterforce, which had crossed Mesopotamia and Persia in small Ford cars. A boat would come each day from Enzeli, to bring us food and take back our report to HQ. The bay itself was surrounded by tropical marshland where mosquitoes proliferated, and after several days I fell ill with a high fever. The doctor attached to the MP HQ at Enzeli gave me some quinine which, on the good advice of the British soldiers in my patrol, I drank with a glass of the potent local brandy, *dji-dji*, and this cured me in no time. In fact, next day I was back at my post. The British certainly know how to cure fevers as well as the curative properties of a stiff drink!

During our stay at Enzeli we made friends with many young men serving in the Military Police, with one glaring exception – a Sergeant-Major Reed. He was a brute and a sadist, despised by his men. The system of justice enforced by the British in Persia was the same as the one practised in India: Persians arrested on suspicion of a criminal offence were brought before the young lieutenant on duty, who would examine each case with the aid of a Persian interpreter and give judgement. Those found guilty were sentenced to flogging – this being the normal practice in the East. It happened quite frequently, and it was always Sergeant-Major Reed who volunteered to carry out the punishment, flogging the miserable wretch with sadistic pleasure, and drenching him afterwards with cold water to revive him.

One day I had a serious confrontation with Reed. He had summoned my brother and me to stand in line in the Barrack Square, along with the Persian soldiers serving under him. I had assumed that we had been summoned to be told the latest order of the day, but no, he was determined to make us join in a routine session of square-bashing and be taught the elementary rules of military drill. I told the sergeant-major that this was not applicable to us since we were Russian liaison officers, not raw Persian recruits. Nevertheless he insisted that it was my duty to carry out his orders without question. My reply was that I was not under his orders. My brother, anxious to avoid an unpleasant incident, tugged at my elbow, muttering in Russian that we had better do as Reed asked to avoid any conflict, for the sergeant-major's violence was well known. But I had made up my mind not to give in, and I told Reed I was going straight to the colonel who would explain to him the terms under which my brother and I were engaged. The colonel then summoned Reed, and told him in front of everybody that my brother and I were attached to the Military Police on special terms. The soldiers were delighted, for they hated the sergeant-major and his brutal ways, and the colonel knew it. Reed was furious but there was nothing he could do. He saluted and stomped off, while the others congratulated us for standing our ground.

Much later on we heard that Reed had died in mysterious circumstances. One of the soldiers had a little dog, for it is a custom for British soldiers to have a mascot that follows the regiment wherever it goes. But Reed brutally killed the dog one day in front of everybody, just to show he had the upper hand. Next time he went on patrol he was killed, though nobody could say how or why.

3. THE ARMISTICE AND BRITISH OCCUPATION OF TRANSCAUCASIA

On 11 November 1918, the Armistice brought the First World War to a close. We had already been two months in Enzeli, and a feverish activity reigned in the city. The Turks were evacuating Transcaucasia, and Baku was to be occupied by the Allied forces. Colonel Cockerell, appointed Chief of the Allied Police Force in Baku, asked my brother and I to stay on as liaison officers, my brother acting as his interpreter.

The colonel and my brother left for Baku at once, but I stayed on for a while, to help with preparing lists of Armenian refugees, and organizing their transportation on board the many ships still anchored in the port of Enzeli. All were anxious to return to Baku as soon as possible, to find out what had happened to the families who stayed behind during the Turkish occupation, and the massacre which ensued, when the Turks had allowed the Tartars to kill and rape, burn and pillage at will. Long queues of refugees formed daily in the barrack square. I knew many of them personally, and each pleaded for preferential treatment. We worked without stopping throughout the day, then I would go down to the quayside to supervise the embarkations and check permits.

Then, one day, I had a message from Baku that Colonel Cockerell wanted me to join him as soon as possible, as there was much work for me there. There was also a letter from my brother with the good news that my father, step-mother and elder brother, as well as my aunt and her son, the surgeon attached to the hospital in 'Black City', were alive and well, the Turks having posted a single sentry at the hospital gate to keep the Tartars at bay. In this they showed the contempt they felt for the Tartars. Nevertheless, many friends and acquaintances had perished at the hands of the murderous Tartar hordes. I went at once to buy a big jar of melted butter and some rice to take with me, as I knew the food supply situation in Baku was still bad.

Colonel Cockerell's offices were in the Governor-General's Palace on Maritime Boulevard. As I walked into the courtyard I saw many agitated people anxiously seeking police protection after all the misfortunes they had suffered. The colonel there and then appointed me his liaison officer with the local government of Azerbaidjan, the most important question being to ensure the security of the Baku-Batumi pipeline as well as the oil supplies of Baku itself. The policy was to establish an independent state of Azerbaidjan, whose government, representing the various ethnic communities, would be easier to negotiate with than a strong military dictatorship. Everybody was in a hurry to make as much money as possible, for everybody knew the respite could not last. It was inevitable that within a year or two Russian armies, White or Red, would be back to reclaim the oil, indispensable for maintaining mobility.

After leaving hospital, my elder brother had not returned to his small flat in the city centre where it was still dangerous for Armenians. Therefore, to avoid it being requisitioned, our cousin, the surgeon, had arranged to sub-let it to a Jewish chemist who worked with him in the 'Black City' hospital, on the understanding that he would vacate the flat when the atmosphere calmed down. When the atmosphere did indeed improve with the arrival of the British, the chemist refused to leave. He liked the flat and wanted to keep it. A lawyer advised us that the best way to speed up legal proceedings was for a member of the family to enter the flat and remain there twenty-four hours. I therefore decided to use military tactics and to attempt a surprise entry. I knew that the flat was fitted with plugs and portable telephones, including one in the hall, so I planned to take an instrument with me to ring my brother as soon as I achieved entry as the chemist would obviously not allow me to use his. One evening, still wearing uniform, I took my brother's key and slowly opened the front door, which fortunately did not have a safety chain. I at once plugged in the instrument but as I began to dial the main telephone in the flat made short-ringing noises as its bell responded to my dialling. The chemist ran out in alarm, demanding to know what I was doing there. I revealed my identity and warned him that I was armed. Total chaos ensued as the chemist and his wife began to scream and shout. They then phoned the police to come and save them from attack by armed bandits.

Within minutes a detachment from the Allied Military Police arrived, headed by a young ginger-haired, freckle-faced Scots captain whom I already knew well. The captain, amazed to see me, asked, 'Where are the bandits?' The chemist pointed an accusing finger at me. The captain was furious to have been called out on a wild-goose chase, all the more so as the alarm had been passed on to Colonel Cockerell. The result was that we were all taken to see the Colonel, who was always in his office, day or night, and slept there on a simple camp bed with an army blanket. 'So, you're the bandit,' he exclaimed with amusement on seeing me enter the room. 'Yes, sir, it is I,' I replied, and explained how the chemist wished to profit from the difficulties the Armenians still found themselves in, by taking illegal possession of my brother's flat. Even though the British had taken over, the Tartars continued to ill-treat the Christians but left the Jews in peace. So he thought he could get away with it. As Christians, Armenians could expect no justice in a Moslem state. That was the sad situation and why we had decided to follow our lawyer's advice.

The chemist, who spoke no English, became increasingly worried at being excluded from the conversation. He tried to interrupt several times, but this only served to irritate the Colonel, who told him in German, which he spoke fluently, that he should wait his turn. When his turn came, it became obvious that the chemist did not really speak German, just a mix-ture of Russian and Yiddish. But he babbled happily away when asked for his version of events and the colonel heard him out in silence before telling him: 'You have no right to occupy this flat. You have raised a false alarm and summoned the police to try to turn the situation to your advantage! You are to vacate it within three days, and if you don't go I will order the police to evict you.' It was a firm decision, taken by a military man in a war situation in an occupied country. The colonel understood perfectly the local tensions and the danger in which the unprotected Armenians found themselves, and he was anxious to avoid having to take the case before a judge whose decision might not be impartial.

The British meanwhile worked to promote arrangements for the formation of a National Government of Azerbaidjan, instructions having come from London that the Tartars should have some sort of Parliament as well as their own national government. Faced with the benevolent attitude of the Allied Occupation Forces, the Azerbaidjani Tartars regained their courage and initiative. They recommenced their acts of terrorism against Christians, albeit in secret, and Armenians were being kidnapped on the street and hustled away to Guiandja, the old city of Elisavetpol, where they were tortured and killed. The local police denied all knowledge of these events and could not explain the disappearances, and the British, too, turned a deaf ear. Official policy was to maintain good relations with Azerbaidjan.

One day, as I was walking down one of the main streets in Baku, a friend riding in a hackney carriage ordered the driver to stop and called to me to get in as he had something important to tell me. An attempt had been made to kidnap one of our mutual friends, Artiusha Sergeyev who was, like us, a former officer in the Russian Imperial Army. As he was walking down the Telefonnaya, a hackney cab drew alongside and two men got out. Together with the driver, they then tried to force him into the cab, all in broad daylight at eleven in the morning. But Artiusha was heavily-built and he fought back, shouting for help. A British 'Tommy', walking nearby, had run to the rescue, and on seeing the soldier approach the three Tartars let go and fled. Artiusha thanked the young soldier and asked him home to join his family and friends in a celebration so they could toast his 'saviour'. I, too, was invited, my presence being essential since I spoke English.

When we arrived at the Sergeyev household everybody was already sitting at table, and I was placed next to the British 'Tommy' whose presence alone had been enough to put the cowardly assassins to flight. Many toasts were drunk to the 'saviour' for delivering Artiusha from extreme peril, but the soldier was a shy young man, unaware of the political background to the events in which he had become unwittingly involved. He simply could not understand why his intervention should be considered a 'miracle'. It fell to me to explain how the Armenians lived in fear of their lives since the terrible massacres of 1905 and 1918, and how the Tartars had recommenced their murderous practices, such as the attempted kidnapping he had himself witnessed. By the end of the evening he understood the reality of the situation, and was determined that his comrades should also be made aware of the terrible truth about the Moslem fanatics' behaviour.

At the beginning of 1919, Colonel Cockerell was transferred, but before he left he took the trouble to ensure that both my younger brother and I continued to work for the British. He arranged that my brother go to work as secretary and interpreter to a Major Brown who was head of the British Control Commission for Shipping, the British having requisitioned all the shipping in the Caspian Sea. I, likewise, was transferred to the offices of the British Control Commission for Maritime Transport and was attached to the personnel officer of the Caspian Merchant Fleet, a Captain Cook. The work here involved accounting and dealing with the salaries of the commission staff as well as of the crews of the requisitioned ships. My brother's duties included accompanying Major Brown on his frequent sea voyages to Krasnovodsk, Enzeli and other Caspian ports. Although the Caspian is not subject to heavy storms, the crossing is often uncomfortable because of the under-current swell which caused the ship to pitch and roll. My poor brother was constantly sea-sick, until the Major persuaded him to apply a cure which was always guaranteed to work – a couple of glasses of whisky downed quickly before departure. This infallible remedy was adopted as standard practice, to the enjoyment of both, and with stomach nerves tranquilized by the alcohol, they would happily set off on their journey.

One day a young Armenian mechanic responsible for the maintenance of our office equipment came to me to plead for my brother and I to intervene with Major Brown to save his sister. The young woman had been kidnapped by Tartars while the city was still under Turkish occupation and somehow she succeeded in getting a message out, begging him to rescue her. He knew she was being held prisoner by a Tartar peasant in a village quite near Baku. The matter was technically not within Major Brown's province but that of the local police. But as everybody knew, approaching them would be useless if not grievous in its consequences for the poor girl. On his own responsibility, Major Brown therefore sent out his sergeant and the young Armenian together in a jeep. The two of them drove to the specified village and returned with the girl unharmed. Both Colonel Cockerell and Major Brown had behaved as truly gallant and courageous British officers, generously unstinting in their assistance to the oppressed and defenceless. Shortly afterwards, the Colonel left Baku, and we bid him a tender farewell, wishing him all happiness and good health, and thanking him for everthing he had done. He was his usual cheerful wonderful self when I saw him again in 1924 in London, where he had a small shop for 'Artistic book bindings', opposite Harrods. We went to a bar nearby, to reminisce about days gone by over a couple of whiskies.

It was about this time that my elder brother's wife and family decided to make their way back to Baku. Far from offering a hoped-for security, the cities along the Volga had been buffeted both by the civil war and by the typhus epidemic, raging through Russia and leaving tens of thousands of victims in its wake. With great difficulty, they got as far as Astrakhan at the mouth of the Volga, by now in the hands of the Bolsheviks, only to find all communication with Baku cut off. Nevertheless, my sister-in-law's cousin managed to find a local fisherman willing to take a small group of Armenians to the port of Petrovsk. Petrovsk was not far to the north of Baku, and at the time still within the zone controlled by the 'White Russian' armies.

There was still a major complication, however, for all fighting-boats in Astrakhan were controlled by the Bolsheviks and authorization needed to be obtained from the local Communist Security (Cheka) Commandant. The price of their exit permit was that they include in the group a Red agent who would pose as an Armenian refugee to enter Petrovsk, where he had an important mission. My sister-in-law and the others were perfectly aware of what would happen to them if the 'Whites' found out. But my sister-in-law was an energetic, decisive woman, and her main aim was to get away as quickly as possible. The Red agent duly appeared, very correct and going out of his way to be pleasant and chatting with my little niece. Everyone tried to behave normally, although they could see that the agent and fisherman were armed. Three days later the boat docked in Petrovsk. The agent disembarked first, and somehow evaded the control of the 'White' port authorities. Clearly the whole operation had been carefully organized. The refugees then made their own way to Baku without further complications.

Meanwhile, because the Tartar-dominated Nationalist Mussavat Party was obliged to ensure that the Russian and Armenian minorities were also represented in Parliament, in accordance with the directives issued by the Allied Powers, my father, well-known for having organized the hospitals established by the Association of Petroleum Producers, had been appointed Minister of Public Health. Simultaneously with my father becoming Minister, a new Director-General of the Association of Petroleum Producers was appointed to replace him – a very rich Tartar industrialist, Mirza Assadulayev. Despite the tense relations between Tartars and Armenians, my father was always highly respected by Tartar industrialists, with many of whom he had excellent personal relations. He had worked closely with them for twenty-five years and he spoke their language. They also admired him for introducing a system of management that believed in conciliation between workers and bosses, thus avoiding endless crisis and confrontation. When he left the association, a solemn meeting was held with speeches eulogizing his achievements and a resolution granting him a handsome pension for life.

Yet, despite the continued presence of the British, sectarian tension between the Tartars and Armenians worsened every day. Rumours were rife that the Tartar Minister of Interior was preparing for another massacre, and when my father asked Mirza Assadulayev if these rumours were true, the old Tartar replied that the planned massacre would be only 'partial'. 'Anyway, you need not worry, for you personally are in no danger,' he added in an effort at reassurance. Father understood this to mean that the Tartar Government did not want to risk another carnage while the British were still in Baku. That must wait until the British left. In the meantime, they would content themselves with limited massacres in a few provincial cities.

My elder brother was so affected by the rumours that he became afflicted with nervous depression. Still weak after an attack of typhus, he found the tense atmosphere and stories of kidnapping and murder quite unbearable. He began to lose his hair, and small round bald patches appeared on his head, but it was difficult to arrange for any treatment in prevailing circumstances. He became so ill that even the return of his wife and little daughter could do nothing to lift him from his state of depression. It was decided to arrange for him to leave Baku, and go to Tiflis in Georgia where all was quiet for the moment under the Menshevik Government. But it would not be an easy journey. Trains from Baku to Tiflis were often attacked by bands of Tartars intent on kidnapping Armenian passengers and taking them to Guiandja for torture and death. So it was arranged that he travel with another Tartar friend of Father's, who was going to Tiflis on a diplomatic mission and would be travelling in a ministerial rail carriage. Tartar bands would never be allowed in a ministerial rail carriage, even if they stopped the train, and besides, with his blond hair and blue eyes, my brother didn't look typically Armenian.

Several days later, my younger brother, too, left Baku, to accompany Major Brown on one of his inspection tours, and shortly afterwards my father also left for Tiflis, again in the ministerial carriage, together with the Armenian deputy who was my elder brother's brother-in-law. The situation in Baku had so deteriorated that it was no longer safe for any Armenian to remain, not even if he was in an official position.

But I stayed on. The British Control Commission had finished its work, and the local staff were transferred to the offices of the biggest shipping line in southern Russia, called 'Mercury and the Caucasus', which operated ships on the Volga and the Caspian. The ships requisitioned by the British had reverted to the ownership of the company and I had a lot of work to do.

The ambition of the Nationalist Mussavat Party was to see Azerbaidjan consolidated as an independent republic, as the Western Allies had promised. But once again, this proved to be a policy of mere words. The Allies were already engaged in supporting the White Armies of General Denikin against the Bolsheviks in southern Russia. The advance of the Red Armies towards the mountains of Daghestan and Baku meanwhile, threatened the independence of the new republic and the government tried to raise and organize an Azerbaidjani national army. The task was rendered almost impossible by the non-existence of any trained cadres, for under Tsarist rule the Tartars had been exempt from military service. Nevertheless, several months later, I watched the new Tartar army march along Merkurievskaya Street, where we lived, towards Petrovsky Square. The Tartars thronging the streets were delighted with this demonstration of military force, but in truth they were a pitiful sight. The bearing of the marchers bore little resemblance to the military gait of a trained soldier, although efforts had been made to instil some military spirit into the raw recruits by making them sing as they marched, in accordance with Russian military custom. The band, too, was Russian, as there were no Tartar musicians available, and a special song had been composed for the occasion: *'Irali, irali, Azerbaidjan Askeri'* ('March on, march on, ye soldiers of Azerbaidjan').

Before long these same raw recruits were used to massacre Christian Armenians when the Minister of the Interior, Djevanshir, sent them to various provincial cities to assist the bands of Tartar thugs, ever-ready to start a fresh carnage. And it was on the Minister's direct orders that the Armenian quarters of Shusha, where our family was born, were set on fire and completely destroyed, only a very few inhabitants surviving the holocaust by fleeing to the mountains before eventually making their way into the neighbouring states of Armenia and Persia. Towards the end of 1919 rumours intensified of preparations being made for a fresh massacre of Christians in Baku itself.

The year 1920 began with the Red Army winning victory after victory, thus precipitating the rout of the White forces. More and more Russian deserters began to appear on the streets of Baku and White Russian families also arrived in increasing numbers, on their way out of the country, though many did not have the means to continue their journey and had to remain. As the 11th Red Army of the Caucasus advanced rapidly towards Baku, there was much talk of an ultimatum issued to the Azerbaidjani authorities. The Government did not even consider the possibility of a show of resistance, the total lack of fighting ability of the army being apparent to all. The high dignitaries, the Ministers and the rich disappeared as fast as they could, only leaving as a 'precious hostage' my old acquaintance the ninety-seven-year-old Hadji-Zeinal Taghiev, still considered to be the symbol of the National Republic who refused to leave his country. An atmosphere of total terror reigned over the city as the Armenians anxiously awaited the arrival of the Red Army to free them from the threat of total genocide.

Early in the morning of 28 April 1920, our Russian maid Fenya, who did not live in the house, came running in great excitement to announce that the Red Army had taken over the city. It was all done simply and quickly: an armoured train pulled into Baku station and the Commanding Officer stepped off and declared that Azerbaidjan was liberated. The Red Army was taking over control. The Christian population, both Russian and Armenians, received the liberators with open arms, for it meant the end of the Tartar massacres.

Within days the streets were flooded with victorious Red Army soldiers mounted on an incredible mixture of horses and camels, some of the units having fought the campaigns in the Kalmuk steppes. 'The beauty and pride of the glorious Revolution', as the sailors of the Baltic and Black Sea Fleets styled themselves, were also represented. The victors had marched south in search of food, their pockets full of money, for there had been nothing to spend it on on the way: the Civil War had devastated Russia, and famine had spread across the land. All at once they found themselves walking down the streets lined with shops full of an infinite variety of goods, for Baku's trade had never ceased to prosper as oil continued to be exported through the Georgian and Black Sea ports, bringing in large revenues with which the traders could import anything they wished.

Two days after the Red Army took control of the city, big posters appeared on the streets with an order issued by the Army HQ, stating that 'all former officers should, without exception, present themselves tomorrow morning at the Opera for registration'. When I arrived at the Opera at nine next morning, the auditorium was already full with ex-officers waiting their turn. Each one was issued with a questionnaire – the famous Soviet *anketa* (from the French *enquete*, which means 'investigation'). After all the forms were completed and handed in, we were told to report at 6 a.m. the following day at the quayside in Petrovsky Square, for transportation to the island of Narghen, situated at the entrance to the port of Baku (where Turkish prisoners had been kept during the war).

When I returned home to relate to the family what had happened, our maid Fenya said I was not to worry. Her husband was a Communist Party member (a fact of which we were completely unaware), and she would get him to intervene on my behalf. Astonished but unimpressed, I decided to make my way to the quayside as instructed, taking with me a small bag with clean linen and a blanket, for the nights were still cold although it was already the end of April. But when I arrived at the quayside, there was nobody there, nor was there a ship in sight. I waited half an hour, but still nothing happened, so I decided to go to the office as usual. On my way there, I noticed people crowding round some new wall-posters. It was an official Communique, this time issued by the Red Army's Special Department ('Osobyj Otdel', or OO for short), listing the names of 190 officers, described as 'the rabble remnants of the White Armies', who had been shot during the night in accordance with the decision of the Revolutionary Tribunal. I was absolutely stunned by this demonstration of ruthless efficiency as practised by the Red Courts. They had examined 190 dossiers, given judgement and executed those found guilty, all in a single night.

It was my good fortune that I had not fought with the White Army and that I had been mobilized in 1918 by the Red Army HQ of the Caucasus. Somewhat reassured by this apparently benign divine control over my destiny, I returned to my office at the newly designated Directorate of Maritime Transport. This had now been transferred to a big building on Olginskaya Street, which before being requisitioned had housed a series of shops. My desk was right next to the shop window which had formerly exhibited the delicious bread and cakes sold by the Stepanian Patisserie, now closed, all such shops being considered just another form of bourgeois self-indulgence!

All commercial enterprises had been nationalized, and whereas the offices of the shipping line Mercury and the Caucasus had operated successfully from only one floor, the nationalised company now took up three floors of an enormous building. I had practically nothing to do all day, as there were now several dozen clerks to do the work which three people easily coped with when the company was in private hands. Yet one of the basic slogans of Communist propaganda was 'Down with Bureaucracy'. The main advantage of having a job was that employees received a guaranteed ration of rye bread each day, white bread having completely disappeared.

At home, too, there were changes. One of the rooms in the house was requisitioned and we now had a lodger, an elderly Russian appointed professor at the newly opened University in Baku. A shy, well-educated man, he was so poorly paid that he could barely afford a decent meal, and our cook had to prepare for him exactly the same meagre dish each day: a small piece of fish with a few boiled potatoes. We put him in Father's study where there was a sofa he could sleep on and a desk to work at. Our own financial resources were also becoming rather limited, but we still had the income of my step-mother, who continued to work as a doctor in the 'Black City' hospital, as well as my own salary and the daily bread ration that went with my job.

Several weeks later we received notification that the whole house was to be taken over for the use of the new 'Commissariat for Culture' of Soviet Azerbaidjan. The entire family, as well as the recently installed lodger were moved to more humble accommodation. The professor was to be found a room elsewhere. Our new tiny flat, in the very centre of the town, had a small drawing-room where my step-mother could receive patients, a dining-room, two bedrooms, a bathroom and small kitchen. We were delighted with this act of generosity on the part of the new administration, until we discovered that the building opposite housed the dreaded Cheka HQ. Every day we saw long queues of unhappy people waiting for the guards to accept parcels brought for detained relatives. The sad spectacle was made even more tragic by the brutal way they were treated by the guards.

The victorious Red Army was in a hurry and people were arrested on the slightest suspicion, regardless of guilt or innocence. There was, for example, the case of my step-mother's cousin, a young married man with a small child. After completing his university studies in Paris, he had returned during the war to help his aged father, who owned a small factory in Baku. He was not involved in politics in any way, but just managed the factory, and was much respected by the workforce. Nevertheless, he was arrested and imprisoned. The factory workers' committee made an official representation that he be freed, while his distraught father tried to intervene through influential Communist acquaintances. He was promised that his son would be freed two days hence, but when the old man presented himself at the Cheka HQ at the appointed time he was told he could have his son's effects since he had been executed 'by mistake' the previous day!

No sooner had we moved in than we were presented with a new lodger. He was installed in one of the two bedrooms, while I slept on the sofa in the small drawing-room. As luck would have it, he, too, was a graduate of the Mikhajlovskoe Artillery School in St Petersburg, now a full colonel serving with the Red Army as artillery inspector. We got on well and he was a great help in supplementing our food rations out of his own more plentiful military entitlement. One evening, as we chatted over dinner, he was appalled to hear that I was wasting my time in the Directorate of Maritime Transport and proposed that I be transferred to the Red Army as chief instructor in a new, much-needed School of Artillery for N.C.O.s that he was about to organize in Baku. At that stage there were no officers as such in the Red Army, all officers being called instructors. I was tempted by his offer and eventually decided to accept.

The Civil War was over, I was 22 years old, and things were bound to improve. At least it would mean an interesting job instead of the senseless, badly paid one I did at the Directorate of Maritime Transport. Moreover, I would start with the rank of lieutenant-colonel as chief instructor, with a good salary, and ample food rations. This latter consideration was particularly important because my step-mother had fallen ill with acute anaemia brought on by malnutrition and further complicated by an attack of boils. We had also, in the meantime, adopted a little orphan girl, and she, too, needed to be properly fed.

The one problem was that I had been mobilized to serve in the 'Water-Transport' sector and could not transfer jobs without official authorization. However, the inspector assured me that he would himself make all the necessary arrangements and so, the following morning, the two of us went together to Army HQ where I was officially entrusted with two tasks: firstly to find a suitable building to house the new School of Artillery of which I would be commandant; secondly, and this was an order of a more military nature given in writing, to go and inspect the fortifications that the deposed Tartar Government had built on the Apsheron Peninsula, around Baku.

I spent the next two days trying to find a suitable building for the new school, but on returning home on the second day I was handed an 'invitation' to present myself to a section of the Cheka in Torgovaya Street. There was no joking with these comrades, so I hastened to the indicated address and showed my 'invitation' to the head guard. He looked at it and said, 'Comrade X wishes to see you.' This mystified me even more, for 'X' was a name quite unknown to me. Upstairs, Comrade 'X' received me most courteously, invited me to sit down and asked if I knew a certain Mrs Y who had the same surname as myself. It was no use pretending otherwise, so I said, 'Yes, indeed, she's my sister-in-law, the wife of my elder brother Sarkis.' 'Oh, that's wonderful,' replied Comrade X. 'I asked you to come along because I did not want to trouble her. I was anxious to have news of her. You see, we met when we travelled together in a fishing boat from Astrakhan to Petrovsk, and I wondered how she was, also her little daughter.' So Comrade 'X' was the important Red agent they had had to take along in the boat as the price of their exit visas! I replied calmly that my sister-in-law and my niece were well and in good health. 'Oh, I am so happy to hear it,' he said 'Please remember me to her and convey my affectionate greetings. Tell her that they come from comrade N.N., for this was the name I used during my journey, and X is the name I use at present. Good-bye, dear comrade, and good luck.'

I left the amiable comrade and ran downstairs and out of the building, hastening to tell my sister-in-law of the impression she had made on the comrade in the Cheka. She was only too delighted to hear that he was too busy to call upon her in person, for she could never forget the fear she suffered throughout that terrible journey with the mysterious passenger inflicted upon them. And now here he was in Baku, inquiring tenderly after her just as her husband was away in Tiflis! And what if she applied to join her husband? It could all lead to very unpleasant complications. Fortunately, we never heard from him again.

But two days later I received another summons from the Cheka. This time it was more serious, for the matter concerned me personally. I had just returned to the flat for a quick lunch. It was a very hot day. My step-mother and recently adopted little sister were also at home, but our lodger was not there as he was away on a job. No sooner had we sat down to our simple meal than a young man in short sleeves arrived and asked me to follow him to the Mor-Cheka (Naval Security HQ) where someone wished to speak to me. It was not very far, he said. I had no option but to accompany him, and left my meal unfinished as we set off towards Maritime Boulevard where the Mor-Cheka had its offices in a pretty house, built in the Oriental style.

We climbed a narrow staircase to the second floor, where I was received by a sailor of the Red Fleet, acting as examining magistrate. He produced the usual *Anketa* and proceeded to fill in my name, age, address and so on before getting down to the interrogation proper. He wanted to know why I had absented myself from my duties at the Directorate of Maritime Transport for over a week and why I had deserted my post without permission. I assured him there was no question of desertion, and told him about the offer made by the artillery inspector and his promise to personally arrange all the necessary formalities for my transfer to the Red Army. Fortunately, I still had on me the written order issued by the Army Inspectorate, instructing me to carry out the inspection of the fortifications on Apsheron Peninsula. The sailor took the paper and put it on his desk, saying gruffly, 'We'll have to check all that.' 'Can I go now?' I asked, and for a while there was no reply. Then he summoned the guard and told him: 'Take the prisoner away!' I was under arrest.

The guard took me down to the ground floor, to a room at the front of the building, facing the Boulevard. At one time it had been occupied by a greengrocer's shop, but now was used as a 'provisional' prison. It was a big room, with two sliding metal grills to the left and right, through which one could see passers-by outside and they could see in. The room contained not a single stick of furniture. There were already about ten people, sitting on the floor or lying, all Tartars who told me they had been arrested on suspicion of being members of the Mussavat Party, which had formed the National Government overthrown by the arrival of the Red Army.

In the evening, the Tartars were brought food from home, but there was none for me since my family didn't know where I was. I was very hungry, having left the flat without lunch, but my companions in misfortune invited me to share some of theirs. It was a typical Oriental meal – rice with chicken – and everybody ate with their fingers, according to Oriental custom. I tried to do the same, but without much success, and noticing my difficulty one of the old Tartars told the others to give me a spoon quickly, otherwise I would starve. Everybody laughed and a spoon was produced at once.

Two days after my initial interrogation, I was called again to face the Red sailor, this time for a confrontation with the deputy inspector of artillery, also an ex-Tsarist officer who had joined the Red Army as an artillery specialist and who was standing in for the chief inspector while he was away at the Front. He confirmed that he had seen me at GHQ with the chief inspector, and that I had been given the written order that I handed to the Red sailor at our first meeting. Nothing more could be done, however, until the return of the chief inspector himself, since it was he who would arrange the formalities for my transfer to the Red Army. I would have to wait patiently for another few days, and so was taken back downstairs.

In the meantime, my step-mother had found where I was and fresh linen and a blanket were brought in. After four days, the guards took us all down to the cellars where beds had been improvised by putting planks down on the floor of beaten earth. The cellar was full of hungry rats, and one night one of the Tartars was badly bitten. The animals were so famished they were not afraid to come out even in the full electric light. Before long the Tartars were taken away, no doubt to be sentenced and shot in summary fashion.

My good fortune was to have been detained not by the Cheka proper but by the Mor-Cheka which took a somewhat more 'professional' approach to detainees. Ten days after my arrest the Red sailor summoned me again and with a beaming smile told me I was being granted 'provisional liberty', until such time as a tribunal could judge my case of 'desertion from duty'. I must sign a document promising not to leave Baku until my case came up in court. I signed, for there was no alternative. Either I signed or stayed in prison.

Back at home I busied myself with arrangements for the departure to Georgia of my sister-in-law with her little daughter, and of my step-mother with the Armenian orphan. They already had Georgian entry visas and were now awaiting authorization from the Soviet authorities to allow them to leave with all their goods and chattels. Arrangement was made whereby a goods waggon filled with their furniture and luggage would be attached to the ordinary passenger train from Baku to Tiflis.

Their departure was finally fixed for the beginning of October 1920, and on the day everything seemed to be going to plan. Their luggage, together with that of other Armenians granted exit visas, had already been loaded into the reserved goods waggon, and we stood on the platform saying our farewells and waiting for the signal for departure. Suddenly the Soviet commissar attached to the station came up to complain that something was not in order. I didn't know what to do, but looking around, I noticed that the customs officer who acted as assistant to the commissar was a Georgian I had got to know well when I was working for Colonel Cockerell. In the hope that he could help I approached him to ask if something could perhaps be arranged by bribing the commissar. I was taking a risk, but he readily agreed to speak to the commissar and told me to have the money ready. It was the first time in my life I had attempted to bribe anybody, and I was terrified, the new regime being implacable. However, he returned to say that all was agreed and that a meeting with the commissar would take place some distance away, between two trains standing in the station. Surreptitiously, I handed over the money, and at last my family got away, albeit with a slight delay because of last-minute negotiations to smooth the path. I was now the only member of the immediate family left in Baku, for my brother had already found a new job with the Tiflis office of the American Relief Association, which was concerned with the distribution of food to the starving population of Transcaucasia, as well as in Russia itself.

Soon after my family's departure I received a letter from my father, who was back in Tiflis after visiting the Armenian capital Erevan. He wrote to say that he was being sent to Europe as Minister Plenipotentiary of the Armenian Republic to discuss sales of oil. His first stop would be Romania, and he would like me to accompany him since this would give me a chance to complete my higher education at a European university. I was to make my way to Tiflis as soon as possible.

I had to think of a way of leaving Baku, and decided that the best plan would be to take advantage of the Armenian Repatriation Scheme. But there was still the problem of the summons I was awaiting to answer the ridiculous charge of desertion from duty. I arranged to be hospitalized for a minor operation, to obtain a postponement of the hearing, and then put my name down on the list of those desiring evacuation by the first available train, due to leave in a few days. My luck held. The appointed day arrived without the summons being presented and I was told to go to the station and embark on the goods train taking Armenian emigrés through Georgia on their way to their homeland. I knew many of them, young people like myself, all hoping to build a new life in the Independent Armenian Republic. Everything went well to begin with, although the train was travelling at an incomprehensibly slow speed, with long stops on the way. Only later did we find out that the reason for this was that the Soviet High Command was busy making preparations for the invasion of Armenia.

When we arrived at the small station of Poily we faced an unexpected calamity. The Georgians refused to allow us entry, even though we were only travelling in transit. We were told that the country was already flooded with Armenian refugees, and that a new war had broken out between Armenia and Turkey, who objected to the terms laid down by the Treaty of Sèvres, signed in August 1920, whereby the Allies demanded that the Turks give up the provinces of Erzerum, Trebizond, Van and Bitlis, to be included in the western part of the new Armenian Republic. The new Government in Turkey, headed by Kemal Pasha Atatürk, refused to recognize the Sèvres Treaty and several Turkish divisions had crossed the frontier on 22 September to retake the ceded provinces.

For us, the direct consequence was that we were stranded in a refugee train at a small frontier post where there were no village shops, no houses, nothing – just the little cottage where the station guard lived. Passengers had only brought enough food to last the two-days journey to Tiflis, and this soon disappeared. One of the passengers tried to keep our spirits up by playing a violin he had with him.

After several days we were told that we could cross the bridge into Georgia. Somebody must have intervened in Tiflis to allow the repatriation to go ahead. But first we had to pass through a check-point where 'Comrade Lyuba', a young snub-nosed Soviet lady commissar armed with a gun, examined our papers against her list of repatriates. I had told no one that I had signed a declaration not to leave Baku and I was fairly confident that the Soviet authorities would not yet have notified any of the border posts. Still, it was a great relief to cross the bridge and leave Comrade Lyuba behind.

Passengers with Georgian visas left the same day on the train to Tiflis. Not having a visa, I asked friends among them to notify my elder brother in Tiflis that I had got as far as Poily and that he should make arrangements for me to join him. In the meantime, I tried to see for myself what the chances were of getting away.

The following day a special train arrived from Baku, carrying British nationals expelled by the new Soviet Republic of Azerbaidjan. I walked along the train and, as I passed a luggage van with its sliding doors open, saw in it two Englishmen, one of whom, Mr Coutts, I knew well. I explained my difficulty and asked him to let me jump into the luggage van as the train started to move. Mr Coutts readily agreed and I crossed to the other side of the train to have more chance of doing this without being seen. No sooner had the train started to move than I jumped aboard through the door especially left open. Unfortunately, I was seen by a Georgian guard who blew his whistle and the train stopped. There was nothing for it but get off again. I was then arrested and locked up in the station-master's office, together with a young Armenian student who had tried the same trick. We were kept under lock and key until evening when the station master allowed us to walk up and down the platform to stretch our legs a bit. It was a hint, probably, that he was willing to let us go free – for a consideration. But neither the student nor I had any Georgian money, and as night began to fall I suggested an attempt to escape and hide in the darkness. Crossing the railway, we ran across the neighbouring fields to get as far away as possible from the station. Then we turned left and followed the line to the next station. We had been told that the first two stations down the line were to be avoided, as they were surrounded and patrolled by Georgian Red guards, but that after that the way was clear. The night was quite dark and we had been marching along the railway sleepers for a while when we were suddenly attacked by large sheep-dogs which guarded the flocks against wolves. We tried to drive them away by throwing ballast from between the sleepers. Fortunately, the shepherds soon appeared, alarmed by the noise and shouting, and called off the dogs.

We passed what we thought were the two stations patrolled by Red guards, until we came to a small station, all lit up, thinking we were safely outside the cordon of troops. Alas, one of the stations we had passed was only a minor halt. We were, in fact, right inside the cordon of armed Red guards, one of whom intercepted us and escorted us to the rail carriage that served as guard room. The officer was not there, so we were interrogated by a corporal who ordered us to remain in the carriage with the soldiers until the following morning. The soldiers paid not the slightest attention to us, drinking and chatting among themselves and finally settling to sleep on the floor. When practically all of them were asleep, I turned to my companion and asked if he spoke German. When he confirmed that he did, I switched to German, proposing that we make another attempt to escape. He at once answered in Russian: 'Why do you want to escape?' I sighed. Obviously I wouldn't stand much chance with such an idiot. Fortunately, the soldier on duty had not overheard our whispered conversation.

I dozed for another hour, then asked the soldier on guard if I could go out to relieve myself. He got off the train with me, and while he was busy chatting to another guard, I ran off into the surrounding darkness as fast as my legs could carry me. He shouted after me, telling me to stop and firing into the air. But it was dark, and I was already too far away, so after a while he gave up. At dawn I arrived at a small river, washed, cleaned my shoes, wiped some of the dirt off my trousers and had a little rest before continuing. Coming to a narrow country lane, I walked along it until I met an old Tartar peasant driving a cart with two oxen. I asked him where he was going, and he replied in broken Russian that he was returning to his village, Kara-Yazi. He would give me a lift by all means. I knew Kara-Yazi had a station, so I climbed into his cart, which continued its leisurely pace to the village, where we arrived about mid-day. He dropped me in the village square, at the tea-house, which was the centre of all village life. I only had some Azerbaidjani money, but the proprietor was happy to accept it so I sat down and ordered tea with fresh bread and cheese.

Soon I was joined by a Georgian wearing a soldier's greatcoat, who sat down at my table and ordered his meal. Seeing I was not Georgian, he confided that he was a deserter who had come to the village to hunt bear. He had already shot one and now hoped to sell the carcass in Tiflis. It was in the large sack he had placed next to his chair. We agreed to walk to the station together to catch the next train going in the direction of Tiflis. We arrived at the station at about five o'clock in the afternoon, and sat down in the station buffet to wait. When a train finally pulled into the station, and we were getting up to go and board it, I suddenly saw my elder brother entering the buffet. accompanied by the train's guard and engine driver! We rushed to embrace. Advised by fellow passengers of my whereabouts, he had rushed to the frontier post at Poily to collect me, but on arrival was told I had disappeared. All he could do was to return to Tiflis.

On the way to Poily he had made friends with the guard, and the two of them had been wondering what to do next. They went to have a drink in the buffet to talk things over and there, by a stroke of incredible luck, found me. There were loud shouts of happiness at this unexpected reunion from the two Georgians, who at once suggested we have some more drinks to celebrate the success of my brother's mission. The train was at our disposal. It could wait until the celebration was over! Everybody joined in, including the deserter with the bear's carcass. Brandy and wine was ordered all round and, as is customary in that part of the world, the jovial Georgians began to sing in our honour songs composed on the spur of the moment.

In the end the station master came to say that he could not delay the train any longer. We all got on, the whistle of departure was sounded, and we were off. Everything was carefully arranged with the guard, and the train stopped at a small halt a quarter of a mile before Tiflis to allow us to get off and avoid the control-check at Tiflis station. And so we arrived, without further complication, at the house where my brother lodged with his family. They were all there to greet me, including his new-born son, delivered on 7 October, on the evening of the same day my sister-in-law arrived from Baku after a two-day journey. My own trip from Baku had taken nine days, but at last we were all together again.

My father had just left on his official mission abroad. My brother had managed to get us all passports and the necessary visas, and thanks to the intervention of the British Consul passages had been booked on the S.S. *Ionic* bound for France. The year 1921 was just beginning and it was a propitious time to be leaving the turmoil of events in the Caucasus, for by the end of February it was Georgia's turn to be swallowed up by the new Soviet empire. The whole of Transcaucasia was about to be reoccupied by its old masters, the Russians, with the exception of the provinces of Kars and Ardaghan. They had been annexed by the Turks, but the Soviets did not feel strong enough at that moment to confront Turkey and also seize those two remaining Armenian provinces.

4. ASSIGNMENTS IN ROMANIA

During the years that followed my departure from Tiflis I graduated from the Berlin School of Economic Studies and then completed a course at a commercial college in the United Kingdom. I left London in February 1925 to settle down to a life in business. First I worked with an oil company in Romania, founded by my elder brother with his brother-in-law and a group of Paris bankers. Five years later, when they resigned from the board and returned to France, I, too, left and went as an accountant to a new British oil-drilling company founded by two Englishmen, one of whom was an oil-drilling expert, Tom Walton, whom I had known well in Baku. The new firm soon operated with some success, and during the next ten years drilled some 115 oil wells for the big companies, at much cheaper rates than the big companies, with their large overheads, could have done it themselves. It operated from Ploesti, the oil centre some forty miles north of Bucharest, and it was there that in 1930 I first met Dro, the Dashnak nationalist guerrilla.

Over the years that I knew him, Dro often spoke of his life in Moscow after the sovietization of Armenia in 1920. When the Turkish army crossed the frontier to retake the provinces ceded under the Treaty of Sèvres, the Armenian Government sent a delegation to Moscow to plead for help. A Soviet mission arrived in Erevan, but they dragged out the negotiations to force Armenia to accept Moscow's conditions, however hard and disadvantageous they may be. They had come with instructions to do a deal with the Turks: Armenia would have to surrender to the Turks and two provinces of Kars and Ardhagan. In exchange, the Turks would withdraw from Alexandropol, and Azerbaidjan would now take over the province of Karabagh. Stalin himself arrived in Baku, and the fate of independent Armenia was sealed – it would henceforth be a Soviet republic.

For a whole month, the small Armenian army had fought fiercely to defend its homeland, but their position became impossible once the Soviet Government agreed with the Turks to allow the Azerbaidjani Tartar units to attack the Armenians from the other side. Threatened by superior forces from all sides, the Armenians didn't stand a chance and had no option but to sign the peace treaty with the Turks.

It was Dro, acting as Armenian plenipotentiary, who signed the final agreement. Stalin, who knew him personally from the days when they were both young revolutionaries in 1904-1905, offered him the command of the Turkestan military region, on the frontier with Persia and China. But Dro did not want to go, and Stalin agreed that he should remain in Moscow. In Moscow, Dro started a small Armenian co-operative and managed a Caucasian restaurant, which was very popular, but he remained virtually a prisoner. Eventually, he decided to ask Stalin's permission to leave the

USSR, using as a pretext the need to persuade the Central Committee of the Armenian National Dashnak Party, whose headquarters were in Boston in the United States, to end its hostile activities against the Soviet Communist regime. He undertook to find grounds for compromise and possible co-operation. Stalin received Dro in the Kremlin, where he lived in a small apartment of three rooms and a kitchenette, in the block formerly used as the servants' quarters in the times of the Tsars. He invited Dro to stay to dinner – a simple meal, the only luxury he allowed himself being some luscious fruit, brought specially from the Crimea or the Caucasus, and a bottle of rough red Georgian wine from Kakhetia, which was Stalin's favourite. Stalin would drink a bottle a day, a habit acquired during his youth in the Caucasus.

To this day, I cannot understand how Dro succeeded in persuading such a cunning and suspicious man as Stalin to accept his proposition, but Stalin authorized his departure. Perhaps it was in the memory of their comradeship in the old days, when they had met as young revolutionaries, or was it that Stalin was already thinking of the war against Hitler, ten years hence? Whatever the reason, one could only admire Dro's ingenuity and guile. He was allowed to leave Moscow in 1929, together with his eldest son Luther (named after a fellow Dashnak killed in Turkey), but his wife and two other sons had to stay behind as hostages. All three were subsequently arrested and deported to Siberia, where they died. Dro knew this could happen, but he had dedicated his entire life to the Armenian cause and family; wife and children took second place.

On leaving Moscow, Dro came to Romania where he got a job in an oil refinery in Ploesti, as a supervisor. He was paid a small salary by the refinery's managing director, who was exceptionally mean, living even more modestly than Dro, though naturally allowing himself a much bigger salary. One day Dro, who was endowed with all the skills of a born merchant, proposed a profitable deal. They would form a new company, with the Managing Director investing some capital and Dro acting as broker, buying and selling 'coupons'. Both the small oil producers and the owners of oil-rich lands who had leased them to the big oil companies for exploitation, would receive fixed dues in the form of these 'coupons', which represented a percentage of the total crude oil output from the oil wells drilled on their land. There were various broker firms in Bucharest and Ploesti who would buy these certificates, re-selling them in lots to the refineries at a good profit as their value was enhanced. It was an expanding, highly competitive market, and Dro entered it determined to outbid all the others.

It was hard, intensive work, and although his Romanian was limited if colourful (to put it mildly) he had a persuasive manner and knew how to create a congenial atmosphere to establish friendly relations with his clients. At the same time, he knew how to establish good relations with the management of the big oil companies, and had the knack of persuading them to grant certain advantages, such as accelerating the pumping or the mixing of various grades of petrol necessary to promote business. In a country like Romania, all sorts of gifts and gratuities at Christmas and Easter, not to mention the greasing of palms with money, were accepted normal practice.

Little by little, Dro became well known in the oil-fields. He opened a small office in Ploesti, and his unfailing energy and initiative helped business to prosper, so much so that in 1937, one of the oil companies in Bucharest offered him the job of manager of their Ploesti Agency for its sales of crude oil. I had by then, in 1937, also joined this company as chief accountant, and it was my task to prepare the monthly balance sheets, showing the profits achieved. All of this gave me ample opportunity to observe Dro's extraordinary talents for sales-promotion, even though he left school early and never studied at college. He could forecast exactly the revenues forthcoming each month as a result of his deals, and his rule-of-thumb estimates were invariably correct.

Dro's astuteness was amply confirmed when he had a major confrontation with the company's three main directors in Bucharest. Clever and able businessmen though they were, they badly underestimated Dro, believing him to be a primitive soul who might easily be hoodwinked. Why, he lacked the ability even to learn the language of the country! They failed to realize that his simple, unceremonious manner was a ruse to conceal intelligence and cunning. And so, one day when he was in Bucharest for the usual conference to compare the end-of-the-month accounts, he noticed that the directors' beautifully typed calculations did not correspond to his own. He asked for a detailed statement, and with his extraordinary memory had no difficulty in pointing out discrepancies between the prices and quantities and the figures entered by the Bucharest accountant. He put on such an act of outraged fury that the three directors were absolutely terrified. Knowing his revolutionary past and what he was capable of, they did their best to calm him down, laying all the blame on the incompetence of a clerk in the accounting office. Their explanations were somewhat vague, but Dro accepted them, realizing he had given them a fright that would stand him in good stead.

In organizing his business, Dro never forgot his old party comrades and gave some of them jobs. There was, for instance, a charming, frail elderly gentleman called Sharafyan, a great Armenian patriot sentenced to ten years' hard labour in Siberia by the last Tsarist Government. Now a refugee in Romania, his health much impaired by so many years' hard labour, he worked in Dro's office as a cashier. Another was Missak, whose entire family perished in the Moslem massacres and who eventually found his way to Constantinople. There in 1921, the Dashnak Party entrusted him with an important mission - to assassinate Djevanshir, the former Minister of the Interior who organized the massacres of Christian Armenians by Azerbaidjani army units and bands of Tartar assassins before the entry of the Red Army into Baku.

When the Red Army took control in Azerbaidjan, Djevanshir had fled to Constantinople, together with other Tartar dignitaries, and set himself up in style in the grand Hotel Tokatlyan on the rue de Pera, in the very centre of the city. Missak spent some time wtching the ex-Minister's movements, and then one day, as Djevanshir stood in the hotel lobby, went up to him and shot him at point-blank range with a Mauser. The Minister fell, mortally wounded, and in the panic and confusion Missak made his way to the streets and out of danger. But as he stood there, he suddenly remembered how the night before he dreamt he had fired at the Minister but the shots had not killed him. His nightmare seemed so real that he decided to go back into the hotel. By now there was a whole crowd round the Minister's body, and the police had arrived. Oblivious to everything except success of his task, Missak pushed his way to the front and fired several more shots into the prostrate body. The Turkish police arrested him, tortured and beat him almost to death in their efforts to get him to reveal the names of his accomplices, but fortunately the Allied Military Court acquitted and released him.

When Dro started his company Missak was not yet fully restored to health, but Dro took him under his wing and did not expect him actually to work. As he was penniless, he was given a small room at the back of the office to live in. It had a bed, a small table and an electric cooker. The room was stuffy and permeated with a variety of aromas, including Missak's favourite eau de cologne called Fleurs de Tabac, for like so many Orientals he loved to use scent. We used to refer to it among ourselves as 'Fleurs de Missak'. For him Dro represented the party to which his loyalty was total.

The three years I worked in the agency for crude oil sales were happy ones for me. The job was interesting, the pay ample for my needs. I made many new friends among the Romanians and foreigners who worked in the foreign oil companies operating from Ploesti. It was a tranquil corner of Europe, and life went on happily, seemingly quite unaffected by the dark storm clouds gathering over Europe as Hitler's troops marched successively into the Rhineland, then Austria, then Czechoslovakia. It was on 24 August 1939 that the Nazi-Soviet Pact was signed, and on Saturday 1 September I was in Sinaia, a beautiful resort in the Carpathians, some forty miles north of Bucharest. The high-society set customarily took refuge there from the stifling heat that engulfed the capital during the summer months. I was staying with friends who had a suite in the best hotel and we were drinking aperitifs and chatting when an odd impulse made me decide to switch on the wireless. I still remember that moment: premonition followed by the stunning announcement that Hitler's armies had attacked Poland at dawn. Although the Allies had guaranteed Poland's independence Hitler had been certain that they would give in and Britain do nothing, but on 3 September the Allies declared war on Germany and the Second World War erupted. A flood of Polish refugees began to cross the frontier into Romania where they hoped to receive a friendly welcome. They came on foot, horseback, by car or in carts, seeking shelter and food for themselves and their horses. Certain

Romanians, always on the look-out for a profitable deal, bought the desperate refugees' cars and jewellery for pittances, despite the fact that Poland was Romania's ally in the so-called 'Little Entente'. The Romanian Government, too, confiscated the gold reserves which the fleeing Polish Government brought with it into exile, on the grounds that they were needed to pay for the maintenance of the thousands of refugees. The Polish Prime Minister and his Ministers wasted no time in making their way to Britain to set up a government-in-exile, and continue to fight against the German aggressors.

At the close of 1939 Dro told me that he must go on an important mission to Berlin. That winter was even more bitter than usual in that part of the world, and it was very cold when I accompanied him to the station. An icy wind blew as we paced up and down the platform, trying to keep warm while waiting for the train from Bucharest. He explained, in strictest confidence, that he had received a letter from the Central Committee of the Dashnak Party in Boston saying that, in America, everyone was certain that sooner or later war would break out between Germany and Russia, despite their protestations of friendship. Poland was merely the first step in Hitler's conquest of the East, and it was imperative that the martyred Armenian nation should ensure she was on the side of the winner – whoever that might be! Although the Boston Committee sided with the Allies, and was certain that the United States would soon be forced to enter the war, it felt it was nevertheless also necessary to establish a link with the Germans – just in case!

Dro was to declare himself a dissident who disagreed with the committee's siding with the Allies. In Berlin, he was to establish a close liaison with the Nazis, presenting himself as the representative of the Armenian people, sorely oppressed by the Communist regime. The German policy of forming 'national legions' was well known, and a precondition of the alliance must be that any national units formed from Armenians among Red Army POWs would not be used against the USSR, but would be kept behind the lines until such time as the Germans occupied the Caucasus. They would then be used to maintain order and support a newly established National Government in a free and independent Armenia.

Dro did not care for the plan, but as a loyal Dashnak Party member he had to carry out the committee's orders. If the Germans accepted the proposals, they would have to allow him to visit POW camps to recruit any Armenians he could find there; and their military training, somewhere in the rear, would be undertaken only by agreement with Dro or his personal representative. They were not to be used without his knowledge or approval. The Germans agreed, and Dro made several trips to Berlin.

The spring of 1940 blossomed, and on the Western front, in France and Belgium, the so-called 'phoney war' continued. My friend from Baku and former employer, Tom Walton, had left Ploesti to work at the British Embassy, where he was attached to a special mission for the Ministry of

Economic Warfare. Always a great admirer of the British, and having worked with them in the First World War, I felt I wanted to do something to thwart the advance of the German aggressor, so I asked Tom if I could be of any use. It so happened that he had already thought of it, and several days later he confirmed that it had all been agreed and I would be working as his assistant.

When I told Dro that I would be leaving to work for the British, he did not want to release me and, for purely personal reasons, begged me to continue to act as his accountant in Bucharest, in my spare time. I reported this to the British, who agreed that the arrangement should continue. The British must have already known about Dro's frequent trips to Germany and his activities there, so it was in their interest for me to maintain contact with him and keep an eye on what was going on. I was now in the somewhat ambiguous position of working as an accountant in a Romanian oil company that exported valuable oil to Germany and, at the same time, assiduously helping my British directors with defending Allied interests. It was, however, very advantageous from the financial point of view, since I was being paid by both sides.

When this work began, Romania was still a neutral country. Her sympathies were with the Allied cause, for the Romanians had never forgotten their suffering during the German occupation in the First World War. The British took advantage of this to carry out some plans devised by the Ministry of Economic Warfare to thwart, by all possible means, the transportation to Hitler's Germany of vital materials such as oil and grain. They formed a private navigation company on the Danube, called the Goeland Transport & Trading Co. with its Head Office in London and agencies in all the main Danubian ports, for the Danube was a declared international waterway. Goeland then took over all vessels flying the Red Ensign on the Danube, including tugs, barges, tankers and so on, and also any available vessels flying the flags of Allied countries, including Romanian ones. The idea was to immobilize in port all the valuable tonnage, leaving practically no vessels for the Germans to use.

Moreover, Goeland took over all local crews and pilots by the simple ruse of paying them twice as much as anybody else. Thus practically all the naval personnel available transferred to the company, which continued to pay them for doing nothing. All they had to do was to clock in at 10 o'clock each morning at the Goeland agency offices to sign the register and then spend the rest of the day playing backgammon at their favourite cafe or going home to do whatever they wished. It was a serious blow to the German war machine. Deprived of the necessary tonnage, they were forced to build new vessels and to recall from other fronts the naval personnel necessary to man them.

The Goeland office in Bucharest was meanwhile full of Dutch, Greek, French, Romanian and other owners waiting to be paid for their vessels, preferably in sterling, on a London bank account. They were all in a great hurry to get away while there was still time. Goeland's managing director, a former chartered accountant now holding the rank of colonel, was William Harris-Burland; his second-in-command was Tom Walton, also holding military rank as is the British custom in times of war. To begin with I was given the job of chief accountant, but as work accumulated and payments became a matter of urgency, I was also appointed chief cashier. And as work increased daily, I soon had to employ my own assistant to lighten my burden. I engaged a young Romanian, whose family I knew to be sympathetic to the Allied cause.

The situation in the country as a whole was becoming daily more unstable. Many people, mostly Jews, were anxious to leave. The Romanian Government was under pressure from Hitler to join the Axis, and though the King remained loyal to the Allies, the National-Socialist movement known as the Iron Guard, or the Legionaries of the Archangel Michael, set about their nefarious activities, encouraged and subsidized by German funds. An atmosphere of terrorism, kidnapping and assassination reigned as Nazi agents penetrated all ranks of Romanian society, in preparation for Hitler's advance through the Balkans, towards Greece and the Mediterranean.

Colonel Burland would arrive at the Goeland offices in the centre of the city every morning at ten o'clock, having spent the first part of the day at the British Embassy. I had to be there at nine o'clock, to receive the various clients queuing to sell boats or to change Romanian bank notes, which they would bring by the sackful, or packed in suitcases. One morning, arriving at my usual time, I was amazed to find the colonel already there. Seeing my astonishment, he laughed and told me not to bother to open the safe and fish out my daily statements of accounts, as they weren't there. Late the previous evening, after I had left the office, he was warned that the Legionaries were preparing a raid so he went straight to the office to burn all files and papers that might have been of interest to them. We had foreseen such an event, and had installed a big stove with an oxygen cylinder to accelerate the burning process. However, as it was all done in great haste, the colonel had not taken any notes of the details on my statement, and he now asked me to do it again from memory, giving approximate figures as close to the actual ones as possible.

The Legionaries, who would stop at nothing to achieve their aims, decided one day to kidnap three Englishmen, one of them being Percy Clark, managing director of a steel cable firm in Ploesti, whom I had first met in Baku. Two or three days after the kidnapping, a short Englishman of a certain age came to see the colonel, and soon after I was introduced to this extraordinary character, who spoke many languages and dialects, having operated as a British Intelligence agent in Persia, Russia and Turkey from the First World War onwards. He knew how to cross frontiers at will, and now he was going to arrange Percy Clark's release. A large sum of money was necessary, for the Legionaries were always willing to trade their prisoners for cash. Burland instructed me to pack two suitcases full of banknotes, and together we left, this real-life 007 and I, to meet the intermediary who would pass on the money to the Legionaries. Sure enough, the following day, Percy Clark and the others were freed and could leave the country to recover from their ordeal, having been tortured and strung up by their wrists during captivity.

Goeland attempted one sabotage operation, the plan being to sink a ship at a double bend in the Danube known as the Iron Gates, thus blocking all navigation. A merchant ship from London, loaded with explosives and a ballast of rocks, her normal crew of merchant seamen replaced by disguised sailors of the Royal Navy, sailed unchallenged in the summer of 1940 through the Mediterranean, the Dardanelles and the Bosphorus into the Black Sea, arriving safely at the port of Galatzi on the Danube. But German Intelligence agents somehow got wind of the scheme, and Berlin warned the Romanian authorities, leaving them no option but to place the ship under arrest for investigation. The irony was that, five years later in the Lubyanka prison in Moscow, I discovered in the prison library a book on British espionage that included a detailed description of the whole operation, identifying Burland and Walton as those responsible. So the Soviets knew about it all along, having presumably shared the knowledge with the Germans in those heady days of the summer of 1940 when the Nazi-Soviet pact still had a year to run.

The arrival of a German military mission in Romania was another indicator of definite changes on the way. In the West, the collapse of France had left Romania isolated from the Western Allies, while in the East Stalin renewed Russia's territorial claims to the province of Bessarabia. In this he sought Hitler's support, and the two dictators presented Romania with an ultimatum demanding the evacuation of Bessarabia in three days, Hitler having specified that all Bessarabians of German origin be allowed to return to Germany. Obviously he did not trust his ally enough to leave his countrymen in his power.

Several days before the ultimatum, King Carol II solemnly declared that he would not cede 'a single plot of our land to the enemy'. Once the ultimatum was given, nobody even considered the possiblity of rejecting it and a massive exodus began. Units of Soviet parachutists were dropped into the area to control the crossings and ensure no one born in Bessarabia be allowed to escape. The following month Hitler decided to support Hungary's claim to the northern part of Transylvania, formerly part of the Austro-Hungarian Empire. He forced Romania to sign, on 30 August 1940, an agreement ceding to Hungary the northern part of Transylvania. But despite ever-increasing pressure from Hitler, the King refused to ratify the agreement and so was forced to abdicate on 6 September.

The moment young King Michael succeeded to the throne, Hitler now demanded that Romania grant a free passage to the German troops he wished to send to help the 'invincible' armies of his ally Mussolini, now bogged down in Greece. The new military government, headed by General Antonescu, advised the king to grant Hitler's demand, to ensure Romania's neutrality. German troops crossed the Danube, and our Goeland agent on the spot hastened to inform us in Bucharest of this latest development, soon to be splashed across the front pages of the Romanian press.

German officers could now be seen everywhere in the capital, and the Germans were starting to ask more and more questions. Why, for instance, was the main part of the Danube merchant fleet kept immobilized in port when they needed it? The Minister of Merchant Marine sent an urgent message asking that the barges navigate up and down river, even if loaded with rocks, just to show they were being used. The Goeland barges and tugs thus began to move up and down river, enabling the Minister to tell the Germans that his investigations showed that the barges were being used to carry freight.

Goeland then approached the Minister to allow the evacuation of the company's best tankers and barges to Turkey, beyond the Germans' reach. The chosen vessels needed to be structurally reinforced to make the journey across the stormy Black Sea, and it all had to be done in the greatest secrecy. Official permission for departure was given only at the very last minute, so making it impossible for the Germans to prevent it. They were in fact destined ultimately for Egypt, where they could be used on the Nile to help supply the British forces.

I had not realized, all this time, the extent to which the Iron Guard had won sympathizers among ordinary people. When my assistant at Goeland invited me to his wedding, I accepted with pleasure. After the church service there was a reception at the young man's flat, and as I arrived I was stunned to see it full of young men wearing the Iron Guard uniform of dark green shirts, black trousers and jackboots. The bride was herself, it turned out, a member of the Legion and here was I, working for the British, completely surrounded by Legionaries singing their martial songs. Towards midnight, with the party in full swing, I asked the young legionary next to me to lend me his richly embroidered cap. I then left the party unobtrusively and hurried to Tom Walton's house. He and his wife were still up, drinking tea from a samovar, Russian fashion, as I joined them wearing my legionary's cap. As a true Englishman, Tom showed no reaction whatsoever to my story, but his wife couldn't get over it. The young man's uncle had been an old and loyal member of the National Peasant Party which abhorred the dogma of the Legionaries. But seeing the calm bearing of my host, it occurred to me that he must have known about it all along. Perhaps, even, it was my assistant who gave warning of the Legionaries' plans to raid the Goeland offices.

The Romanians did not like the Germans, and they were not received in society circles. Ardent Francophiles for generations, many Romanians had completed their university education in Paris. France had been a close ally during and after the First World War, and the news of her defeat in 1940 caused great distress throughout the country. The Press was still sufficiently free to openly declare where its sympathies lay, and few believed in

Hitler's ultimate victory. Even when Romania was forced to ally herself with Germany and enter the war by sending troops to fight against the USSR, many people refused to conceal their true feelings. At the height of the war on the Eastern front, in 1943, everybody was talking with admiration about the story entitled 'The Baron', which the great Romanian writer Tudor Arghezi had published in his Review 'The Torch' ('FACLIA') expressing so vividly this hatred of the Germans, for it was clear to everybody that the Baron was, in fact, Baron Killinger – the Nazi Ambassador to Romania.

The Prime Minister – General Antonescu – himself was well-known for his pro-French sympathies. He had graduated from a French Military Academy, and although the international situation was such that he was forced to co-operate with the Germans, he refused to give in to all their demands. A shining example of this was his reaction over the incident of the French POWs. Nineteen French POWs had somehow managed to escape from a camp in Germany, and after weeks of privation, had managed to make their way through Poland to Romania. When the Germans found out, they at once demanded that the French POWs be handed over to them, to be sent back to Germany. But the general refused, saying that Romania was not at war with France, Romania was a neutral country, and as such, could give asylum to POWs. I know this from one of the French officers himself, who subsequently married the daughter of a Russian émigré friend of mine.

Since my move to Bucharest I had been living in a small flat on the fourth floor of a new apartment block which had a big restaurant and brasserie on the ground floor. Early one morning in October just as I was sitting down to breakfast, the whole flat began to shake. The table and the cups and plates on it moved from side to side so much that the tea I was pouring missed the cup and spilled. It was the first tremor of an earthquake. I hurried to the office where there was much agitation among the local staff. Although they soon settled down to a normal routine, at lunch-time a delegation of secretaries came to see me in a highly emotional state, saying there had just been a news-flash on the radio that a second earthquake was expected at two o'clock. They feared the worst and were panic-stricken. I tried to reason with them, arguing that science had not yet devised a means of forecasting earthquakes, but all to no avail. The offices were in one of the old buildings in the city, and they were convinced it would be one of the first to collapse. I consulted my two directors, who were in the middle of a conference. They roared with laughter but were willing to allow the staff to leave until such time as the situation became a bit clearer. Obviously, in their present state, they were incapable of concentrating on their work.

On the evening of Saturday, 3 November, I dined with some friends but had to leave them at ten o'clock to finish a job in Dro's office, where I usually worked weekends. I had to complete a balance sheet up to the end of October for the monthly directors' meeting, due to take place at ten the following morning. Dro's offices were in the very centre of the city, on the eighth floor of a new twelve-story apartment block known as the Carlton Block after the luxurious cinema on the ground floor. I finished what I had to do at 1.30 a.m., locked up the office and hurried back to my flat which was only some 300 yards away. I was so exhausted that I fell asleep as soon as my head touched the pillow, but a mere two hours later I was woken by my bed shaking and jumping and the noise of walls cracking. I switched on the bedside lamp. It was exactly twenty past three. The telephone had fallen off the table, and so had the books. The quakes continued several seconds, and then the lights went out. I made the sign of the cross and said a quick prayer, but did not move from the bed. The building continued to shake for several seconds until the shaking stopped as abruptly as it had begun.

I could hear voices and shouting on the landing outside. My pocket torch was fortunately still in its usual place, and I put on my dressing gown and opened the door. The landing was crowded with people from neighbouring flats – men, women and children shouting and crying. Gradually, as they realized that the earthquake seemed to have stopped, they calmed down a little. Some went back to their flats and, having dressed, hastened down to the street, dragging their children out of the building to safety. Others, less afraid, decided to go back and get some sleep. The lights came on again, and I returned to my flat to find large cracks in the walls and everything strewn all over the place. But, exhausted as I was, I did nothing about clearing up and went straight to bed where I fell instantly asleep again.

At nine in the morning I was woken up by loud ringing at the front door. Outside there stood the daughter and son-in-law of the friends I had dined with the night before. They knew that I had gone to work at the Carlton and were very concerned because the Carlton was now nothing but a mass of concrete slabs and dust. Again I made the sign of the cross and thanked God that I had not stayed on at the office a couple of hours longer. Now I must go to see if the office safe could be salvaged for it had over 2 million Lei in it.

We decided to go together, and as we turned the corner we were faced with a mountain of debris to which nobody was allowed to get too close. Little by little, the events of the night began to fall into place and we heard first of the miraculous escapes. A fireman on watch on the roof in case of air-raids had slid down to the street, riding on the roof as it fell. He had run off shouting with joy, unable to believe his luck. A well-known group of actors who specialized in satirical revue had been celebrating the success of their performance, eating, drinking and dancing the night away in one of the flats. But as the wine ran out, they decided to transfer the party to a flat further down the street where the wine cellar was full. Hardly were they out in the street than the earthquake began and they watched with horror as the whole building fell like a house of cards.

Of those who were in the building, only the owner of a smart ladies' fashion shop escaped alive, as her bed with her in it was thrown out of the falling building into the street. Her husband, lying in the bed next to hers, perished. But the most tragic story concerned the servants and maintenance staff, who slept in the basement and survived under the debris. They managed to telephone for help and before long firemen and sappers had started to dig a tunnel into the basement from a cellar across the narrow street. Then, all at once, a detachment of Legionaries arrived and chased away the experts. The Iron Guard were now in charge and would organize everything. Doubtless they had their thoughts on the chance of spoil and plunder amid the rubble and corpses. In their inexperience and haste, they used oxy-acetylene torches to cut through the metal rods in the concrete blocks and failed to recognize the smell of fuel-oil leaking from damaged tanks for the central heating system. In no time the oil was on fire and the poor souls in the basement were burnt alive or died from asphyxia. In the disaster overall, about 200 people perished.

The commission of inquiry set up to investigate the disaster found there had been criminal tampering with the architect's original design. The real cause was greed, the owner of the cinema himself having ordered the removal of several columns in the auditorium, there to support the weight of the ceilings and the twelve floors above. They had impeded the vision of some spectators, and their removal allowed him to sell several dozen extra tickets. He had actually sought planning permission using very persuasive arguments, and while there might have been no danger in normal conditions, a force 7 earthquake had not been foreseen. Fortunately the earthquake came in the middle of the night, when the cinema was empty. Had it happened during an afternoon or evening, the cinema would have been full and over 1,000 people killed.

After the earthquake Dro's offices moved into a quiet street near Rosetti Square. As soon as he heard that the company safe was found he went to the ruins, accompanied by a German officer to make sure there would be no nonsense from the Legionaries. The safe was handed over at once, without formality and with the usual salute of 'Heil Hitler!' I watched the scene from across the road, marvelling at the close relationship Dro had established with the Germans less than a year after his first visit to Berlin.

By December 1940, it was known that in two months' time the British Embassy would leave Romania. Towards the end of the month I fell ill with a severe attack of lumbago. Fortunately my doctor, a Turkish Armenian, was a specialist in rheumatology whose extensive researches had shown that rheumatism needed to be treated individually. What was required in my case was a course of Vitamin B injections, to be made every two days. Although it was difficult to obtain these injections in war time, he somehow always managed to get some for me.

On one of those cold winter days in January 1941, I lay in bed in agony waiting for him to arrive with my injection. When the front door bell rang I found standing there, instead of the doctor, the nice twelve-year-old who served as lift-boy in the apartment block and whom I used to spoil with frequent tips. He told me that fighting had broken out in the streets. The Iron Guard had staged a *coup* to overthrow the government of General Antonescu, and their troops, having attacked and occupied the Police HQ, were moving towards the Central Telephone Exchange quite close to the apartment block which now found itself right in the centre of the shooting. The lift-boy was worried about my being alone and ill and wanted to know if I needed any food. If I liked, he would run down the street to the small dairy to get something to eat and drink. I protested that I did not want him to risk his life, but he assured me it would be all right, there was no real risk and he was not afraid. He would run down the street in the opposite direction, out of the direct line of fire. I gave him enough money to buy some food for himself as well, for it was obvious that he hadn't had anything to eat either. The brave youngster dashed off and returned a quarter of an hour later bringing fresh bread and yoghurt which we shared.

The street fighting continued for three whole days until the army succeeded in clearing the city of Legionary groups. They, meanwhile, had taken advantage of the turmoil to massacre several Jewish families, killing and looting the more prosperous households while simply stringing the poor ones up, still alive, on meat hooks in the local abattoir. They had moved down the street methodically, according to a list given to them.

When my doctor finally got through to me, he prescribed another two or three days in bed, so I was still at home when the front door bell rang again, and an officer, accompanied by several soldiers, asked permission to search the flat. Having re-established order, the army was now carrying out a methodical house-to-house search to root out any concealed Legionaries or arms caches. The officer apologized for disturbing me, and as soon as they left I returned to bed to nurse my lumbago.

Two days after the visit from the army, I felt well enough to return to work. Military controls still being enforced in the streets, and in the office there was feverish activity in connection with the imminent liquidation of the Goeland company. It was general knowledge that Romania was about to enter the war on Hitler's side. Hitler needed the Romanians as allies, but he did not specify whom the alliance was against. Clearly he was already preparing the invasion of the USSR eight months later, which Stalin alone refused to believe would happen despite many warnings to the contrary from both Western and Soviet agents. One day, Colonel Burland asked me to go with him to the Soviet Embassy to act as interpreter at a meeting with Ambassador Vinogradov, even though the USSR was still Germany's ally. At the last minute the visit was cancelled, the colonel saying that the message had already been passed through other channels. I have often wondered whether this was another attempt by Churchill to warn Stalin of the approaching danger.

When all British nationals were advised to leave, a general evacuation having been arranged to Turkey, I, too, was asked by Burland whether I would like to leave with them. I did not know what to say. It could be wise to do so, but I sought the advice of my cousin Ruben who was older than me and who had replaced my elder brother as head of the family when he returned to Paris. I also consulted friends. Should I go or should I stay on? They all advised me to stay, saying, 'What are you, an Armenian, going to do in Turkey? Even with the protection of your British friends, it is too great a risk!' Still I hesitated, but their insistence was so strong that I finally decided to decline the colonel's generous offer, and told him I thought it better to remain in Bucharest. It was an error of judgement that would have grave consequences.

One friendship that was of great importance to me was that with a true Romanian, Mishu Porumboiu. Having been a judge and prosecutor known for his integrity and independence of judgement, Mishu had left the legal profession after a while to join the State Security Service as an inspector. Eventually he became a man of independent means, an uncle having died and left him a small vineyard at Mizil, some eighteen miles east of Ploesti, on the southern slopes of the Carpathians, as well as his small house in Bucharest. The vineyard produced enough wine for his own family as well as enabling him to supply some of the best restaurants.

Mishu's duties as inspector involved frequent travels about the country in his old battered Ford, to keep a watchful eye on the activities of police and security service agencies in the provinces. We would often meet whenever his journey took him to Ploesti, where I was then working, and when I moved to Bucharest to work for Goeland, we became even closer friends. He would phone me practically every day when he was in town, to invite me to join him in what he referred to as his 'office', but which was, in fact, the well-known Brasserie Mircea in the city centre, where a table was always reserved for him. The other guests might include a lawyer attached to the Supreme Court, a retired general, a journalist and so on – all people of like mind and anti-German. These meetings were of great interest to me, and through them I was able to keep my directors informed of latest developments in the political life of the country. Several times a week he would also persuade me to join his family for a delicious meal at his house, accompanied by wine from his own vineyard. Like most Romanians he was a gourmet, and he actually accompanied the cook to the market each morning to choose the food before going on to the office. Those were happy times, and his friendship proved truly invaluable.

One evening, late in 1940, I invited Mishu and his lawyer friend to dine with me at his favourite restaurant, the Modern, where the diners were regaled with gipsy music played by a famous band. The meal was to be specially ordered by Mishu – dishes not on the menu – and the wine, too, would be his own, this being one of the restaurants supplied from his vineyard. It was a gay, enjoyable evening, and the wine flowed, for despite the war in Europe night life in Romania continued to flourish as though nothing had changed. Some wine was sent up to the band, and a bottle of beer went to the talented cymbals player, who thanked us with a solo performance.

At about two o'clock an elderly gentleman entered the restaurant and sat down at the next table, having greeted Mishu as he passed. I suggested to Mishu that we ask him to join us. It seemed a shame to let him sit alone while we were having such a good time. Though obviously embarrassed, Mishu agreed, provided I did the inviting. And so, not in the least shy after all the wine, I asked the solitary gentleman to join our party. He accepted graciously and proved to be most agreeable company. At half past three, our new companion suddenly stood up and said he must return to his office.

Greatly intrigued by this character who arrived at two in the morning only to return to his office an hour and a half later, I asked Mishu about him. Mishu revealed that the mystery man was his chief, the Inspector-General of the Security Service, a Macedonian called Maimuca. He was subordinate only to the Director-General, but it was he who ran the service, working an eighteen or twenty-hour day! He would now remain back in his office till 5 a.m. to read the reports coming in from all over the country. Then he would sleep awhile, but be back at his desk at ten o'clock to work another full day.

A week later, a desperate telephone call came from the Goeland Agency in Braila to say that our man there, Captain Dickie McNabb, had been arrested by the local police on a charge of spying. We knew he used a small motor-boat to inspect and control our barges and tugs in port, but obviously this was a put-up job on the part of the Germans. When Colonel Burland asked me what we could do to get McNabb out of this mess, I at once suggested getting in touch with Mishu. I was certain he would not refuse his help, although I had never before approached him in this way.

I found Mishu at midday, sitting at his usual 'office' table at the Brasserie Mircea. When I told him what had happened, he burst out laughing and said: 'But, my friend, you are now more powerful than me. It is you who can exert the necessary influence.' At a loss to understand his merriment I asked him to explain. It appeared that, after our dinner at the Modern, his chief had several times mentioned me, saying how much he liked me. Mishu was therefore certain that Maimuca would be only too willing to help, especially now he knew I was working for the British. And so, without further ado, we set off to the State Security offices, and as Mishu had predicted were received at once. We were ushered into an immense room where Maimuca sat at his desk, surrounded by telephones and large transmitting and receiving radio sets. He was in excellent spirits and the meeting proceeded according to Oriental custom: Maimuca rang for some coffee and we chatted awhile before actually broaching the matter. Then I explained and gave the name of the Goeland agent in Braila. 'Braila did you say? Just a moment,' Maimuca interrupted me to call the state security officer there on his direct line. After listening to the man's report, he gave instructions that McNabb be released at once. It was all a misunderstanding. Then he turned to me and said: 'There, it's all settled. Is there anything else you would like me to do?' 'Yes,' I replied, 'I have a much more pleasant but equally pressing request. When can you come to have dinner with me again, now that we know each other better?' That same afternoon, McNabb was released.

In February 1941, the British Embassy closed its doors. Goeland was forced to cede to the Romanian authorities the remainder of the Danube fleet which it had been impossible to evacuate to Turkey, and this was inevitably handed over to the Germans.

Before leaving Bucharest, Colonel Burland had given me a large sum as a bonus. This, together with the savings I had accumulated, made it possible to contemplate buying a small flat. Dro, being indefatigable in his business activities, had taken over a construction company which had gone bankrupt leaving a particular building unfinished. It was only a concrete shell, but Dro and his friends invested sufficient money to turn it into a luxury apartment block. It was he who urged me to join the scheme, and buy one of the flats, having already decided for me and set the formalities in motion. He did this because, he told me, my father had been like a father to him. 'Your father,' he said, 'always gave me and my comrades the support we needed. Now it is my turn to take care of you, who have no business sense whatsoever, just as your father before you had none either.' Laughing uproariously, he recalled how my father had helped a group of penniless Dashnak Party members. As head of the Petroleum Producers Association, father had no difficulty in finding them work, but several weeks later he summoned Dro and said: 'You asked me to help those ten lads as a favour. Now it is my turn to ask a ten times favour – please take one of them back. He is quite impossible and I simply can't keep him on!'

I accepted Dro's offer and moved into a flat on the fourth floor which had a beautiful view towards Parc Bonaparte. It was a quarter of an hour's walk from Rosetti Square, where Dro's office was located, so was really very convenient. I was now working full time for Dro and, as a result of his German connections, the company was soon involved in exporting crude oil to Germany. Dro never neglected to use his political connections to enhance his business activities.

In June 1941, Hitler attacked Russia, and Romania was forced to join in. The war was not at all popular, and people listened to the BBC broadcasts, even though this was forbidden. Walking down the street in the hot summer, one would often hear through an open window the famous BBC signal. The Romanians were defiant in disregarding the ban, and everybody anxiously awaited the latest reports from the Eastern Front. Even Germans passing by would stop to listen, for they also wanted to know the truth. I bought myself a small German Saaba short-wave radio that enabled me to listen at one in the morning to broadcast reports being sent from Istanbul by American correspondents to their newspapers in the USA. Turkey was a neutral country without censorship, and the news reports were very detailed and contained many items on Romania that the local authorities were anxious to suppress.

Just before the commencement of hostilities, Dro left Bucharest for Berlin, presumably to prepare for his mission of evacuating Armenian soldiers in the Red Army who were taken prisoner by the Germans. But I had no news of him until, months later, as the German and Romanian armies reached the Crimea, he returned to Bucharest for a short visit. He spoke then of his trips to POW camps in the rear to arrange for the release of all Red Army soldiers of Armenian origin. He had been appalled by the terrible conditions the prisoners were kept in, but when I asked him how the war was going or what he thought the final outcome would be, he brushed my question aside. All he would talk about was the absolutely bestial treatment inflicted by the Germans on Soviet POWs and the Russian population as a whole. It had been a great shock to him, although everybody in Romania was already aware of the savage way the Nazi forces treated vanquished nations.

Tens of thousands of prisoners never reached the POW camps in Germany. They died on the way, as they were being marched across the land, without food or drink. It was the simplest way of killing them off, without having to waste any of the valuable ammunition needed to mow down those still putting up a fight. Dro's shocking stories of German inhumanity were later reinforced by the equally distressing incidents witnessed in the Ukraine and Southern Russia by a Romanian friend – Nina Calatorescu, the wife of a colonel in the Security Service. At the beginning of the war she had enlisted as a nurse and was appointed Matron in charge of the Red Cross train doing the shuttle between the Eastern Front and hospitals in Bucharest, to evacuate wounded Romanian soldiers. When the train stopped at the main railway station of Shepetovka in the Ukraine, she saw across the railway lines a camp crammed full of Soviet POWs, shouting and begging for water to drink. She at once ordered several of her Red Cross orderlies to take some buckets of water to the unfortunate wretches, but when they reached the barbed wire fence surrounding the camp, they were stopped by the threatening German sentry-guards who pushed her back, cursing and forbidding them to hand over the buckets, saying that they had been given strict orders 'to ensure that these Soviet dogs should perish....!'

In Romania itself, life continued unchanged. Prices on imported goods did go up a bit, but, as a rich agricultural country, Romania did not depend on imports to feed her people. The country had everthing needed for a comfortable life, and soon the German soldiers stationed there began sending food parcels to their starving families at home – so much so that an alarmed government issued a regulation restricting the sending of parcels abroad to one per month. I also sent parcels to Paris for my brother and his family.

The one obvious change was an inevitable insistence on 'racial purity'. The pact signed with Hitler included a clause which stipulated the introduction of restrictive measures against Jews and gipsies, but these were not too strictly applied. Centuries of Turkish occupation had left the country with an ingrained tradition of *baksheesh*, as the 'greasing of palms' was known, and something could usually be arranged. To begin with, several Jewish families were deported to the occupied territories beyond Dniester, the river marking the old frontier with the USSR, but after a while some of them returned to Bucharest and continued to live as before, a suitable arrangement having been made with the authorities. Even German officers stationed in the country soon learned how to use the system, doing profitable deals with Jews, in order to ensure the necessary Army supplies, as well as arranging the export of foreign currency, and so on.

The year 1944, however, brought the first Allied air-raids on the Ploesti oil-refineries. Even before the surrender of Italy, the Americans were assembling squadrons of Flying Fortresses and training the pilots by bombing a model of Ploesti, specially built in the North African desert for the purpose. But when the real air-raids began, it soon became obvious that the distance was too great, for almost half of the planes were lost while the pilots of others were interned in Turkey when they had to land there to refuel for the return journey to Libya. Subsequently the Americans organized the raids from a base in southern Italy, and now the planes could carry enough fuel for a return flight to base. Even so, it was still a dangerous mission, as it meant flying over German-occupied Yugoslavia, whose observation posts could warn the Romanians of the direction the Flying Fortresses were taking, thus indicating whether the raids were aimed at Bucharest, Ploesti or Brasov.

The first American air-raid on Bucharest took place on 4 April 1944. It came without warning. It had been announced that an anti-aircraft defence exercise would take place at one o'clock that afternoon, but nobody paid much attention to such announcements. I had been invited to lunch at Mishu's house together with an Armenian ex-general. Knowing that Mishu's family were partial to chocolate cake, I bought some before catching a tram. When the piercing sounds of air-raid sirens began to wail, the driver stopped the tram and told the passengers to get off and run for the nearest air-raid shelter. But most people refused to do so, being in a hurry to reach their destinations. They protested so loudly about all these air-raid exercises being futile and a disgrace, that he finally gave in and agreed to continue. But not for long, for the tram was soon stopped by a traffic policeman who announced that this was no exercise but the real thing.

Once again, I disregarded the warning, as Mishu's house was only about a mile away. I decided to continue on foot, still carrying my carton of cakes. But when I was about half-way there I heard the deafening roar of rapidly approaching planes, and as I looked up saw wave upon wave of Flying Fortresses. I stopped and began to count them. There were about 250 planes flying towards the Gare du Nord, the principal railway station about half a mile away. Then all hell was let loose as bombs and explosives erupted all around. Fragments of debris from shattered buildings flew in all directions, and I hastened to take cover in a small newspaper kiosk. There were already several people there, instinctively huddled together under the cover of a roof, however thin, to protect them from the showers of debris. After the waves of bombers had passed, I ran all the way to Mishu's, into the courtyard and entered through the back door into the kitchen, which opened straight on to the dining-room. All the houses in the street were exactly the same size and, whereas the back door was always open, the front door was kept firmly locked, according to Romanian custom.

The other guests had already arrived and were standing round the table discussing the bombardment, which was about to be resumed. Mishu told the girls to open all the windows, so as not to be hit by flying glass, while I strongly advised the ladies to go down into the cellar, which was very small so there was not enough room to fit everybody in. But they refused, and insisted on staying with the men. None of us realized the real danger; everybody was convinced that the Americans would concentrate their bombs on the railway station only. But soon we heard fresh waves of Flying Fortresses and, amidst the deafening roar of the planes, the sound of explosions coming nearer and nearer. Then the house itself shook as bombs fell all around us. Pieces of plaster rained down and the dining room was engulfed in dust. Mishu shouted at his daughters to cover the table with newspapers to protect the dishes, so we could all sit down to lunch as soon as the bombardment ceased. He did this not because, as a true gourmet, his first thought was for the food, but so as to give them something to do and take their minds off the danger.

The raid continued for some time, but gradually the sound of bombs became more and more distant. Then total silence fell. Mishu and I went out into the courtyard to inspect the damage. It was, indeed, a miracle that we were still alive. Mishu's house was the only one left standing in the street, all the neighbouring ones having been reduced to rubble. The tram lines in the road and the wires overhead were twisted like bunches of macaroni. A horse lay dead, next to its overturned cart, and there was a deep crater some four yards across right outside Mishu's house. The whole neighbourhood had been destroyed, and wherever one looked all one could see were craters, craters everywhere. It had been our introduction to the American system of 'carpet' bombing by scattering bombs over a whole area – a system later explained to me as not requiring the long training of individual pilots.

Having confirmed our miraculous survival, we sat down to lunch to celebrate our unbelievable luck. It was only then that we noticed all the bread had disappeared. But this mystery, too, was solved when one of the guests, an Armenian friend, confessed that as the bombs fell nearer and nearer he had paced nervously round and round the table, taking and eating the bread rolls laid out on the side-plates without realizing what he was doing. Everybody roared with laughter and teased him mercilessly, but the incident served to break the tension.

It was obvious that the bombing would continue, so Mishu and his wife moved to the country house at the vineyard. He did not mind driving the sixty-five miles into town each morning, and whenever the radio announced that Flying Fortresses were again coming in the direction of the capital, he would return to the safety of his vineyard. His daughters, however, stayed in Bucharest as they were both working.

On Easter Sunday I went to Mishu's house, concerned about his girls for the telephone hadn't worked when I tried to ring. On the way I was held up by another air-raid warning but there was no cause for alarm this time as the planes were returning from a raid on Brasov, their bomb-bays empty. As I walked along the Boulevard Bonaparte, I could see the terrible destruction, but when I turned into the street where Mishu lived I stood rooted to the spot in dismay. Mishu's house was no longer there – just a mass of debris, bits of broken furniture and an enormous hole where the dining room had been. It must have taken a direct hit. But where were the girls? Were they at home when the bombs fell? The street was completely deserted, but I was too stunned to move. After about a quarter of an hour, a woman emerged from the ruins of one of the houses that backed on to the street where Mishu lived. I hurried towards her, fearing she might be a mirage. But no, she was real enough and reassured me at once, saying 'Please calm yourself, all is well!' When the raid started, Mishu's youngest daughter and the maid, who were alone in the house, took shelter in the cellar. The bomb fell a mere nine feet away but the force of the explosion spread out like a fan above the cellar and so they escaped unharmed. All the wine was destroyed, including a barrel of good red wine which Mishu had specially reserved for us to drink over Easter. I had given up drinking for Lent so we did not have it when it first arrived from the vineyard. Everybody had teased me for my abstinence and now Mishu teased me all the more, saying that, because of it, we had lost the chance to drink that very good wine. Yet he never spoke of the loss of his house.

So long as the raids lasted, Mishu continued to live at the vineyard in the firm belief that one should not tempt fate too often. I spent several weekends at his vineyard, on the slopes of Mizil, only twenty miles from Ploesti, where the oil fields were one of the prime targets for Allied bombers, the Americans coming over by day, the British by night. One weekend we witnessed the awe-inspiring sight of a night raid on Ploesti by the RAF, enjoying a perfect view from the hillside. We could see the refineries burning fiercely as the petrol flowed out of storage tanks hit by bombs, the red flames rising high in the sky, accompanied by the bursting shells of the German anti-aircraft guns, the entire scene further illuminated by flares and searchlights. After the last plane had left, the beams of the German searchlights, which had been criss-crossing the sky, suddenly went vertical and then went out as suddenly as they had been switched on, as if marking the end of this magnificent spectacle.

Despite the intensive air-raids, I went to the office every morning to do a normal day's work. But we kept the wireless switched on, listening for the next official air-raid warning, based on news of approaching bombers flashed from Yugoslavia. This gave us half an hour to reach the air-raid shelters. Human nature being what it is, there were many who rejoiced whenever a raid was directed 'not at us' in Bucharest, but on Ploesti or elsewhere. As soon as the wireless broadcast an air-raid warning for Bucharest, people would jump into their cars, and drive off at speed into the countryside to get beyond the danger zone, for although the raids were mainly concentrated on military targets, it sometimes happened that, to show their absolute mastery of the air, pilots would drop their bombs at random, often in purely residential areas.

Many of my friends had followed Mishu's example and moved into the countryside as far from any military target as possible. They would drive into town and start work very early in the morning, dashing off to the country at the first air-raid warning. Among them was the Bishovsky family who had taken a house in one of the southernmost suburbs of Bucharest, and I was looking forward to going there on 7 May for the wedding of their daughter Vicky. The problem was that, the night before, the RAF had carried out another of their precision raids on the southern part of the capital, and all transport was disrupted as a result, the tram lines having been seriously damaged during the bombing. So what to do? I decided to telephone Mishu's daughter who was working at the Cabinet Office. She too had been invited to the wedding, and was bound to have a solution to the problem. As indeed she did. An energetic girl, she at once arranged for one of the Cabinet Office cars to be put at her disposal. She would come to collect me in good time, and on the way we would also pick up two other mutual friends - Michael and Arthur - who were also going to the wedding.

We arrived safely at Ferentari, and went straight into the small church for the religious ceremony, while the driver turned round and went back to Bucharest. But no sooner had the service started, than another air-raid warning was sounded - the American Flying Fortresses were coming to complete the work begun by the RAF the night before. Unperturbed, the priest continued the service, amid the deafening noise of the Flying Fortresses passing overhead and the AA batteries firing off all their guns to try to bring them down. The American pilots then replied in kind, dropping off some of their bombs to silence the guns, before flying on their way.

Greatly relieved that the alarm had been so short-lived, everybody sat down to celebrate and drink the health of the newly-weds. Then someone noticed fires burning fiercely to the north, in the city itself. Worried, Mishu's daughter rang the Cabinet Office to find out from her colleagues what was happening. Fortunately, the lines had not been damaged and the telephones were still working. But the news was bad. The Americans had changed tactics. They had bombed this time, not only the airport and the surrounding neighbourhood, but the entire northern part of the city, using incendiary bombs. So, on leaving the air-raid shelters as soon as the all clear was sounded, people found their houses burning fiercely and all their belongings destroyed.

Both my friends and I lived in the northern part of the city. We were anxious to know if the apartment block we lived in had also been hit. The Cabinet Office didn't know but very obligingly offered to send an army motor-cyclist to have a look and report back. Half an hour later they rang to say that the block I lived in was still intact, although the hospital opposite, which was run by nuns, had been destroyed. As for the house where my friends lived, it was still intact for the moment, but other houses in the street were on fire, so theirs too was in danger.

We decided to get back to town somehow, even though there was no transport. We started to walk down the main Giurgiu – Bucharest motorway and had not got very far when suddenly we saw a Romanian tank driving slowly in the same direction. We waved at the driver to stop and begged the tank crew to give us a lift, explaining the urgent need to get back into town because of the raging fires and promising a handsome reward. Full of sympathy and understanding, the nice young soldiers didn't hesitate for a moment. Inviting us to climb aboard, they made a special detour to stop us at the indicated address, before continuing on their appointed journey.

When we arrived the street was already full of fire engines and my friends' house had already started to burn, the strong wind having blown the flames over from the house next door. Familiar with the old Romanian custom requiring financial reward for all services to be rendered, my friends went straight to the chief fireman and agreed a sum with him to support their argument that their house required priority attention. He, at once, gave orders to his men to concentrate all their efforts on my friends' house, to stop the fire from spreading further. Thus all was quickly settled and everybody was satisfied. I relate this story as an example of the happy-go-lucky atmosphere in Romania at the time.

Whenever there was an air-raid I always followed the same simple routine. As soon as the warning was broadcast I would leave the office and return to my flat, a quarter of an hour's walk away. I never went down to the air-raid shelter in the small basement cellar of the apartment block. The one time I did go down I found it filled with women and children huddled together, and the crying and moaning made the atmosphere so insupportable that I very soon came up again. At least from my flat I could witness the spectacle of the raid itself, whereas down in the cellar I would see nothing. I would stand on my fourth-floor balcony, watching through binoculars the waves of bombers coming over the airport, dropping their bomb-loads and leaving. The spectacle at night was even more magical as the rocket flares dropped by the RAF slowly descended by parachute, interspersed with tracer-shells from the German anti-aircraft guns, the whole scene illuminated by flashes of fire shooting out in all directions as bombs exploded in mid-air.

One day, hurrying back to the flat, I bumped into a former colleague from Goeland, a Captain in the Merchant Navy. Delighted to see each other again, we went into the Cafe Nestor nearby for one of their famous iced-coffees. He told me how for some months past he had been in radio contact with the British GHQ in Cairo. The British had sent him a W/T set, which had been parachuted into neighbouring Yugoslavia. When it finally reached him, he installed it in his flat on the top floor of the apartment block where he lived. This was a most suitable location, being opposite the Central Post Office, so he could safely send out his messages at the same time as the Post Office was transmitting and no one was any the wiser. He communicated regularly to the British the effectiveness of their air-raids, the damage inflicted to the target area, and how long it would take for the refineries, pipe-lines or railways to be put back into operation. Unfortunately, one of the raids by American bombers had tragic consequences for his family. As often happened, on their way back after a raid, the Flying Fortresses dropped their remaining bomb-load at random over the city centre. The family had all gone down to the air-raid shelter in the basement while he remained in the flat to send his message to Cairo. By chance, one of the bombs exploded on the pavement right outside the basement entrance, and all in it were killed or badly burned, including his wife, whose face was badly burned. After that he could no longer transmit from the flat and had to conceal his W/T set elsewhere. He also told me, in the deepest confidence, that King Michael was negotiating a separate peace with the Allies, and had sent a small delegation to Cairo for this purpose.

Dro, who had remarried in Romania, told me one day in the spring of 1944 that he was sending his family to Vienna, from where they would go to Semmering, *en route* to Italy. He was still travelling everywhere in the small plane placed at his disposal by the Germans, and was accompanied everywhere by a Russian-speaking German officer who was invaluable in smoothing his relations with the Romanian authorities. But his relations with the Germans were not always so easy, and he needed to spend a lot of money to sweeten the mood of his protectors. As there was a great shortage of food in Germany, and coffee in particular was practically non-existent, Dro would always take a large supply of coffee for Major Braun, the head of Counter Intelligence for the Eastern Front, every time he went to Berlin, in order to ensure favourable treatment for any Armenians there might be amongst the vast numbers of Red Army prisoners taken by the Germans.

Because he was so often away, Dro had given me Power of Attorney – the right to draw certain sums of money from the revenues earned from exports of oil to Germany so as to make payments to his family while they remained in Bucharest. But when he was at home he often entertained German officers, and one day, while his interpreter was away on another mission, he asked me to come to dinner and stand in as interpreter. His guests that evening were to be high-ranking German officers, so I was not to mention that I had worked for the British. He had already told them that I was a personal friend, an Armenian who had studied in Berlin and spoke fluent German. My role was to keep the conversation going, encourage the guests to eat, drink and have a good time, but I was not to intervene in the discussion or take part in any way.

Dro's wife had prepared a superb meal of Armenian national dishes and there was more than enough to drink – vodka, wine and liqueurs. When I arrived I was introduced to three German officers: a colonel on the general staff who was in charge of a sector on the Eastern Front, a lieutenant-colonel and a captain on his staff. All were regular army officers of the old school, who spoke fluent French and even some English. Conversation became more and more lively as Dro's talents as the perfect host were extended to the full. His brief speeches in the little German he had acquired during his trips and the endless flow of drink all contributed to a relaxed atmosphere, and it soon became obvious that they knew Dro well.

As regular army officers, they despised the SS and did not hesitate openly to criticize the Nazi Party's conduct of the war and the disastrous consequences of the short-sighted policy being enforced on the Eastern Front. The *blitzkrieg* had completely failed in Russia. They were professionals, fashioned in the mould of the old, traditional army officer, and as such they were strongly opposed to the atrocities committed against the civilian population on Hitler's personal orders that the SS so enthusiastically enforced.

I was amazed at the extent and boldness of their criticism. It was obvious that this was not the first time they were expressing such sentiments, and Dro's presence did not seem to restrain them in the least. It was an indication of the widespread feeling among German army officers, a prelude to the July plot – that botched attempt on Hitler's life.

The last time I saw Dro was in the summer of 1944, during an American air-raid. He told me he had made arrangements to leave the country for good, travelling in his small plane, loaded, as usual, with ample supplies of food and coffee. The Red Army was already too close for comfort and he must get away before they arrived. Later I learnt that he had gone to join his family in Austria, from where the Dashnak Committee in Boston arranged for them all to go to the United States, his mission to save Armenian POWs having been completed.

Throughout August 1944 the Red Army continued its relentless advance through the Ukraine. The inevitability of the defeat of Hitler's forces was not obvious to all. Romania had no option but to withdraw from the German alliance into which she had been so brutally coerced. The Allies, likewise, were anxious to end the fighting on the Eastern Front to complete the defeat of Germany.

On the night of 22-23 August I dined with a friend and his colleagues in the German pharmaceutical firm of Schering. It was a delightful party, with lots of pretty young girls, and after dinner we danced to the music on the radio. All at once the music was interrupted for an important announcement: the King was going to speak to his people. Shortly afterwards the young King's voice could be heard saying that, at his request, the Allies had agreed to a separate peace with Romania. We all went out into the street where the general rejoicing had to be seen to be believed. As if by magic the blackout vanished and lights blazed in all the houses and in the streets. People sang, shouted and hugged each other in delight. No more bombs, no more killing. Peace had come at last.

The King now offered the Germans the chance to withdraw all their forces in peace, and guaranteed they could do this without any resistance from the Romanian forces. But the King had no illusions about the Führer's reaction to his offer. He knew it was bound to be negative and that Hitler's fury would be unleashed against him personally. He left the Palace before the German bombers arrived, but fortunately Hitler's order to destroy Bucharest could not be enforced as thoroughly as he had hoped. The Germans had no bombers at Baneasa Airport, only several fighter planes. Nor did they have any big bombs in stock. Therefore, to carry out the Führer's orders, three or four small bombs had to be tied together in bunches to be dropped on the Palace, the Central Post Office and other important buildings.

Meanwhile the Romanians did not remain idle but organized a ground artillery attack against the airport to prevent the planes taking off. The Allies, too, were informed of the changed situation, and a famous Romanian pilot, Prince Byzou Cantacuzene, flew his tiny private plane to an American base in Italy to give the USAF Commander there all practical details of the German attack. The very next morning American Flying Fortresses were back over Bucharest to bomb the German air base on the northern outskirts. Having completed their mission they flew over Bucharest itself in a salute to the city. People crowded the streets to wave and acclaim the liberators. There was an air of general rejoicing, and before long the Romanian crowds were joined by American and Soviet POWs, all released from their camps. They were greeted with open arms, given cigarettes and presents, and invited into people's homes as honoured guests. Several Soviet POWs who expressed the wish to continue the fight against the Germans were given arms and joined Romanian troops in the attack launched against Baneasa Airport.

At night I had watched it all from my little balcony: the duel between the two artilleries, the German and the Romanian, as tracer shells exploded. But the German attempt to occupy the capital failed, and on the third day the German air-raids ceased. The German troops in Romania were now forced to beat a hasty retreat. The Red Army was advancing at great speed in considerable numbers, while the Romanian Army units in Transylvania cut off the German escape route through the Carpathian mountains and 50,000 Germans were taken prisoner. The Führer's vengeful order proved fatal for his own army.

The Red Army actually marched into Bucharest on 27 August 1944, though the official communique gave the date as the 30th. It was on that day that the deep baritone voice of the Radio Moscow news reader Levitan announced that 'after fierce fighting, the invincible Red Army occupied the Romanian capital Bucharest'. In fact there had been no fighting. Presumably the ever-cautious Red Army command wanted to be sure there would be none of those unpleasant surprises that sometimes occur when total victory is announced too soon. To begin with, we in the capital saw little of the victorious Soviet troops, the order having been given to by-pass Bucharest and race on for Hungary so as not to lose any time in catching the retreating Germans. But we had plenty of opportunity to see the Soviet Military Police, who were everywhere with their red arm-bands and cap-bands. There were both men and women MPs controlling the traffic and giving directions to any army convoys that happened to be passing. Discipline was very strict and wide-ranging. There was a war on, and the MPs represented the Law. Everybody, whether officer or private, was subject to their control.

In the old days, when I was an officer in the Imperial Russian Army, no soldier in the MP would dare to arrest an officer. This could only be done by the Adjutant or the local Military Commander. But in the Red Army, things were different, and in Bucharest, any soldier in the MP could stop and demand to see the papers of captains, colonels, or any other high-ranking officer, and he would be obeyed.

One evening I witnessed an alarming scene in the centre of the capital: a Soviet officer, obviously drunk, had decided to stop all circulation in the street. Brandishing his revolver, he threatened passers-by and trams alike, forcing them to stop while yelling at the top of his voice in Russian. The poor Romanians couldn't understand a single word, nor did they wish to. But this only made him brandish his revolver all the more threateningly, until suddenly a jeep full of Soviet MPs appeared from nowhere. Seeing their red arm-bands, the officer gave himself up like a docile child who had at last found his parents. Order was restored as if by a miracle. There was no argument, nothing. He simply climbed into the jeep as ordered, and it sped off out of sight.

After experiencing years of total war and desolation, the Russians suddenly found themselves in a rich and prosperous country that had scarcely been touched by the war. The front line was far away, and they arrived with their pockets stuffed full of roubles that they could exchange for the local currency at a favourable rate of exchange fixed by the Soviet authorities to their own advantage, the Romanian National Bank having no option but to agree. Everything was cheap and plentiful, and soldiers and officers profited alike, taking full advantage of the situation. In their rapid advance on the capital, they had found time to call on the local branches of the National Bank and obtain hundreds of rolls of new banknotes which they then crammed into brand-new suitcases.

There were many so-called 'heroes of the rear' who could arrange such things, while the real heroes were busy fighting at the front. Well-organized, and with good local contacts, they were people who were always willing to act as intermediaries and help the victors by indicating where the required goods could be found – for a small financial consideration, of course. One day, I was by chance in one of the big textile shops on Lipscani Street when a Soviet officer came in and bought everything in sight. First he pointed to a whole shelf of rolls of woollen cloth, then to another shelf of rolls of silk, then to one of velvet material and so on. And when he had chosen all he wanted, he just asked, 'how much?', and paid with notes that he took from a suitcase crammed full with row upon row of carefully bound rolls of new banknotes. He paid without querying the price or bargaining. 'A lorry will come and pick them up,' he said briskly, and left, obviously in a great hurry. The visit had probably been arranged in advance by one of the intermediaries, who had also negotiated the price.

The situation began to change rapidly as a shortage of goods set in and prices began to rise. For example, over the course of several weeks, the price of wine doubled. Goods were either being exported, or hidden for an emergency. It became too expensive to eat out, and so my cousin Ruben and I, together with two Armenian friends and business colleagues, Michael and Arthur, organized a Mess in the latter's house where we would meet regularly to eat and talk. We called it the *Majlis* after the Iranian Parliament. I was, after all, the proud bearer of an Iranian passport, our family having originated from Persia. Soon, others joined our Mess, and one day, as I was having a pre-lunch drink at a bar, I noticed two Soviet Air Force pilots sitting at the small table next to mine: one was a big blond Russian, while the other was short and dark – a typical Armenian. They spoke cultured Russian, not the usual illiterate jargon of Soviet soldiers, and when I approached them and spoke in Russian they were absolutely delighted. We soon became great friends, and they would often come to our *Majlis* for a meal, bringing along other Soviet pilots who happened to be passing through. They soon came to regard it as their 'base' and meeting place whenever they were in town.

One evening they arrived with another Armenian – a much older man, a full colonel who was Officer Commanding the Artillery Army Corps advancing into Hungary. We discussed artillery matters, exchanging views on a subject we both knew well. He too was now fighting on the Austro-Hungarian front just as I had done twenty-two years earlier, and our talk brought it all back to me. I asked him to explain how the Soviet artillery was being used as a support to the infantry, in preparation for an attack. I could not forget the miserably scant resources available to the Russian Army in the First World War, as a result of which German artillery always had the supremacy. The Soviet colonel assured me that, despite the terrible losses suffered at the beginning of the war, incredible efforts were made to replace lost equipment, and Soviet forces now had the supremacy in the air as well as on the ground where artillery and tanks had been brought up to required numbers. He had fought mostly on the Northern front where there was now no longer any shortage of artillery or tanks. The Romanian front was not really considered to be of great importance, the main thrust of the Soviet mass attacks being directed on the Northern front. Nevertheless, when the time came to launch an attack against Bessarabia – defended jointly by German and Romanian forces – he concentrated at the central point of attack some 300 artillery guns of different calibres, placing them in depth and width along every kilometre of the attacked sector. To me, remembering our scant resources in the First World War, this was something really fantastic.

Our meetings and conversations made it clear that Soviet superiority on the land and in the air was now a formidable fact. No doubt the young King Michael had been aware of this when he decided to negotiate a separate peace. Had he not done so, Romania would have been utterly destroyed and pillaged by the victorious conquerors from the East. By his action, he was at least able to save his country as well as considerably facilitating the Allied victory, and so he more than deserved the award of the Soviet Order of Victory, not that it was to make much difference in the long run. It did not stop Stalin from forcing his abdication three years later when he refused to agree to an imposed, non-elected Communist government. Bucharest was full of the story how the Soviet Ambassador in Bucharest was so furious at the King's refusal that he thumped the table and walked out of the throne room, shouting: 'I'll show you who is master here,' banging the door so violently against the wall that it left a dent in the plaster, which the King wanted framed as a memento of Soviet diplomatic tactics.

Following Romania's surrender in August 1944, foreign military missions began to arrive in Bucharest one after the other. One day, I was invited to meet an officer of the French Air Force, who was attached to the French mission sent to arrange the repatriation of French POWs liberated from German camps in Eastern Europe. He brought me good news of my elder brother and his family in Paris. They had all survived the war and the German occupation; my niece had married a Frenchman and my brother was now a grandfather. It was to be the last contact I had with them for twelve long years.

The British mission arrived at the end of 1944, the new head of the Commercial Section being an old friend who had left the country with the British colony in their hasty evacuation. I asked him for his opinion, now that Romania had been 'liberated' by the Soviets. What did he think of the country's prospects for the future? He was under no illusions whatsoever. He saw the future as gloomy indeed, now it was known that Churchill and Roosevelt had signed a secret agreement with Stalin, leaving the entire Balkans in the Soviet zone of influence, with the exception of Greece. I also called on my former Goeland boss, Colonel Burland. He, too, had no good news to offer, nothing to encourage or cheer. The Soviets were now in total control, well-organized and determined to keep Romania within their orbit. Knowing that the British were helping certain people to leave the country, I asked the colonel if it would be possible to arrange that I should also leave, going to Turkey to rejoin Tom Walton, now attached to the British Embassy in Istanbul. The colonel replied that this would be rather difficult. Nevertheless he promised to make inquiries and asked me to stay in touch. These tentative approaches were, alas, to come to nothing.

5. THE COILS OF THE SOVIET STATE

There was much political activity in Bucharest. The King appointed a new coalition government, including members of the Liberal, National Peasant and Socialist parties, and one Communist, but the Soviet Union was determined to have things done her way. With the Western Allies persuaded into signing the secret agreement dividing Europe into spheres of influence, preparations began in earnest for Romania's permanent inclusion within the Communist fold. The plan was carefully thought out. The local Communist Party, though small to begin with (a mere 2,000 members) was well organized, and with the arrival of the Red Army it moved into action. General (now Marshal) Antonescu was arrested and transferred to the Lubyanka Prison in Moscow, and, once the situation was organized to the Soviets' liking, brought back to Bucharest to be tried and shot.

So-called 'spontaneous demonstrations by the workers and the people', organized by Communist Party leaders and infiltrated agitators, demanded the inclusion of more Communists in government and the resignation of the Prime Minister, General Rădescu. There was talk in Bucharest of how each demonstrator had been given 100 lei and a loaf of rye bread that could have come only from the Red Army bakeries. The Communist Party grew in numbers daily and many former Iron Guard legionaries hastened to convert to the Communist dogma in an effort to conceal their compromised past. All new members were received into the Party with minimal formalities, to help swell membership as quickly as possible, and provide the necessary 'rent-a-mob' crowds to be manipulated at will.

The end of hostilities had brought peace to Romania, but not freedom. The Prime Minister, General Rădescu, was forced to resign and, on 6/7 March 1945, a new Government was installed in the face of an ultimatum from Moscow. It was headed by Petru Groza of the Communist-dominated movement known as the Ploughman's Front. Communist Ministers occupied the most important posts, including that of Minister of the Interior which controlled the Security Service and the Police, and the Ministry of War where Emil Bodnaras – a former Army deserter who had fled to Russia in the early 1930s was now installed. The new Minister for Foreign Affairs was the notorious lady Komissar Anna Pauker (who had her own husband executed, having denounced him for deviation). She too, like Bodnaras, had returned to Romania in Red Army uniform. It was the classic move to be followed later in Czechoslovakia, to ensure the elimination of all opposition, especially of the Socialists who represented a viable alternative to a left-wing electorate. The Soviet State Security and its SMERSH agents, long installed in key positions throughout the country, now embarked on a series of arrests of all those considered dangerous to the new regime. Their lists were passed to the Romanian Ministry of the Interior, which then executed the actual arrests.

First to be arrested were the Socialists, and so all those recently released after years of imprisonment under Antonescu promptly returned to gaol. Next followed the heads of all the other political parties – the President of the National Peasant Party, Juliu Maniu and the Liberal statesman, Bratianu. My friend Mishu Porumboiu suffered the same fate, interned in the notorious Tirgu-Jiu political prison where he died of starvation.

With the problem of the Socialist opposition settled, the next step was to annul the elections to the Trade Union Council and announce new elections, which the Communists won with a crushing majority. Trade unionists who did not vote for the Communist-nominated candidate were sent to the camp at Caracal, where I met some of them when my turn came. The process of cleansing the country of all undesirable elements was set in rapid motion. All former Russian officers who took refuge in Romania after the 1917 Revolution were to be arrested at once. But events did not always work out to plan. It all depended who you knew. One day I was amazed to meet an old acquaintance, a White Russian Army Officer, a fervent monarchist, who, rumour had it, had already been arrested. He told me he had indeed been arrested, but subsequently freed after a strong intervention by the Belgian Consul. He was fortunate to be married to an energetic Belgian woman who achieved the impossible and arranged an intervention by the Western Allied Missions to save him. But now he was free, they must leave Romania as soon as possible.

I took courage from this fact. After all, I had spent the first years of the war working for the British, with whom the Soviet Union was linked in 'close and loyal alliance'. But I knew my turn would come soon. Next in line after the White Russians were the Armenians, and in the first week of March 1945, I heard that an old Armenian merchant, called Israelyan, had been arrested. There had initially been a mix-up when the younger brother was arrested by mistake, but this did not perturb the Soviet Commandant. As soon as he realized he had the wrong man, he warned the family that the younger Israelyan would remain in detention until the elder brother surrendered. The old man therefore had no choice, and had to give himself up to save his brother, but since he held an Iranian passport, perhaps a subsequent intervention could be made.

The Israelyans originated from the province of Van in Eastern Turkey. At the outbreak of the Russo-Turkish war in 1914, when the Turks surrounded the city of Van to massacre the Armenians, who were Christian and formed the majority of its inhabitants, the population organized the defence so well that they managed to hold out until the arrival of the Russian armies, after which the Armenian inhabitants of the region were evacuated and thus saved from annihilation. It so happened that the advance party of Russians consisted of the Legion of Armenian Volunteers commanded by Dro, who after the relief of Van came to know the Israelyan family quite well. But as soon as Romania was occupied by the Red Army, the KGB began to search out all friends and contacts of Dro, since he was known to have collaborated with Hitler's occupying forces.

The Soviet Counter-Intelligence Services had a thick file on Dro, having maintained an interest in his activities since long before the outbreak of the Second World War. Dro's promise to Stalin on leaving Moscow was not forgotten, and besides, the KGB always had a network of agents planted in Romania to watch over the Armenian colony; and, to prove their loyalty, these agents would include in their regular lists various people who had nothing whatsoever to do with Dro's anti-Soviet activities. The more the names on the lists, the greater the credit due to the agent, and both the KGB and SMERSH accepted the lists as genuine. The plan was gradually to arrest everyone on the lists, and transport them to the Soviet Union where they would be tried and sentenced by the Moscow courts, a fact of which we innocents, never involved in any political activities, were totally unaware.

The only explanation to emerge for the release of the White Russian on the intervention of the Belgian Consul was that the Romanian police had not as yet had a chance to hand over 'the goods' to the Soviet authorities. In those early stages the services of the Romanian Security Police were still not re-organized under the new Minister of the Interior, so an intervention remained possible, the Romanians being more than anxious to be of service to their old allies in the West. In Israelyan's case, however, it was naive indeed to think that a simple diplomatic intervention on the grounds that he was, after all, an Iranian subject with a valid Iranian passport, might bring about his release. It was already too late. He had been handed over to the Soviets, and all intercessions by the Swedish Consul, representing Iranian interests in Romania, proved to be fruitless.

Several days after the Israelyan incident I had a phone call from a clerk at the oil company asking me to go to the office at once. Michael and Arthur, the joint managing directors, who were also close personal friends, needed my help urgently. He could not say more on the telephone, and as my small flat was no more than ten minutes' walk from the office, I hurried over, only to find it occupied by two inspectors from the Romanian Security Police and a civilian, who turned out to be a Party member set to watch over the inspectors sent to arrest the two directors.

My friends had been woken very early that morning by the inspectors demanding to search their respective flats. The search continued for several hours, after which they were told to accompany the inspectors to Police HQ to sign the official report on the search and its outcome. They understood at once what this meant; they were being arrested and would disappear without trace unless they did something. They therefore asked the inspectors for permission to go to the office on the grounds that it was essential for them to talk to the staff and give instructions to cover their absence. The inspectors agreed all too readily, being also anxious to search their office and perhaps find something incriminating. The company chairman also needed to be summoned, to be put in the picture. Of course, it was only possible in the circumstances to say what was strictly necessary. The inspectors were in a hurry; the driver of the police car parked outside was blowing his horn. Shortly after I arrived my friends were led away.

When I went into my own office the chairman's nephew bravely warned me that my situation was equally perilous as an Armenian and ex-officer of the Imperial Russian Army, working for a company in which Dro was a principal shareholder. 'Don't go back to your flat', he advised. 'You will be safe if you come to stay with me for the time being, until we can think of something else.' It was good and sound advice indeed, but like a fool I remained blindly convinced that my work for the British during the war would protect me from any accusation of being 'an enemy of the Soviet State'. How could I be an enemy of the Soviet State when I was working with their Allies in the war against Nazi Germany? I promptly went to the British Mission to speak to Colonel Burland again and told him what had just happened to my two friends. Colonel Burland advised me to stay in touch, assuring me that, in case of need, the Allied Mission would intervene on my behalf. With a clear conscience and no feelings of guilt and reassured by my talk with the colonel, I forgot the wise advice to hide, and, far from hiding did the contrary. I started to make inquiries to try and discover where my friends had been taken.

Three days later, news reached me that they were in the 'Special Prison' of the Ministry of the Interior, near the Arsenal. Since this prison was not yet completely 'Sovietized', they had managed to get a note out through the Romanian guard to their housekeeper-cook, asking for clean linen and blankets and something to eat. The science of prison management as perfected by the Communists had not yet come into force here, and so the prisoners were allowed food cooked at home and could send the guards out on errands. They were not kept in cells but could walk freely in the big court-yard, taking full advantage of the good weather. If a visitor came to the prison gates and asked to speak to a prisoner, one of the guards would call the prisoner, the conversations then taking place through the iron railing surrounding the courtyard. Ten days after their arrest, I learned, they had still not been given any reason. I sought the opinion of my cousin Ruben, with whom I discussed latest developments each day. We were perplexed to know what to think and what else to do about it.

It was early in the morning of 23 March that my own front-door bell rang, well before seven o'clock. In the light of recent events I didn't react as normally but kept quiet, gave no sign of life and didn't open the door. But, wide awake by now, I decided to shave, take a bath and dress. I had almost finished when the bell rang again and the porter shouted through the closed door, asking to speak to me. I hesitated, knowing this could well be the old police trick, but then asked who it was. I should have stuck to my first instinct and said nothing, but now there was nothing for it except to open the door and see what the porter wanted. And as I had rightly assumed, he was not alone. Standing next to him was an inspector of the Romanian Security Police and the young Party member to watch over his every move: the same team who arrested my friends Michael and Arthur. Producing a search warrant issued by the Romanian State Security they proceeded to search the flat before the inspector invited me to accompany him to Security HQ, to sign the official report. Following the example of my friends, I requested permission to visit the office first, to hand over the keys of the company safe, and so forth. Events then followed the same course. In no time at all I found myself at the gates of the prison near the Arsenal, and there, too, completing the formalities at the reception desk, I saw my cousin Ruben, brought in a few seconds earlier and already signing a piece of paper listing the various objects taken from him on arrival: his gold watch and so on. I did the same and we were led together into the prison courtyard to join Michael and Arthur among the others.

The first day in prison passed very quickly. We discussed our situation, and what we could do to arrange a defence. At midday the cook arrived, bringing some food that we divided between the four of us and, since we had permission to write, we sent through her messages for the chairman of the company and the company solicitor to explain what had happened. At nine in the evening we were told to pack and be ready to leave in an hour, each having a small travelling case to carry the bare essentials.

Our particular group, numbering between 150 and 180, was put on a bus, one of the ordinary buses of the municipal service, and taken to the small railway station of Mogoshoya in the northern quarter of Bucharest. The main railway station had been destroyed by the American air-raids, but the railway line itself had been repaired, so it was for reasons of secrecy that we were taken to this little-known station where three closed goods waggons already awaited us. The station was packed with police and guard-dogs, and powerful flood-lights illuminated the scene as we were loaded into the train. It was almost midnight before the embarkation was completed, and once the guards had counted us several times to make sure no one was missing, the train finally left.

Since the train stopped several times on its journey, I took the opportunity to ask the friendly Romanian guard on our waggon to buy me some postcards (this being the usual infallible system for tipping). He agreed to post a card to the company in Bucharest that said we were *en route* to Caracal on the Danube, a fact he had himself revealed.

Arriving at Caracal next day, we were marched straight to the old camp where Soviet POWs had been held until their release the previous August. There were already 1,000 people in the camp when we arrived, the majority, about 700 of them, being workers from the Bucharest Railway yards who had refused to vote for the Communist-nominated candidate in the local union elections. The remaining 300 were made up of the old cadres of the Security Police and ordinary constabulary, or anyone else who could be identified as a Socialist or Social Democrat. Among those arrested, the intellectual classes were well represented: lawyers, judges, professors and so on, all considered dangerous elements. None of them had received any official communication explaining why they had been arrested and deported to Caracal. We found there several acquaintances who we had supposed to be still at liberty, and others who had recently disappeared.

The camp was filthy, the wooden barracks furnished with row upon row of wooden bunks, one on top of the other, to save space. The place was crawling with bed-bugs, and column after column of these disgusting insects crawled all over the place, even in full daylight. Sanitary installations were at their most primitive, the sort of lavatories to be found at the front during the war, the difference being that during a war with a constantly moving front line, the lavatories are purposely built on a temporary basis, whereas these were meant to last! Taps were installed in the narrow spaces between the barracks and prisoners had to wash quickly in the open air, whatever the weather.

The food consisted of *mamaliga* - the Romanian porridge made of maize, similar to the Italian polenta, and boiled white beans. There was no bread. Those prisoners who had managed to bring some money could order food to be bought from the local restaurant, a privilege granted as a great favour on the part of the camp administration. The vast majority of detainees, like ourselves, had no money, and so were condemned to an endless diet of *mamaliga* and white beans.

We passed the time in talk and telling stories. One of the detainees was a Jewish lawyer, a true phenomenon with an endless fund of jokes and stories, he would sit telling one after the other, hundreds of them without ever repeating himself. He was very popular since he made everybody laugh. It was as good as having a live theatre, and he was always surrounded by a large circle.

One day Michael and Arthur were summoned to the guard-room at the camp gates. A visitor had arrived. It was Mr Popescu, the company clerk, who had travelled in haste from Bucharest as soon as he received the postcard the kindly guard had sent off as promised. Mr Popescu had brought them some money, but he still couldn't tell them why they had been arrested. Nobody knew, and there was still no official notification to give a reason. Another visitor was a Romanian lady, a good friend from Bucharest whose country estate was not far from Caracal. The camp commandant, a pleasant captain in the Romanian Army, gave her permission to speak to us, even though regulations forbade such meetings without the prior permission of the Bucharest authorities.

With the money brought by Popescu, we ordered food from the local restaurant. Famished after a month's meagre diet of *mamaliga* and white beans, it was the first time for a month that we could satisfy our hunger. Several days later the camp commandant allowed a group of detainees to go into town accompanied by an escort, to buy some food. Everybody made out a list, and we went off with our escort of two soldiers. We gave them some money to have a drink at the local pub while we completed our purchases, and then, at the appointed hour, made our way to the pub to meet up with them for the return journey. Of course, it would have been very easy to escape, but, naively and foolishly, we preferred to await the outcome of the application for our release, submitted by the company solicitor. Several detainees in the camp had been visited by their lawyers and, several days after the visit, had been allowed to return to Bucharest. Thus there was hope. Things were beginning to move and our turn would come. After all, we four Armenians had no political past. We were confident the solicitor would succeed in securing our release.

On the afternoon of 27 April, just over a month after our arrival, we were all four summoned by the camp commandant and told to prepare for departure. The other detainees began to congratulate us, believing that our case, too, had been satisfactorily settled. As night fell, we were escorted to the police station in town and told we would spend the night in one of the offices there, with a policeman to guard us. We asked him to go to the local restaurant and ask the waiter to come to take our order for dinner. A small tip can work wonders, and before long the waiter arrived. We ordered a good dinner, with wine, and half an hour later settled down to a thoroughly enjoyable meal. We were in excellent spirits, confident of being back and free in Bucharest next day. Our police guard joined us, and shared our food and wine. Dinner over, we lay down to sleep on the desks, happy at last to be free of the infamous columns of bed-bugs that prevented sleep in the camp.

Woken at five the following morning, we were told to go down into the courtyard, where we saw an army lorry with three Soviet soldiers standing by. They were instantly recognizable by the red bands on their caps, as dreaded MVD (Ministry of the Interior) troops. Only then did we realize the true seriousness of our situation. We were ordered into the lorry and to sit on the floor. At the back of the driver's cabin was a bench on which the three soldiers sat and faced us, Kalashnikov sub-machine guns on their knees. Already lying on the floor was a soldier, his hands and legs tied with rope. We were told he was a deserter being taken to be tried and sentenced. As the lorry started on its journey we exchanged few words. Our thoughts were the same; we were no longer in the care of the Romanian authorities, but had been handed over to the Soviets. Our destinies were out of our hands.

As the lorry swung round the corners at great speed, the poor deserter was thrown violently from side to side. I turned to one of the soldiers to say, 'I understand that you have to take him to be sentenced somewhere, but why ill-treat him so on the way? It's a savage inhuman thing. You could at least untie his hands so he can steady himself.' The soldier did not reply, but at the first stop one of them bent over the deserter and untied the rope round his hands so he could sit up and hold on to the side of the lorry as we were doing.

Not one of the three soldiers had said a word, but my remark had had an effect.

The lorry stopped twice, and each time we were given something to eat and drink, always, it seemed, the identical piece of black rye bread and salted fish. We had left Caracal at 5.30 in the morning; we arrived in Bucharest at nine o'clock that night, our first stop being a rich villa near the Park Bonaparte, in the northern quarter of the city. The villa was now occupied by the Red Army, and here the deserter was dumped. The driver then asked for directions to the city centre where we were to be delivered to our fate. It was eleven o'clock by the time we reached Victoria Street, on which the Palace stands. We were driven past the Palace gates and along Victoria Street until finally the driver stopped at a building on the corner where Grivitza Road branches off to the main railway station. Once again we were surrounded by MVD soldiers as we were ordered off the lorry and made to go down some steps into a basement divided into two small rooms, where the central heating boilers were installed.

The place was already full with some forty to fifty prisoners, some standing, some sitting on the floor. There was no room to lie down. We soon learnt that all the prisoners were Armenians – schoolmasters, lawyers, journalists. We recognized several, and saw among the others the eldest son of the tailor Arutik, whom we knew to be a member of the Dashnak Revolutionary Party. The boy told us how the Soviet soldiers had come to arrest his father, but since he had gone into hiding weeks before they arrested the son instead. That was how the system worked. If they couldn't find the father, they took the son. It was all a question of fulfilling your quota. The soldiers were ordered to arrest a certain number, and if the right person wasn't there to be arrested, they took another member of the family, thus ensuring that they had the specified number. The boy had never had anything to do with Armenian politics. He had never worked. Terribly spoiled by his parents, he had turned into a problem child whose parents couldn't control him. Now he had become a hostage of sorts for his absent father.

We were no longer under any illusions about our own fate. All the people in the basement, whether guilty or innocent, had been declared 'enemies of the Soviet State'. They were Armenian nationalists who had links with the Dashnak Revolutionary Party, which, since it had collaborated with Hitler's National Socialists, was invariably labelled by the Soviets with the umbrella term 'Fascist'. As we greeted others we knew, we were told how they had been locked in the basement for several days already. They were completely cut off from the outside world and had no idea what was happening.

At around midnight, each of the four of us former inmates of the Caracal camp began to be summoned in turn. My name was the last to be called, and a guard took me to an office on the ground floor where a Soviet colonel sat behind a large desk. He asked me in Armenian what language I would prefer to use in the course of interrogation. It was a clever move to have an

Armenian interrogator, since most of the Armenians locked in the basement spoke no Russian. I therefore assumed that he had been specially delegated by the KGB to interrogate this particular group so that it could be done without the intermediary of an interpreter. I chose to speak Russian, and he asked me all the questions listed in a questionnaire, the preliminary formality for an examining magistrate, which the Soviets call an *anketa* (probably derived from *enquete*, the French word for investigation). He carefully wrote my replies in the appropriate slot, making no comment. And when he came to the question of nationality, he did not even bother to wait for my answer and started writing 'Nansen passport for refugees' (the identity papers issued to all Armenian, Greek and other refugees fleeing from persecution in Russia and Turkey). I interrupted him to point out that I held a Persian (Iranian) passport and handed him my identity card (Residence Permit registration), certifying that I was an Iranian national. The colonel replied that it was of no importance! And it was, indeed, a fact that the Soviet authorities arrested and deported people without bothering about their nationality. So obviously, for him, it was a matter of no importance. But it was important to me, and I refused to sign the questionnaire unless my nationality was stated as such. The colonel gave in and entered my nationality as Iranian and we both signed the document. I was not to know it, but my insistence was to have decisive consequences eleven years later.

And so, half an hour after being ushered into the room, it was all over. After all, half an hour is long enough for an affair of no importance. He told me that I was now free to leave, and that we could continue our conversation the following morning. It was a lie, of course – the usual trick practised by the KGB to keep you in suspense. I returned to the basement, where all those who had managed to find sufficient room on the floor were already asleep. I tried to squeeze into a small place near the door, and to lie down, but it wasn't for long. At five o'clock we were woken and told to 'prepare to leave'.

There were altogether forty-five Armenians in this particular detachment of prisoners, or *etap* as the Soviets termed it. As we were shepherded into the courtyard, we saw four army lorries – the same sort that had transported us to the Caracal camp. Separated into three groups of fifteen prisoners each, we were ordered to climb aboard. The fourth lorry was loaded with barrels of fuel, oil and provisions for the trip – a sign that we were in for a long, unpleasant journey. These lorries were also fitted with a wooden bench, fixed to the back of the driver's cabin, and on it sat four KGB guards, armed with Kalashnikov sub-machine guns and facing the prisoners sitting on the floor.

Our little convoy then left the courtyard, the three lorries with prisoners first, the provisions lorry coming last. The convoy turned left along Victoria Street and the Kisseleff Highway, then right in the direction of the airport and the north – a clear indication that our final destination was the USSR. In the rush of embarkation we became separated and I found myself in the second lorry with Michael, while my cousin Ruben was in the third lorry with Arthur. We had been separated by pure chance, but the separation lasted throughout the journey.

Dawn was breaking as we sped along the beautiful Kisseleff Highway, along which my friends and I used to drive to the racecourse almost every Sunday afternoon. We had loved these afternoons, when the colourful stands would be filled with excited people as the horses paraded to be weighed and assessed by the punters before they went to place bets at the Tote. Now, looking around, I could no longer restrain my feelings, and turning to Michael said, 'Take a good look, my friend. It is probably the last time we will see this beautiful highway!' Michael agreed, and, indeed, he was destined barely to survive two years of imprisonment in the USSR. A year of detention in prison awaiting trial followed by another year of terrible conditions in a forced labour camp would bring on his early death.

Once we were out of the city and past the airport, the lorries picked up speed and soon we were in Ploesti, the centre of the oil fields, and here the lorries stopped outside the Town Hall. The driver didn't know the way and had to go in to ask directions. Although it was only 7.30 in the morning, the streets were already crowded. Desperately we searched the faces of passers-by, trying to spot a familiar face among them, but luck was not on our side. We could recognize no one we knew, and the passers-by, seeing Soviet lorries full of prisoners guarded by 'fraternal Slav comrades' armed with Kalashnikovs, hurried by as fast as they could. No one wanted to complicate their existence further.

The necessary directions having been obtained, the convoy moved off again, and henceforth the journey always followed the same pattern. The convoy never stopped in towns or villages during the day. It stopped only at night, and then only somewhere well out of sight. The Soviet policy was always to be discreet; they had no wish to attract the attention of the populace to what was going on. And, once out of the cities, the drivers seemed familiar with the route. It became obvious that this was not the first time they were ferrying prisoners along this route. They always knew where to stop, near a small river, so as to fill the flasks with fresh drinking water. We were then allowed twenty minutes to eat our ration of black bread and *kamsa*, the very small salted fish, and so were lucky indeed to have plenty of fresh water to drink!

Towards evening of the first day we arrived in Focsani, a big city in the eastern part of the country. The lorries drew up in the courtyard of the local police station, and we were told to dismount, go to the toilets, and then eat our meagre rations. All forty-five of us were then herded into two small cells, with just enough room to sit down, the only ventilation being the grill in the door. Only those sitting near the door could breathe, and before long an old Armenian, squashed in the back of the cell, was taken ill. We called the guard, to ask him to allow the old man out into the yard for a while to get some fresh air, but not a chance. The cell door must remain locked until the morning. Nobody is allowed to open it till then. That is the rule. One is not allowed to break the rules. Shuffle around a bit and let someone near the door give up his place to the old man.

We left Focsani very early next morning, travelling in a northerly direction, the convoy of lorries stopping only outside inhabited areas in the middle of nowhere. Towards evening we approached the frontier with Bessarabia, but stopped some distance from the frontier, in a desolate village in a sort of no-man's land. It made a melancholy scene: not a villager in sight; only the frontier guards patrolling the area with specially trained dogs. When the Red Army marched in, in August 1944, and Romania was forced to sue for a separate peace, everyone in the border villages had fled and so all the small peasant houses stood empty. But when we were told to get down from the lorries we were only too happy to do so. After spending two terrible days huddled together on the lorry floors we could at last stretch our legs and lie down on the floor of a peasant house. There was plenty of room, and we fell asleep at once, exhausted by the long journey and the heat and dust.

We resumed our journey early next day, passing through no-man's land, on and on through the beautiful rich Bessarabian landscape with its rolling green hills and valleys that resembled gigantic green waves chasing each other across the countryside. In the afternoon we arrived in Kishinev, the capital of Bessarabia, from where we were to continue our journey by rail. It was quite hot, and we were glad to be finishing with our journey in the lorries. Although it was 1 May, Labour Day, the streets were almost empty. All the buildings were decorated with the Red Flag, but the town looked deserted, its people probably preferring to stay hidden inside their houses, just to be on the safe side. You never knew with the Red Army.

The four lorries drove into an empty compound specially allocated for transports of detainees. There we spent the rest of the day sitting in the lorries, not allowed to move except to go twice to the primitive lavatories built for the detainees in transit. And, as night fell, the lorries moved off again in the direction of the railway station, driving through the deserted, badly lit streets. It was like a ghost town, with no passers-by to witness yet another embarkation. And that was the way the Soviet authorities wanted it. Any initial curiosity there may have been to watch such a spectacle had vanished completely, and after several months of occupation by the Red Army, nobody wanted to know what was going on!

The passenger coach awaiting us discreetly in one of the sidings was an antique Russian rail coach of the sort used for transporting convicts in the nineteenth century, even before the introduction of the old Stolypin coaches at the beginning of the century. It was an ordinary three-axle 3rd Class carriage, not divided into compartments, and with grills over the windows and doors, designed to hold fifty passengers. There were wooden benches with superimposed bunks, and we were lucky indeed that each could lie on his own bunk for the three days it took to reach Moscow. It was the most luxurious of all the journeys I was destined to make with detainees across the USSR. Each day we were handed our food rations, always the same, and we were allowed to drink water only twice a day, or not even that, depending on whether the guard on duty was willing to exert himself sufficiently to refill the water bucket at the station pumps on the way.

We had left Kishinev in the middle of the night, our coach being attached to the regular train going to Odessa, where we arrived the following morning to be shunted at once on to one of the sidings amid rows of empty carriages so as not to be seen by ordinary travellers. The next evening, 2 May, our coach was attached to the Moscow Express, and as the train sped on its way, we saw scenes of total desolation, with station after station in utter ruin. The retreating German armies had dynamited whole cities, railway stations, factories and all important buildings on the way, determined to leave nothing but ruins behind them. Now the Soviets were repairing only what was strictly necessary to allow the victorious advance of the Red Army towards Berlin.

We arrived in Moscow on 5 May 1945, at the Ryazan Station. Once again our coach was detached and shunted into a depot siding – a place specially reserved for the so-called 'guests of the NKVD'. As the train entered the station I glimpsed the clock. It was eleven in the morning, but not until seven in the evening did the guards order us to prepare to leave the coach. We were marched out of the station, through a side-door giving on to a dark side-street, on the far side of which there waited two of the small closed vans known in Russia as 'Black Ravens' (the equivalent of Black Marias). The vans were painted black, and on the sides they bore the inscription in large letters KHLEB, which in Russian means bread, as though these were ordinary bakery vans. Although the vans were built to carry twelve, all forty-five of us were pushed in like sardines into a tin, some sitting, others standing. The few possessions we had managed to bring with us from Romania were also thrown into the van, thus further increasing the misery and discomfort.

The vans set off almost immediately, the driver driving very fast. At every turning, those who were standing were thrown against those who got in first and so had a chance to grab a seat on the bench. There was no ventilation, the atmosphere airless. Fortunately, the journey lasted no longer than thirty to forty minutes, otherwise we would have suffocated. As soon as the vans stopped the rear door was opened and the guard told us to get down. We looked around to find ourselves under an arched gateway leading to an enormous building. As we very soon learnt, we had arrived at the Lubyanka – one of the most infamous prisons in the world.

6. A GUEST IN THE LUBYANKA

The large reception hall was surrounded by small cells, each the size of a telephone booth, but with no windows. As each prisoner was locked up separately, all hope evaporated. It was probably the last time any of us would see our friends again – the end of all communication between us. But having foreseen how this might happen, my cousin Ruben, my friends Michael and Arthur and I had agreed on the train from Kishinev to Moscow that, should we be allowed to send letters, we would all write to the address of my cousin's family in Baku. It was a well-known fact that, once the preliminary interrogations were completed, we would be allowed to do this, but not before. And, indeed, so it proved, and it was thus that we would manage to re-establish contact a year later. Throughout the interrogation period in the Lubyanka, however, which lasted nine months, we saw each other only in the course of confrontation sessions in the room of the interrogating magistrate, when we could neither speak nor communicate freely.

The Lubyanka building, originally the Head Office of the Rossya Insurance Company, was transformed into a prison at the end of 1917, at the height of the bitter conflict between the Bolshevik Communist Party and the Social Revolutionaries of the Left. The Bolsheviks declared their Socialist enemies as counter-revolutionaries, and an Extraordinary Commission (Chrezvychajnaya Komissya, or Cheka for short) was formed to combat the counter-revolutionaries first, the speculators second, and thirdly all other so-called 'enemies of the people'. These two initials, 'Che-Ka' became the dreaded symbol of the Soviet terror, and although its initials have changed over the years, first to the GPU, then to NKVD and the MGB (Ministry of State Security – established in 1943), and finally to the KGB (the Committee for State Security), it has remained unbending in its task of annihilating the enemies of the Soviet system and all those who seek to contest the power of the Bolsheviks. For convenience, I shall use the term 'KGB'.

I was personally under no illusions as to what lay ahead. There was only one possible outcome to the confrontation of an individual and a pitiless state-machine. We emigrés of the old Russian Tsarist regime did not need the revelations of a Solzhenitsyn to tell us about the existence of the vast network of camps known as the Gulag, and were only too aware of the terror reigning in the USSR. One of the first books I read on the Soviet forced labour camps had appeared in the 1920s, written by one of two brothers called Solonevich and published in Russian, so not many people knew about it. Its description of life in the Karelian camps, east of the Finnish border, and of the brothers' escape through the surrounding forests to Finland, remained vivid in my mind. Long before my own arrest I had had nightmares after reading it, nightmares that I, too, might wake up one day to find myself in a camp similar to those that were described in the book.

Now, shut in my tiny cell-cabin in the Lubyanka, I knew that my destiny was already decided and that, being already fifty years old, I could put up little resistance to the KGB's relentless interrogation procedure. I, too, would be crushed by it, like millions before me. But, determined to survive, I decided to do everything they asked, to sign any confession put before me. I told myself again and again that my only aim now was to safeguard my health and resist with every means at my disposal the suffering that lay ahead. I must survive all the humiliations and suffering, and live to see the day when I could rejoin my family in France.

An hour after arriving at the Lubyanka, I was led to the bath-house for a shower, then to the barber to have my head shaved, like any army recruit. The body hair was also shaved, to remove any lice one might have acquired during the long journey to prison. The next move was to be photographed and to have finger-prints taken, all of this taking place in the basement. Then it was back upstairs for a thorough body search in a specially equipped small room, escorted by a guard in white jacket, like a medical orderly in hospital. He went through the small suitcase I had brought with me to Moscow, packed with clean underwear and various toiletries, then put me in a corner and told me to take off my clothes. Each item of clothing was then closely examined, every single seam of the jacket, trousers and underwear checked inch by inch to make sure nothing was concealed or sewn inside. It was the same with the shoes – the heel and sole carefully checked, the laces removed. My belt and braces were also taken away from me. That done, he told me to lift my arms and then get down on all fours so he could check I had nothing hidden between my legs, my fingers or my toes. He cut off all the buttons on my jacket and trousers, presumably to ensure that I didn't swallow anything during interrogation.

I was asked what I wished to keep, the rest then being put back in the suitcase which was placed on the luggage rack. My wristwatch, my gold christening cross and chain, my wallet with my documents and some Romanian money, were all sealed inside a large envelope and the list of contents signed by myself and the guard, the gold objects being described as of 'yellow metal'. The guard explained that all my personal possessions would be returned to me when I left prison or camp, and so they were, nine years later.

These formalities had all lasted till long after midnight. Once they were completed I was led along various corridors to a very small cell, 1.5 metres wide by 2 metres long. It was no more than a box – the actual name given to it by the prison authorities – and half of it was taken up by a raised shelf, the bed.

On the shelf there lay a man fast asleep. As the noise of the door opening awakened him, I recognized my friend Arthur. He had been brought to the box a short time before me but, thoroughly exhausted by all the formalities, had fallen asleep at once. I lay down on the floor beside him as best

I could. We chatted a bit, but not for long, and soon were both fast asleep. Several hours later, I could not say exactly when, the door of the box opened and the guard ordered Arthur to follow. Years later, I learnt that he was taken to Lefortovo, the most modern prison in Moscow, built in the time of the Tsars, and from there brought back to the Lubyanka every day for interrogation.

The so-called box in Soviet prisons is used as a transit cell, and a prisoner stays in a box only a few hours, usually alone, this system having been designed to prevent him meeting other prisoners. One leaves the box only to be taken to another cell, and so, an hour after Arthur's departure, it was my turn to be conducted to a new place of residence. The guard marched me along several corridors to a lift up to the fourth floor. We were now in the internal prison in the courtyard, the old hotel for the insurance company's agents, and on the landing was a small table with an open register and a guard on duty. My escort handed me over to his colleague who recorded my arrival in the register, and they both signed. My spectacles were taken away, it being explained that they would be returned when I was summoned for interrogation. It did not worry me. I am short-sighted and only need spectacles when crossing the road, to avoid being hit by traffic! Shoe-laces, belt and braces were also removed, as a precaution against a detainee attempting suicide or damaging his health in any way before interrogation could be completed.

The guard then escorted me along the old hotel corridor, opened a door and ushered me into a small room, just large enough for one or two people but containing six beds in two triple bunks facing each other along the side-walls. The wall facing the door had a large window, but hardly any light entered since the window was blocked from the outside with wooden planks slanting outwards, so that all one could see was a small piece of sky. By the window was a small table and two benches, on which the six occupants might sit to eat or read. A strong electric bulb lit up the cell, and as the door shut I saw five bunks were already occupied. My new cell-mates were wide awake, having been woken by the noise of the key in the lock and the opening of the heavy door. Nobody said anything to begin with, but once the guard disappeared they all began to ask questions in Russian. Having noticed my foreign clothes, the soft hat, the smart overcoat, so obviously purchased abroad, they wished to know when I had arrived in the Soviet Union, how long it was since I was brought to the Lubyanka. The questions came thick and fast. I answered them all, and then it was my turn to find out about my cell companions – this group of 'enemies of the people'. They turned out to be highly educated people from the professions – a mining engineer, an architect, a university professor from the engineering faculty and two Red Army officers.

The famous *parasha*, the metal bucket used as a lavatory, stood in its usual place beside the door, despite the fact that the building has been designed as a hotel and had all the usual sanitary conveniences. There it stood on the beautiful old parquet floor, a filthy bucket more than two feet high whose lid did not control the terrible stench – the portable lavatory of all Russian prisons for centuries. It had reigned in the time of the Tsars, and continued to fulfil the same mission under the Communist regime.

In every prison every cell has its roster for emptying the *parasha*. Each morning and evening the inmates take turns to carry it to the main lavatory, where it is briefly washed but never disinfected. In the time of the Tsars, the use of carbolic disinfectant was obligatory throughout the Russian prisons, which then held no more than 22,000 to 23,000 people; not so under the Soviets, whose prison and camp population totalled millions. Ever-present, with its all-pervading stench, the *parasha* became the eternal symbol of Soviet prison life. Serving the natural needs of the detainees, it is known by a woman's name – 'Praskovia Ivanovna' or *parasha* for short. There it stands by the cell door, saturated with the stinking filth accumulated over the years, which nothing can eliminate. The surrounding wooden floor is germ sodden, filthy and permanently stinking, for the organs of the KGB and MVD are not in the least bit concerned with human rights or the humane treatment of prisoners. Human rights are regarded as mere 'bourgeois theories and inventions', outmoded principles not to be applied to enemies of the Soviet people, and the more that die – the better. Over-populated prisons? Not enough beds? So what?! Let the prisoners lie on the floor between wooden bunks, under the bunks, or next to the stinking *parasha*.

For the first two days after my arrival, I remained in the cell. The guard would come from time to time to summon one of my companions, each of whom had been under interrogation for months already. The guard never called out the full surname of the person summoned – only the first letter. He would enter the cell and say 'the letter B', or 'the letter S', as the case might be. Thus there was no danger of the guard inadvertently calling out the name of a prisoner who was in another cell and so revealing his presence. The prisoner whose name began with the initial called had to reply, giving his full name. If this was indeed the name indicated on the list, then the guard would tell him to 'get ready to leave'. Sometimes it happened that two people in the cell had names that both began with the same letter, and if one answered, giving his full name, but it did not correspond with the name on the list, the guard would not reveal the name of the person he wanted but merely said: 'Does the name of anyone else here begin with the letter X?' He then invited the identified man to follow him. Thus were all possible risks of errors and revelations foreseen and eliminated in advance.

The moment the key was heard turning in the heavy lock, everyone became alert. And once the guard had left with the unfortunate prisoner, the others relaxed, happy that this time, at least, it was none of their names that had been called. It was on 7 May, just after ten o'clock at night, that the guard entered our cell and called out the initial letter of my surname. Not yet familiar with the procedure, I did not react until one of the other detainees told me: 'It's probably you he's calling. You must acknowledge it and tell him your full name!' I replied as directed, and my name was indeed the one the guard wanted. So now it was my turn to be told 'get ready to leave', only ten minutes after the ten o'clock signal for 'lights out'. As I was to learn, this was the usual procedure: the signal for bed and lights out and then, ten minutes later, once you had relaxed a little and were feeling sleepy, the summons came for your interrogation.

It took me five minutes to get ready to follow the guard. At the small table in the corridor, the guard responsible for the floor handed me back my spectacles, but not my belt or braces, and another guard, specially sent to fetch me, escorted me to the interrogation room. Once again we took the lift descending two floors. Along a corridor a covered bridge linked the internal prison with the main building of the KGB HQ, and in the corridor sat another guard at a table on which lay open a big register into which he meticulously marked the time a prisoner arrived for interrogation and left once it was over. This book was nicknamed by the prisoners the 'Iron Book' since it was kept open at the page for the day by an aluminium plate. It was simpler to call it an 'Iron' rather than an 'Aluminium' book – the type of metal is immaterial. In the middle of this plate a slot allowed one to see just a line at a time. Thus, when the prisoner stopped to have his name registered, he saw only his name and no others.

My guard signed the book, confirming the handover for the onward journey, and the new guard and I continued on our way, I holding up my trousers. The guard ordered me to walk with hands behind the back. I protested that this was impossible. 'If I do, my trousers will fall down since there's nothing to hold them up, neither belt nor braces, and all the buttons are cut off.' My sojourn in the Caracal camp and the journey via Kishinev to Moscow had resulted in a considerable loss of weight and my usual plump outline had melted away so my clothes no longer fitted. Obviously I was not the first to make such a protest for the guard agreed that I should continue holding up the front of my trousers, but must do so with only one hand, the other to be kept behind my back as ordered!

All along the corridors were the tightly shut doors to small cubicles. As we approached the end of one corridor, and before turning the corner into another, the guard gave a signal, clicking his tongue as a warning of approach. Suddenly, a similar sound was heard from the other corridor. The guard escorting me ordered me to turn about and we quickly retraced our steps to the cells just passed. He locked me into one, leaving me in total darkness. The rapid manoeuvre had been essential to prevent me seeing another escorted prisoner. Apparently no one here had yet discovered the 'one-way' traffic system.

(Throughout the nine months I spent in the Lubyanka, I only once met another prisoner in the corridors. It happened as we were waiting for the lift to come up to take me for yet another interrogation, and as the lift doors opened there stood another prisoner accompanied by his guard. The man was completely unknown to me, but the panic on the faces of the two escorting guards was a sight for sore eyes!)

As soon as our journey could continue, the guard marched me up a handsome grand staircase – the main staircase of the KGB HQ. Stopping in front of a door on the landing, the guard knocked softly, opened the door slightly and announced that he had brought the ZK (the abbreviation for *zaklyuchennyj*, the Russian word for a detainee). We entered a large room whose two big windows overlooked Dzerzhinsky Square (the old Lubyanka Square renamed after the first head of the Cheka, Felix Dzerzhinsky). At the far end, near the window, at a big desk sat my interrogator – a young major of the KGB, aged about thirty-five. Near the door, to the right as one entered, was a small table and a chair, where the guard told me to sit. The interrogator's desk was at least six yards from where I sat, to give an idea of the size of the room.

Again I was asked if I preferred the interrogation to be in Russian or Armenian. I chose Russian. I did not want an interpreter distorting whatever I said. And so began the sacred procedure of the Soviet Judicial Investigation: the famous *anketa*. Again and again I was asked the same questions, to check whether my answers would diverge in any way from those given previously. This part of the interrogation over, I was told to sign the detainee's sheet, a single sheet of paper, containing my answers. I noted that it was dated 8 May 1945 and pointed out that I was arrested in Bucharest on 23 March. But I was told that time spent in detention abroad did not count. 'It is today that your investigation proceedings begin: 8 May 1945 at 0.00 hrs.' In the West, VE-Day was just beginning.

The Major spoke the correct Russian of an educated person. And, since I had answered all the questions listed in the form on his desk, I asked if I, too could ask a question. Might I know his name? Without hesitation he replied, 'Major Guitzenko'. I assumed that this was not his real name, but what did it matter, this name or another? The name he gave is Ukrainian, but his features indicated that he was more probably of Jewish origin. He was very polite. He addressed me, as is customary in Russian, by my first name and patronymic, and I replied, addressing him as 'Major'.

The main point of the indictment was that I was an important member of the Armenian National Party of Dashnaks, which was opposed to the Soviet Government of the USSR. I protested at once that the accusation was totally unfounded. I was never a member of the Dashnak Party, never took part in politics and, above all, never participated in any activities directed against the USSR. On the contrary, from the very beginning of the Second World War, I had worked for a British company operating under the aegis of the British Embassy in Bucharest. In other words, I was working for the British – loyal allies of the USSR. Consequently the accusation was groundless. For although it was true that the Dashnaks did fight with the Nazis during the Second World War, the British were fighting against them, 'They were on your side', I told the major. I could see, from the very first words I spoke, that the major was delighted with my statement. On my own admission I had denounced myself as a British agent! 'Ah,' he said, 'so you are an agent of the British intelligence service. Good, good! So you are a

British spy! Therefore, in accordance with paragraph 6 of Article 58 of the USSR Penal Code, I hereby accuse you of being a British spy!' 'But, major, I protested, 'whatever gave you that idea? The agents of British intelligence services are highly qualified professionals, whereas I was nothing more than a simple clerk working in a British shipping company with barges on the Danube. Our aim was to maintain as high a tonnage of navigation as possible, so as to decrease the availability of transportation for the German armed forces. The company was operating in a neutral country. It was the most we could do to help the war effort in the circumstances. So how could I possibly be a spy operating against the interests of the USSR – in a neutral country moreover?'

The major, however, stuck firmly to his position. He repeated confidently that the KGB would prove me to be a British spy! It was a tune I was to hear over and over: 'We, the Soviets, do not arrest anyone until and unless we have irrefutable proof of their guilt and involvement in criminal activities! We have all the time we need to keep under surveillance suspected enemies of the state, and once their crime is proven, and not before, they are brought here to the Lubyanka, from where there is no escape!' And so that there should be no doubt in my mind as to what he meant, so that I should better understand my situation, he handed me a booklet entitled *The Penal Code of the USSR*, telling me to study Article 58, paragraph 6, which concerned 'spies'.

He stopped talking to let me read in silence while he continued to study my file. I read to reassure myself. It said that punishment for the crime of spying is 'detention for ten years in a forced labour camp', or, in more serious cases, the death penalty. Since he had already made it clear that my fate was sealed and that I should never leave, I told Guitzenko that there was no point in continuing this farce. Further discussion was useless since the outcome was already decided. He could give me the Act of Accusation according to Article 58, paragraph 6, and I would sign it, confirming I have taken note of its contents. It would then be up to them to prove the extent of my activities against the USSR, since they refused to accept my denial.

The major added a note, recording my declaration that my activities in Romania were directed in favour of the Allies. He informed me that my contention that I was therefore also working in the interests of the USSR was totally erroneous as Great Britain had been only briefly an ally of the Soviets, for the duration of the war against Germany. The interests of the two countries were completely opposed, Great Britain being a capitalist country whereas the USSR was a Communist democracy. With the war against Germany nearing its end, the war between Communism and capitalism was about to recommence! The logical conclusion to this was that, in working for the British during the war, I was in fact working against the interests of the USSR. When I persisted with my argument that my activities in Romania were directed solely against Nazi Germany, the major replied that there would be plenty of opportunity to see and check the truth of what I was saying.

This is only the gist of the nine-hour interrogation to which I was subjected during this session. It lasted from 10 p.m. on 7 May until 7 a.m. the next morning, the 8th. The major's assertions, my answers and explanations, were hardly the simple matter of a few exchanges. To all my protests at his accusations, he invariably found an unexpected answer based on party-line doctrine, which I, of course, found totally unacceptable. I tried not to give way, but he wouldn't accept my answers and renewed his attacks and accusations. From the very beginning I knew I would have to sign whatever paper he put in front of me, but I refused to give in without a fight. The accusation was so stupid and unreal. I wanted to place on record my protestations, even though our conversation was a sort of dialogue of the deaf with no basis for mutual understanding.

And so at exactly seven in the morning the Major rang for a guard to escort me back to my cell. At the desk of the 'Iron Book', the guard recorded the time of my return journey. Back in the cell, it was reveille time: the morning wash and brush-up accompanied by emptying of the *parasha*. Then we had to wait a while before the arrival of the tea canteen, except that no tea, no milk and sugar, are involved, only boiling water. No doubt somebody pocketed our ration. As well as having our enamel mugs filled with hot water, each of us was also given a piece of black rye bread, very badly baked. The water and bread is consumed at one go, even if one isn't hungry. There is no point in keeping the bread for later. It would be bound to be stolen and eaten by another hungry inmate.

At ten o'clock the guards did the rounds again, to summon the various detainees for the day's interrogation. Again it was my turn to be called for an interrogation that would continue until seven in the evening, and so it went on without respite for a whole week: no chance to rest at night, and none during the day either; no rest between the return to the cell and being summoned for the next interrogation; no rest at all for a whole week. The interrogation dragged on and on, always with the same questions: 'Tell me what anti-Soviet activities were you engaged in while working for the British during the war?' My reply, too, was always the same: 'What sort of activity could I possibly have undertaken against the Soviet Union? I was living in Bucharest, in Romania – a neutral country. There was no communication whatsoever with the USSR! I was working as an accountant in a British shipping company which owned barges on the Danube. How – in this situation – could I possibly engage in anti-Soviet activities? The accusation you are making is not logical. Besides, I was working with your great ally – Great Britain.' But always at this point the major interrupted to say sharply: 'Not so! The British were our allies only while we were waging a war against Hitler! That was only a temporary arrangement and, historically, we are in opposing camps because we are Communists and the British are Capitalists. The war-time alliance against Hitler did not alter this fact, even during the war we remained enemies under the apparent friendliness. That was the basic position, and it remained unchanged.'

We talked of many things, the major and I, but always he reverted to the same issue, the oft-repeated question: 'And now, why don't you tell me something about your anti-Soviet activities in Romania?'

On the evening after my final interrogation, we were sitting in our cell on the fourth floor when, at almost nine o'clock, we suddenly heard a loud rumbling noise and the whole building began to shake. We sat looking at one another wonderingly. It could not be an earthquake because it went on and on for some thirty to forty minutes. Then, just as suddenly, everything was calm again. We simply could not understand what it could have been, Nobody could think of a suitable explanation, and I continued to sit, waiting for the evening's summons for interrogation.

A little after ten o'clock the guard came to escort me to the major's office, and as I entered I greeted him before asking him to explain the meaning of the tremendous noise and shaking to which the building had just been subjected. He laughed and exclaimed: 'It's peace! The Germans have finally surrendered. There will be a grand Victory Parade in Red Square tomorrow. The noise you heard was our tanks passing on their way to Red Square to take up their positions for tomorrow's ceremony.'

That said, we returned to work, to the questions already becoming very familiar: 'And now, tell me about your anti-Soviet activities,' and so on, and on, and on! I tried to reply as good-naturedly, as patiently as I could, trying to distract his persistence by turning the conversation to the happy life we had in Romania, with the lively restaurants, night-clubs and cabaret shows continuing into the night. I could see that he enjoyed all this and gradually I succeeded in establishing a more friendly atmosphere. There were fewer of the enervating questions which he had persisted in throwing at me all the time. We chatted like this for a while but sooner or later he reverted to his set routine, the same old questions. Day or night, it was always the same.

On another occasion, I tried to change tactics again. I told him: 'My dear major, I am too stupid for all these complicated games you play. Just give me a blank piece of paper and I will sign it. You can then fill it in as you please!' 'No,' he exclaimed, 'I can't do it that way. I need facts, full details of your life and your activities in Romania.' It seemed that he wanted to give me another chance, wanted to continue our talks about the Bucharest night-life which he seemed to relish. Yet however much I could change the atmosphere of our conversation, he would suddenly pick on a detail and pounce, pleased to be catching me out over an interesting point that would come in useful for interrogation records.

On my guard, I continued during these sessions to relate my *dolce vita* existence in Bucharest, trying to present myself as a not too serious character, as someone who loved the good life. The conversation grew more free, more agreeable and friendly, for we were becoming well-acquainted with one another's ways by now. And then there came the moment when the major, as if suddenly noticing how exhausted I was from lack of food and sleep, asked if I was hungry. I realized that he was trying the well-known method for making the subject being interrogated more pliable and easier to manipulate. But I replied without hesitation: 'Of course I'm hungry, and I need some sleep!'

He lifted the telephone and gave the order: 'Bring some food for a ZK' (as detainees are called). In ten minutes a tray arrived with two slices of bread, some cheese, a small dish of *kisel*, a jelly made from fruit juice and cornflower, and a glass of tea with sugar. 'You can eat in peace and when you have finished we will continue our conversation,' said the Major. I did not wait to be invited a second time. I started to eat slowly, savouring every morsel and hoping thus to delay as long as possible the inevitable return to our so-called 'conversation'.

The Major was perfectly aware of the food the ZK's normally ate, of our breakfasts of hot water and rye bread, of our suppers consisting of a plate of watery soup, known as *balanda*, in which floated two or three pieces of frost-blackened potato and some fish bones (though never any fish as such), followed by a lump of boiled buck-wheat – a sort of porridge, but lacking any butter or fat. That was all. Then back to the interrogation.

As I was eating another KGB interrogator of junior rank – a captain – entered to consult the major on another case. He handed him a file to study and asked for his comments. It appeared that my major was Chief Interrogator, head of a Section of Interrogators, and had very strong views on how things should be done. He read through the file and commented: 'No, no, you've got it wrong! You must change the wording of the evidence and re-edit the ZK's statement, which must aim to prove that ...! Take it back and be sure you change it all the way through ...' As I realized only too clearly, it was the major who decided how the accused must confess, how his confession should be worded so that the accusation should prove to be well-founded! And when my turn came, I, too, would be subjected to the same experience as this unknown ZK.

When we eventually continued I described the activities of the Goeland Shipping Company on the Danube, activities aimed at thwarting the Germans' supplies of fuel, wheat and other necessities. I explained how the company's tugs, barges and tankers, flying the Red Ensign, remained inactive throughout the years of Romania's neutrality, and the difficulties this created for the Germans. Unable to use any of the barges and tankers already there, they were obliged to build others and to man them with sailors who needed to be withdrawn from other fronts. Furthermore, the company's agencies along the Danube ensured the execution of a plan for 'passive resistance'. Although nothing was moving, the crews continued to receive high salaries and had to report each morning to the agency's office to sign the duty register. The agency directors travelled regularly to head office in Bucharest, to report to the director-general, an Englishman attached to the British Embassy, who was thus kept well informed of all events along the river. For example, when Mussolini's armies failed to defeat the heroic Greek people, Hitler decided to rush German troops to his aid. But to do so he had to pass through Romania. The poor Romanians, abandoned by the Western Powers even as the Poles and the Yugoslavs had been abandoned before them, had no option but to agree to the Germans' demand. They were forced to allow Romanian territory to be used for the transit of German troops to Greece, but the director of the company's agency in Turnu Severin informed the director-general in Bucharest the moment the Germans began the transit of their troops through his area of the Danube.

No sooner had these words left my lips than the major pounced on them and, rising from his desk, he came towards me, shouting in triumph: 'Aha, I've got you. You were the British Resident there. You have just given me the proof I needed!' Naively I protested that I didn't understand. 'What is a Resident?' I asked. But the major was very pleased with himself and told me I was a self-confessed important spy, one who resided in the centre to collect the information gathered by junior spies.

His brusque outburst seemed funny, it was so ridiculous it was only another trick to intimidate me, but precisely because it was so funny, instead of frightening me he made me laugh. I had truly neither heard the term Resident nor knew what it meant. 'But it's not I who received the various agency directors' reports, it was the director-general,' I said. 'I have already told you, I was only a humble accountant who sent the agencies money for the salaries due to be paid to the crews, and to cover the main-tenance costs of the immobilized craft. Besides, the transit of German troops had been openly reported in the Romanian press, and everybody could read about it there even as I did. The passage of German armies through Romania was no secret, and the fact that I was working as an accountant with a British company does not mean that I was working against the Soviet Union. On the contrary, all my sympathies were with the Russian people fighting against the German aggressor.'

Not once did those long days and nights of tortuous interrogation suc-ceed in forcing me to deviate in any way from the pattern of behaviour I decided upon right at the start. I remained determined to show myself as a good-natured and good-tempered person, to prove to the major that, far from being the VIP spy he tried to make me out, I found all his accusations ridiculous and groundless. Again and again I offered to make his task easier by signing whatever declaration he wished, for what was the point of going on after he had told me that my fate was already decided and that 'a sincere confession on my part might lighten the envisaged sentence', to use his very words!

At the end of a week's interrogation, and despite all my willingness to co-operate, he had little material to support the chief accusation that I was a spy working for the British Intelligence Service. He ceased insisting on the oft-repeated question about my anti-Soviet activities. In fact, I was allowed to sit in peace in my corner. He did not speak for hours on end but spent most of his time studying the papers on his desk, not only the papers in my file but also others brought to him by junior interrogators so that he could 'tidy up the case and comment on it'. Again, he ordered that a meal be brought up to me, the same menu as last time, and as I ate he continued to work.

I concluded that each case under interrogation was assigned a set number of hours for which they were paid a bonus. This applied to all interrogators, and my major, too, must remain at his desk, studying my file for the whole time allocated.

He told me that my statements had been sent to Bucharest for verification and comments by the Romanian Security Service. I also noted that the major himself changed tactics. He questioned me in detail about Dro, his activities and connections with the Germans during the war. I repeated all that I knew on the subject, giving him, as a start, a general outline of how Dro left Romania at the beginning of 1941. My British employers knew about Dro's connections with the Germans, but allowed me to continue working as an accountant for the company in which Dro was principal shareholder.

On Dro's rare appearances in Bucharest, he would be accompanied by a German officer, a certain Captain Klir – a fluent Russian speaker who acted as interpreter between Dro and the German Mission to Romania on his travels through Russian provinces occupied by German troops. Dro and his companion had at their disposal a small military aircraft. I knew that, as part of his anti-Soviet activities, Dro had the authorization of the German High Command to visit Soviet POW camps to arrange for the release of all officers and soldiers of Armenian origin so they could be sent to join the so-called Armenian Legions. These military units were being formed by the Germans in the rear of the front line, somewhere in the Ukraine. They were not to take part in actual battles against the Soviet armed forces. That was one of the conditions made by Dro in his agreement to co-operate with the Germans, who regarded him as the official representative of the Armenian Dashnak National Party. The Legions were being kept in reserve for the day when the German armies reached the Armenian frontier in Transcaucasia, the plan being to use them as the basis for a Free Armenian Government and administration.

Whenever I saw Dro on the occasions when he came to collect his share of the company profits, he would speak at length of the atrocities committed by the German armies in the Ukraine. 'You cannot even imagine the extent of the terrible war crimes committed by the Germans against the civilian population and the POWs in the Ukraine,' he used to say. He was so horrified himself that he could not bear to describe the details. He told me that his sole mission and duty was to save at least the Armenian prisoners from a similar fate. He could do nothing for the others. The Germans would not allow him to intervene for anybody who was not an Armenian, on the grounds that the fate of the other Soviet POWs was no concern of his. He could visit the camps and release Armenian prisoners from certain death from hunger by arranging their dispatch to the rear to join the Armenian Legions, but that was all.

The major made careful notes of all my statements concerning Dro, and when I had finished handed me a booklet entitled *Dro Kanayan* saying: 'Take it and read it, for everything you told me is already known to us. This proves that you have indeed spoken the truth, and that you did not try to conceal anything from us. That is good!' I studied the booklet carefully, taking my time to prolong the respite from interrogation. It was a summary of Dro's activities, having been written up as a sort of manual for KGB interrogators. Indeed, everything I had said corresponded exactly with what was in the booklet, except that it labelled Dro a great criminal and enemy of the Soviet people. It also named several of his collaborators, though fortunately my name was not listed among them.

Having thus failed to obtain sufficient proof to substantiate the accusation against me, even after a week of ceaseless interrogation, the major gave me the 'Official Report on the Case' to sign. I was delighted to read that the accusation of espionage (in accordance with paragraph 6 of Article 58) was anulled for lack of material evidence. I certified that I had read the document and taken note of its contents. I was now being detained without any formal accusation, but this minor detail changed nothing so far as the KGB were concerned. The major then sent me back to my cell, warning me that the interrogation would be resumed as usual at ten o'clock. But this was a trick, the usual method of keeping detainees in a constant state of apprehension. Ten o'clock arrived and nobody summoned me to the major's office. What could it mean? I asked the others, but they didn't know either. One could never say what would happen or what to expect. I took advantage of the fact and tried to catch up on my sleep. But I couldn't stop worrying, I didn't know what to think, what to expect next. Only after several days had gone by in peace with no summons, could I finally relax and sleep at night, like my companions in the Lubyanka cell.

Who were these companions who shared my cell? I met many interesting people during my stay in the Lubyanka, but will mention only a few as typical cases demonstrating the unscrupulous methods used by the KGB and Soviet justice. There was, for instance, an old gentleman in his seventies, so short-sighted as to be almost blind. He had to hold a book two inches away from his eyes to read. A former professor at the Engineering Faculty in Moscow University, the most important factor in his life was his marriage to the sister of the infamous Menzhinsky, the Old Bolshevik revolutionary appointed to succeed the butcher Dzerzhinsky as head of the dreaded Cheka. The professor himself had had a rich revolutionary past. After the October Revolution he was appointed Director of the Taganka prison in Moscow, and he assured us the official figure for the *entire* prison population throughout the whole Tsarist Russian Empire in 1917 was only 22,000 to 23,000. Of the many things he had to tell, the one which struck me particularly was this statement. We could not believe it could be such a small number, especially when compared to the hundreds of thousands filling the prisons and the millions wasting away in the concentration camps of the Communist regime. But he assured us, as prison governor he had had access to all the records of prisoners detained not only in his day but also in the days before the Revolution. He knew what he was talking about.

Later, he lectured at Moscow University as a professor for many years, and as a member of the old Revolutionary cadres considered himself to be above suspicion – a fatal assumption. When talking to colleagues at the university, he let slip a few remarks that did not correspond with the current Party line and was inevitably denounced. The old man was arrested and was subjected to a merciless interrogation, the accusation being that he had participated in a plot against Menzhinsky, despite the fact that his brother-in-law died many years before. I often wondered how long he could survive this terrible ordeal.

Another cell mate was a mining engineer who had graduated from the famous Institute of Mines in Leningrad. Aged about thirty-five, he was highly cultured and spoke very educated Russian, which was rare among the younger generation in the Soviet Union. He was knowledgeable not only in Russian literature but also in the literature of other countries as well as in international politics. His story was a familiar one. Part of his job as director of an industrial complex in Central Asia involved regular trips to Moscow to report in person to the Ministry. He was an able manager and had good relations with all the important people. Each time he came to Moscow he brought gifts for various officials, since nothing works in the USSR without such 'gifts'. Then, all at once he was arrested and accused of being a Trotskyite, an accusation probably based on the denunciation of a jealous comrade intriguing for his job. But there was no way for him to defend himself. As my friend, the major, kept assuring me, 'whoever enters the Lubyanka is brought there because he is already known to be guilty.'

We became close friends, speaking the same language, and tried to talk whenever possible without being overheard by others. He warned me not to be too open with our fellow prisoners. He was afraid of them, especially of a young architect whom he suspected of being a 'stool-pigeon'. I described to him the book written by Solonevich twenty years before on Soviet prison life, as he had never heard of it. After several such talks, he tried to cheer me up by saying: 'Now that I know you better, I am sure you will survive all the difficulties of our Soviet way of life with its inhuman camps system. I am certain your courage will never fail you, and that you will be able to adapt yourself to the terrible ordeal awaiting us all. I am sure you will survive!' I often had cause to remember our conversation, his dire prophecies and his confidence that I would survive all hunger, sickness and suffering with the help of my indomitable spirit. It's true that, twice, I succeeded in cheating death of her prey, that twice I reached the very limits of all possible endurance and suffering. It's true that I had the necessary will to resist, the courage and the spirit, but it is also true that I was very lucky each time to find someone to help me survive the terrible conditions of prison and camp life.

A second mining engineer in the cell was a younger man, a typical product of the Soviet system. He had not graduated from the Leningrad Institute of Mines, but had studied at one of the new polytechnics specially created to help produce at speed the technical cadres so desperately needed to complete the programme of technical and industrial reconstruction after the ravages of the Civil War. The polytechnic graduates were specialists in their own narrow fields and nothing more. Their general knowledge was of a purely Soviet character. That is to say, they had received thorough instruction in the political dogmas of the Communist Party creed.

At the start of the war, the young engineer had been called up and commissioned. Shortly afterwards he was taken prisoner by the Germans and forced to work for them, the Germans denying their Soviet prisoners the rules of the Geneva Convention. Even the officers were forced to work in factories to make more Germans available for despatch to the front, but most Soviet POWs were glad to do it, conditions for a factory worker being much better than those in the camps, where they were starved and persecuted and died in their thousands.

Having admitted the nature of his speciality, the young officer engineer had the good fortune to be seconded to work as an assistant to the chief German chemist in a laboratory, and here he saw how the Germans had discovered a new chemical powder compound for welding together metals, the formula for which was completely unknown to the Soviets. As a good patriot he managed to conceal some of the powder so that the formula might later be examined and identified. With the Red Army's advance across Germany, the POW camps were also liberated. At the earliest opportunity, the young engineer presented himself to the Soviet Commandant to inform him how he had succeeded in discovering various secret methods used by the German metallurgical industry, and that he now wished to offer them to his country for the benefit of the Motherland.

Alas, it was the worst mistake he could have made. His story was listened to with grave attention. He was thanked for his devotion and requested to write down a detailed scientific report on the powder compound stolen and hidden on his person. He was given the chance to write his report in peace, but as soon as it was finished he was arrested and told brusquely: 'Thank you for your devotion, but you are a self-confessed traitor. You have broken the oath of a Red Army officer which says you should kill yourself rather than surrender to the enemy! What is more, you became a collaborator of the enemies of the Soviet people.' This was how he came to be in our cell in the Lubyanka, probably destined to receive the sentence meted out to all Soviet POWs who dared to surrender rather than kill themselves – ten years in a forced labour camp!

A third engineer in our cell, a young engineer-architect, was the one of whom the mining engineer had warned me to be wary. He did not trust him at all. The architect had been employed in the offices of the General Administration of Reconstruction, specially set up by the Soviet Government to deal with the immense programme of reconstruction which would have to be organized after the end of the war when all the principal cities in

European Russia would be in ruins, destroyed by aerial bombardment or dynamited by retreating German armies. This young man, like many friends and colleagues, believed that the end of the war would bring great political changes in the country and there would be a new life of freedom and patriotism. They spoke much of this, exchanging ideas among themselves. But there were some security people in their group keeping everything under close surveillance, watching and listening. There was no plot as such, no organized movement, only ordinary discussion among intellectuals. But it was of too liberal a character and enough for the young architect to be arrested and accused of anti-Soviet propaganda.

As usual, he knew nothing about the fate of the others. It was enough for two people to be suspected together, even if they were husband and wife, for them to be arrested and accused of organizing a counter-revolutionary group. The young architect was dragged off for interrogation day after day, and one evening he returned in a state of complete dejection. From the questions put to him by his interrogator he realized that his wife had also been arrested and that she, too, was in a cell in the Lubyanka.

Another occupant of our cell was an old general aged seventy-three, General von Stern. Although his name was of German origin, the family originally came from the Baltic countries annexed by Peter the Great and had become completely Russified. Before the First World War, the general had been a brilliant young professor at the Artillery Academy in St Petersburg. He was a specialist in Ballistics, and it was he who designed and supervised the construction of the two fortresses on the shores of the Finnish Gulf in the Baltic, near the Kronstadt Naval Base. Their batteries of modern cannon were able to provide a volley of cross-fire to deter any enemy intruders in the Kronstadt approaches.

In July 1914, just before the outbreak of war, the French President Raymond Poincaré was on an official visit to Russia, and young Colonel Stern, then aged only 42, was given the task of demonstrating the efficacy of the new fortress guns in the presence of the Tsar and the French President. A convoy of barges was to attempt an entry into the gulf, in the guise of ships of the enemy fleet. Colonel Stern gave the order to fire. Any artilleryman will tell you that it's practically impossible to hit the target bullseye with the first shot, even if all the distances had been carefully calculated beforehand, and the zone divided into well-defined target sectors. But von Stern scored a spectacular direct hit with the first salvo. The Tsar was delighted, and congratulated the young colonel, addressing him as 'General'. In addition to this instant promotion, Stern was also awarded the order of St Vladimir 4th class.

When the 1917 Revolution broke out, von Stern was transferred to Odessa as Professor at the School for Heavy Artillery, called the Sergeevskoe. And thus, after October 1917, found himself in the zone occupied by the White Army of General Denikin, who at once appointed him Comptroller-General of the White Armies. When the Whites were defeated in 1920, he was evacuated with the others to Turkey, where the remnants of the retreating White Armies were maintained by the Allied Forces at Gallipoli. Later the Whites were allowed to leave and settle in Bulgaria and Yugoslavia - Slav countries where they were well received. General von Stern, already famous for his expertise in his own field, was at once taken on by the Yugoslav Ministry of Defence and given the very important task of reorganizing the defences of the ports and fortresses along the part of the Dalmatian coast annexed by Yugoslavia after the fall of the Austro-Hungarian Empire.

When the Second World War broke out, the situation of Russian emigrés in Yugoslavia became both tragic and intolerable. In the ever-intensifying struggle between the nationalist units led by Mihailović and the Communist Partisans under Tito, it was always the Russian emigrés who were suspected, persecuted and assassinated. Miraculously, the general succeeded in fleeing Yugoslavia when the German troops entered the country and was helped to make his way to Germany, together with other Russian refugees. In Germany, he found work in one of the Zeiss factories for optical instruments, now installed underground to protect them from Allied air-raids. As the Allied forces advanced into Germany, precipitating collapse and chaos, a mass of refugees clogged roads, desperately trying to reach the safety of the American Zone. The old general, now ill and exhausted, also succeeded in finding refuge with the Americans after several days of marching on foot. He was nursed back to health, and with rest and good food gradually regained his strength. The Americans offered him a job in the United States where his knowledge would be very useful. But von Stern was already seventy-three. What could he do in America at that age? Moreover, he had heard that the Soviet government had proclaimed a General Amnesty for all Russians living abroad, inviting them all to return home. 'Your Motherland awaits you,' ran the proclamation. The old man thought it over and decided it was preferable to return to Russia. At least that way he would die in his own country and not be buried in some foreign land.

The Americans could neither dissuade nor prevent him. As he wished, they escorted him to the Soviet Zone, where the Soviet authorities greeted him with open arms: 'But of course, your Excellency, you are free to return to Russia, free to go wherever you please. Where would you like to go?' 'I have an old sister living in Moscow, I would like to go and see her, and stay with her, if possible,' said the general. 'Ah, unfortunately that will not be possible. We regret it, but the capital is already over-populated. Perhaps you could choose somewhere else,' was the ingratiating reply. 'Well, yes, I have another sister living in Rostov-on-Don,' said the general. 'So that's agreed, then. Here is your rail ticket. You can travel on your own, through Kharkov. All is in order, your Excellency.'

And so his Excellency boarded the train to Kharkov, stopped there a day to catch the connection to Rostov-on-Don and then continued his journey. But the authorities at Rostov had been warned of his arrival. He was met at the station by two officers of the KGB and, as yet unaware of who they were, was delighted to see them. They took him to a car outside the station and asked him to get in. The car drove through scenes of total devastation and stopped outside an imposing ruin. This was the local KGB HQ, and without further ado the general was escorted to the cellars, already crammed full with detainees, some sitting, others lying on the floor. The cellar windows were broken.

After several days in the cellar he was put on the train to Moscow, in a first-class carriage, but this time under the escort of a young KGB officer. Two days later he arrived in Moscow, where he had asked to go in the first place, but instead of seeing his sister was taken straight to the Lubyanka. As one discovered, the KGB were not lacking in a sense of humour, albeit of a somewhat peculiar brand! At the Lubyanka he was accused of high treason, his list of crimes going back over twenty-five years to 1920. But the old general had returned to die and be buried in his homeland, and the KGB were doing everything to respect his wishes and expedite the event. He was dragged to endless interrogation sessions and questioned about other emigrés, on whom the KGB were anxious to obtain more information. To impress on him how all-powerful and all-knowledgeable they were, they showed him a big dossier with his name on the cover. 'So you see, we know everything about you. You must tell us the truth and conceal nothing,' they told him again and again. It is a method as old as time. They knew a few facts about his past life which they kept throwing at him to frighten him and convince him that they knew far more than he was prepared to tell.

None of the detainees had the right to correspond with his family, or to communicate with them in any way until the interrogation was completed. And yet, among the detainees in our cell were some who still had families living in Moscow, and who, from time to time, received parcels containing no letters but food or cigarettes. For the general, cigarettes were far more important than food, which did not really interest him. He was a heavy smoker and without his daily dose of cigarettes he felt quite ill. So anyone in the cell who received cigarettes or ordinary *makhorka* (tobacco made from the stalks rather than the leaves of the plant, chopped into little bits) invariably shared them with the general. It was customary among detainees to share out whatever they received. But as time went on, the parcels became smaller. The absence of the head of the family was cutting resources and each parcel represented an immense sacrifice. And so, despite this sharing, it sometimes happened that there were periods when nobody had any tobacco left at all. And one day, during such a period, the general suddenly fell to the floor. He had not had a cigarette for several days and the lack of the, to him, indispensable stimulant had precipitated his collapse. As he once explained to me, he started smoking at the age of twelve, and his body had become so used to tobacco that he could not live without it.

As one's interrogation approaches its end and your fate is being decided, your spectacles are returned to you. That was a good sign. It meant that the interrogator had succeeded in arranging the evidence to his satisfaction. Also, having your spectacles back meant you could read or play chess. There was a set of chessmen in our cell and we were allowed one book each a week. The prison library was well stocked so the six of us in the cell agreed among ourselves to take out six books each week so they could be passed round and read by each in turn. One morning when the young woman librarian came to our cell with the catalogue from which to choose a book, I asked for Dostoyevsky's *The Possessed*. My cellmates gasped at my audacity. Dostoyevsky's books had been banned since the Revolution, the Party having decided that this author had been making fun of the heroes of the Revolution! But no, she raised no objection and through some inadvertence it would seem that the detainees in the Lubyanka were allowed to read *The Possessed*. Or was it that the authorities thought it didn't really matter since we were already 'contaminated' and removed from circulation?

I witnessed on several occasions how well trained and disciplined the guards were for their delicate task and their ability to cope. They were always calm and polite, like nurses in a psychiatric hospital, which was not really surprising when one considers that some of the detainees were in a highly abnormal state of tension after all the pressure and suffering to which they had been subjected in the course of interrogation sessions.

One day a new detainee was brought in to occupy a bunk recently vacated. He was a Russian Jew of about forty-five, born in Russia at the end of the century. He emigrated to the United States after the 1905 Revolution and the pogroms that followed. As a US citizen he had travelled far and wide, so regaled us with stories of his trips to India, China and Japan. At the time of the Civil War which followed the 1917 Revolution, he was working as a taxi driver in Constantinople during the period of the great famine in Russia when the Americans were busy organizing famine relief for the starving Russian population through the American Relief Association (ARA). By an extraordinary stroke of fate, two ARA personnel got into his taxi and he overheard them discussing preparations for their imminent departure to Russia. He offered to accompany them, saying he could be very useful to them. After all, he spoke fluent Russian. The offer was accepted and off he went, back to Russia. After the Americans left, he stayed on, first working for the ARA, then employed by the Soviets themselves, and finally getting a job with the newly established Ford motor car factories in the USSR. But everywhere he went he was regarded with suspicion and envy by his Russian comrades because of the privileges accorded this 'American' Jew. Watched all the time by his mates, as well as by the KGB, it wasn't long before he was arrested on charges of 'economic espionage', the formula frequently used for arresting foreigners working in the USSR.

The poor fellow arrived in our cell in a terrible state of nerves. God knows what treatment he had been subjected to. He shouted, cursed, picked quarrels for no reason, even with us, his fellow sufferers. One day as we were all sitting at the table trying to eat our usual menu of *kasha* (baked buckwheat) and black bread, he exploded in hysterical rage and started shouting: 'How can you eat *kasha* with bread? Whoever saw anyone eating bread with bread! It's just not done, you bunch of savages, you ... I don't even know what you are any more!' All our attempts to calm him down and stop his hysterical outburst were to no avail.

At nine o'clock each evening the lights were dipped for a moment: the signal for everybody to get to bed, though one could still read in bed till ten o'clock, when the signal was given for 'lights out'. One evening, after nine o'clock as we were lying in bed, each reading his book, suddenly 'our American' started to shout and tear to shreds the book he had been reading. His shouting became so loud that the guard heard and came into the cell to investigate and at once saw the miserable fellow tearing up a book, the property of the prison library and therefore of the State. He grabbed the book and ordered us all to hand over our books as well. 'You will be given no more books after this,' he declared. This was a catastrophe, a terrible punishment, our sole diversion taken away from us.

My friend the mining engineer tried to persuade the guard to relent. He explained that the poor fellow suffered from a nervous illness which gave rise to uncontrollable outbursts. We all joined in and pleaded with the guard not to punish us all because of this incident. The guard thought it over and said, 'All right, for the moment I'll leave your books. But this is a grave situation and I must report it to my superiors. In the meantime, watch over your comrade and make sure nothing like it ever happens again!' We all thanked the guard for his kindness and he left.

This was one incident which showed the human side of this simple soldier-guard and the relations between prison staff and detainees. The guards did not try to persecute us, or in any way to abuse their power. They simply enforced the strict discipline of the Lubyanka system, and in that, as I learnt in due course, they were unusual. It was a different story in the other Soviet prisons I passed through, and a very different story in the camps.

The KGB made no exceptions in enforcing punishment on all those who dared criticize the Soviet system. One day, a Red Army officer was brought to our cell – a young Second Lieutenant who had fought with the partisan groups organized by the Soviet Government to fight behind enemy lines, as soon as Hitler's armies invaded in 1941. As the unprepared Red Army retreated before the invader's tanks, special units were left behind to organise the Resistance movement, which would maintain constant liaison with the various Red Army HQ and receive regular supplies of arms and ammunition, dropped by small low-flying planes, which could land almost anywhere. The Resistance waged a cruel and implacable guerrilla war against the German forces of occupation. The young Second Lieutenant described to us how they attacked enemy transports and lines of communications, killing the enemy mercilessly wherever they encountered them, without bothering to take prisoners, thus avenging the murder of parents, wives and children, ill-treated, persecuted and killed by the conquering Nazi barbarians. Lightning attacks on small German units were made, and then the partisan group would rapidly disappear into surrounding forests. The entire Ukrainian and Russian population sympathized with the partisans, and helped them in every way they could. For his bravery he was promoted head of a large group of partisans and, after a truly spectacular feat of courage, a plane was sent to take him to Moscow where he was decorated with the Gold Star of Hero of the Soviet Union, at a special ceremony arranged at the Kremlin. This was the highest order, created specially for great feats of courage during the Great Patriotic War, as the Second World War is known in the Soviet Union. After such a momentous occasion, he went into town to celebrate with congenial drinking companions. Totally drunk, he thought he was back amongst his partisans, and there followed the inevitable punch-up. The Militia arrived, and he was arrested. This extraordinary phenomenon stayed with us only for one day, and after that he too disappeared, but from what we saw of him, he should have been awarded the order of a Hero of Soviet Vodka Drinkers.

His place in our cell was taken by a 19-year old German soldier, still wearing his German Army tunic. A theological student at the University of Konigsberg in East Prussia when he was called up, he was sent for training to a military school for WT communications. There, he was chosen, together with another soldier, for an important mission on the Eastern Front. They were told that a large German unit in Byelorussia (the Russian province on the border with Poland) had been completely encircled by the Red Army, but had refused to surrender, and continued sending messages to the Eastern Front HQ, until two days ago, when all radio contact ceased. It was essential that the link be urgently restored, and the two young WT operators would be parachuted in that very night, to see what had gone wrong. They were to be dropped into the zone indicated in the last location given by the encircled unit. They were to be issued with W/T equipment and a secret code they had to memorize, for communicating with Eastern Front HQ. That same night, the two young German soldiers were parachuted over a large forest, where signal flares could be seen directed at their plane from amongst the trees. Although his companion fell badly and became entangled in the trees from which he had difficulty in freeing himself, our new cellmate landed safely. He quickly undid the straps of his parachute, and hid it. Just then a group of soldiers in German uniform arrived led by a 2nd Lieutenant, and they led him through the forest to the officers' camp, where he was ordered to hand over his arms, because no one was allowed to enter the camp armed. The young parachutist did as he was told. He then presented himself to the Duty Officer to report on his mission, after which he was sent to bed to get some sleep.

In the middle of the night, he was suddenly woken up by the sound of shots being fired. The camp was overrun by Russian soldiers, and being unarmed, he was at once taken prisoner. It was only then that he realized that it was all a farce. The German military unit he was dropped to make contact with, did not in fact exist. It had long ago surrendered to the Red

Army. The camp was now occupied by Red Army soldiers wearing German uniforms for their own reasons. They had been waiting for him to be parachuted in, and he was disarmed to prevent him from some mad gesture of defiance when he realized that he had fallen into a well-prepared trap! Next, he was taken to a Soviet officer speaking perfect German who ordered him to behave as though nothing had happened, he would re-establish the W/T link with the German Eastern Front HQ which had sent him on his mission. He would send the messages he would be given and no other, otherwise ...! Was that clear? In the meantime, his companion on the mission had also been found and taken prisoner. He was slightly wounded, and had already agreed to do everything the Soviets asked. Probably, they had each been told that the other one had already agreed, this being the usual procedure.

His instructions were to send a message to HQ every day, indicating a new position 'as though the unit was fighting its way westwards towards the German lines'. He was told: 'You will be given the details of the message to be sent, including new codes for signalling the planes which must come over to drop more supplies. The message would ask for more provisions of food and ammunition to be parachuted to us each day!' Thus for the next ten days, the German HQ on the Eastern Front received signals drafted by the Red Army. All the requests in the messages sent were carried out and the food and ammunition dropped by pre-arranged signal. And as the Red Army group advanced westwards each day, the young German soldier went with them, sending messages as he was told, while the Soviet officer acting as his escort would laugh and say: 'You see, we have a very good agent in the German HQ on the Eastern Front. He forewarned us of your arrival, so we were well prepared to receive you!'

Then after ten days, the drops of supplies ceased. The Germans had probably become suspicious. Soon after that, a Soviet general arrived to visit 'the surrounded German unit'. He thanked the young German for his collaboration and promised that he would be well taken care of. But this generous promise by the general had quite different consequences from the expected ones, and the young German now found himself thrown into the Lubyanka prison, accused of espionage. Several days later, he was taken away from our cell altogether, and not brought back. Probably, like other Germans, he would be sentenced to 10 years' hard labour. But at least, his fate would be better than ours, for German POWs were better treated, better fed than we, the so-called 'enemies of the people', and for a very good reason. The Soviet Government had certain plans for them: to indoctrinate them thoroughly prior to their repatriation so that they would form the main support base for the future Communist administration in Democratic Republics. The same applied to all prisoners from Eastern Europe, whether East Germany, Hungary or Romania.

After a respite, my interrogation sessions resumed with the major, who warned me I was to be confronted with my friend Arthur. I sat quietly in my usual place close to the door. When it opened a small, emaciated man was ushered in and told to sit at another little table to the left, and in front of mine, specially placed there for the occasion. The distance between the two tables was a bit over four yards. The major asked if I knew this man. I looked at him. I had been warned to expect Arthur, but this man didn't look at all like my friend Arthur. As I hesitated, not knowing what to reply, the man suddenly turned to me and asked: 'What's the matter? Don't you recognize me any more?' The voice was Arthur's. It was his physical appearance that had changed so completely. He had lost so much weight he was unrecognizable and his large head was no longer in proportion with his frail body.

The interrogation commenced and the major asked Arthur what he knew of my activities as an enemy of the Soviet people and a British agent in Romania. Now it was Arthur's turn to burst out laughing and he said: 'What on earth are you talking about? I have known him well for more than thirty years and know what he did. I know he worked with the British to sabotage the German shipping on the Danube, but he is not, and never was, a British spy. I refuse to make any such declaration!' And when the major said: 'But your friend has admitted his activities as a British agent and has already signed a declaration to that effect,' Arthur replied simply: 'That proves nothing! You force people to sign, and they do it to please you, but that doesn't prove it is so!' Obviously irritated by the categorical denial, the major said nothing. There was nothing more he could say.

It was now my turn to speak. I told Arthur, yes, I did sign a paper confirming I had taken note of the accusation against me, but that was all. There was no proof to support the accusation that I was a spy. That was why he, too, could sign something on these lines, saying he had taken note of the accusation against me. It would not alter anything in our situation. There was no point in arguing, I told him, because one could change nothing here. One is already condemned before entering the Lubyanka. But Arthur persisted in his refusal to sign anything and left the room without having done so.

Several days later I was subjected to another confrontation, this time with Michael whom I recognized at once. He hadn't changed much, except that he had lost a lot of weight, like all of us, but he held himself well. He was a less excitable character than Arthur and talked calmly while puffing away at the cigarette the major offered him, whereas Arthur refused to accept anything throughout his interrogation, whether cigarettes or food, saying every time an offer was made: 'I cannot accept anything from an enemy, except a glass of water!' Michael also declared that the idea that I was a British spy was absolutely ridiculous, but the major remained displeased that my dossier still lacked the necessary proof for the accusation. So far as I was concerned, I was happy to have this chance to see and speak to my two friends again, but their refusal to support the accusation against me altered nothing. It only meant that another accusation would have to be found to substantiate the prosecutor's case and complete the dossier, for the interrogators didn't give a damn for the niceties of the Soviet Penal Code. If the original accusation – in my case, accusation of espionage under Article 58, paragraph 6 – had to be annulled for lack of proof, any other would do just as well to condemn the declared 'enemy of the people' and ensure he was sent to a forced labour or 're-education' camp. So my major didn't give up and continued the interrogation, but now without asking me to sign any piece of paper indicating the accusations against me. I assumed that the original indictment accusing me of being a member of the Dashnak Party still stood, even though that of a British spy had been dropped. In fact, it took the KGB five years to find a suitable paragraph to fit my case and justify my imprisonment.

One evening, the guard brought into the cell a young man, aged about twenty-five, who wore the uniform of a Red Army officer. When my cellmates asked his name and where he came from, he replied, 'my name is Krjijanovsky and I am from Paris.' I was amazed, for Krjijanovsky was the name of an old friend, a fellow student at the Mikhajlovskoe Artillery School in St Petersburg. Could this be his son? I approached the young man to explain that, in 1916, when I was at the Military Academy, the Adjutant of the first battery I was attached to was an NCO also called Krjijanovsky, serving in the famous Pavlogradsky Regiment of Hussars, immortalized in Tolstoy's *War and Peace*. The young man confirmed that the adjutant was indeed his father, who was still alive and lived in Paris. By extraordinary coincidence, twenty-nine years later, the son of my former adjutant had become my cellmate in the Lubyanka.

After the Revolution, his father, like many Russian officers, fought with the White Army against the Bolsheviks. He stayed with them throughout the retreat to Crimea, and was then evacuated to Turkey from where he emigrated to France. During the Second World War, his son joined the French Army as a second-lieutenant and fought against the Germans. After the German surrender in 1945, the Soviet Government sent to France a military mission to negotiate the repatriation of Red Army POWs interned in camps in West Germany and subsequently liberated by the Allies. As young Krjijanovsky spoke fluent Russian he was attached to the Soviet Military Mission as an interpreter for the French. The Soviet officers at once took an interest in the young French lieutenant who spoke such fluent Russian, and the naive young man told them everything about himself and his family, never even concealing that his father had fought with the Whites. What a stroke of luck for the Soviets: there, before them, stood the self-confessed son of a traitor! The only question was, how to trap him? First, to gain his confidence, they told many tales about the glorious new life in the USSR and the brilliant prospects open to anyone embarking on a military career. They said his chances of promotion would be far better there than in France. The Soviet people, now being free, were starting the great programme to rebuild the beloved Motherland. Moreover, the Soviet Union had declared a General Amnesty and all political refugees living abroad, and all former POWs, could return to rejoin their families in Russia. When he told them how much he was paid as a French second-lieutenant they laughed with delighted astonishment. Why, they said, a Red Army officer earned twice as much, quite apart from many other privileges and perks.

The process of seduction continued throughout his tours of the Soviet POW camps with the Soviet delegation. He was invited to go to the USSR, to visit Moscow and Leningrad and see for himself his father's country and then decide for himself. He was assured he could enlist in the Red Army at a higher rank than the one he held in the French Army without any problems once the task of repatriating POWs was completed. Young Krjijanovsky succumbed totally to the spell so carefully woven, though when he spoke to his father about it the old man was not so easily convinced. He warned the son that all these promises sounded like the sort of lies told by *agents provocateurs* determined to entice him into danger. 'You don't know the perfidy of which the Bolsheviks are capable,' his father told him, but the son, as though hypnotized, was full of the new ideas and possibilities revealed to him. He refused to listen to his parents' warnings, renounced his French nationality and enlisted in the Red Army. He was kitted out with the uniform of a Red Army lieutenant, paid a large sum in bonuses for his services as interpreter and his war service abroad and so forth, and given full tickets to Moscow, Leningrad or wherever he might wish to go.

The naive young man was spellbound and told all his French friends and brother officers, one of whom also happened to be the son of an old Russian Army officer who had taken refuge in France. He, too, was spellbound and asked Krjijanovsky to ask his Soviet friends whether he might also be accepted as an officer in the Red Army, on the same terms. To begin with, the reaction was uncertain. It might be difficult, he was told, but nevertheless they would try to obtain the necessary authorization. The farce was well played, the bait duly swallowed. Eventually the Soviet military mission informed the new victim that he, too, was considered good enough. And so the two young men cheerfully embarked for Leningrad and Moscow, on arrival to be taken straight to the Grand Hotel Lubyanka and relieved of all luggage and possessions as they began to pay the price for the 'crime' of their fathers and give, free of charge, the labour so lacking in a Soviet Union ravaged by the terrible war. For the Soviet Government had worked out a good system for cheaply acquiring able-bodied citizens to provide the manpower necessary for rebuilding the country.

Several weeks passed without any change so far as I was concerned. Like all my cellmates, I felt in the depths of despair, frail and weak after months of imprisonment to which one could see no end. We could scarcely move, but tried to economize our strength. We no longer exerted ourselves in any way, but were like flies trapped under glass, listlessly crawling about with no air left to breathe. Each day we were forced down to the prison courtyard for daily exercise and in this little courtyard, about fifteen by eight yards, obliged to march in a silent circle, in single file, round and round for twenty minutes. We were not allowed to use the lift, but were marched down the stairs and only climbed back up slowly with great difficulty. When

I first came to the Lubyanka, my cellmates and I profited from any free time by playing chess, but now lack of proper food had so weakened us that we decided on only an occasional game. We were given almost nothing to eat. Our heads ached from exhaustion, and none of us felt well. We could hardly walk on our enforced daily march round the dark, filthy courtyard.

My friend the mining engineer, so much younger than me, refused to give up. He did PT for ten minutes each day and advised me to do the same. He showed me how to do Swedish exercises, just moving the arms to improve breathing, standing or lying on the floor, lifting the torso to strengthen the muscles of the abdomen and chest. He told me that this was very important for my health, that I must do the exercises every day for at least ten minutes. I tried to do as he said every day for a week, then I gave up. I had no strength left , I was completely exhausted and overcome by a feeling of complete indifference. Prison and hunger were killing me slowly but surely. We had no strength left, and our moral resistance was slowly fading away.

Of the six occupants of the cell, two were allowed an extra ration of *kasha*, just a small lump, but all the others avidly watched them wolf it down. This extra tit-bit was only for those whose interrogation was completed, and its arrival was a sign that they would soon be leaving the Lubyanka. But for the remaining four of us there were still many months of waiting. My cellmates knew all the grim procedures enacted by the KGB. They warned me that, at the end of the interrogation, there would be another formality to be faced. In the presence of the famous *troika* made up of a prosecutor detailed by the Ministry of Justice, an officer of the Ministry of the Interior and an officer of the KGB, forming the so-called Special Council ('Ossoboye Soveshchanye', or OSSO for short), the detainee would be presented with the formal act of accusation and the sentence recommended by his KGB interrogator. The detainee then had to declare that he had taken note of all the proceedings, but was told nothing else. He would never know the rest of the contents of his dossier, now handed over to the OSSO, who would come back with their final decision in two or three months. It was a simple administrative procedure. There was no trial as such in a Court of Justice, which was considered unnecessary. Besides, a trial involved a lot of work and there were millions of people to be tried. In fact, the Communists had adopted the convenient procedure brought into force when the judicial reforms, first introduced by Tsar Alexander II, stipulating trials by jury, produced such uncomfortable results, the juries invariably acquitting all the revolutionaries brought to trial. With the assassination of Alexander II, all this changed. The Tsarist Government quickly found a new method to combat the revolution, and the Soviet Government thereafter used it to combat their own counter-revolutionaries!

I had now spent some five or six months in the Lubyanka, though there was no way of knowing exactly how much time had elapsed since my arrest. My depression was all-enveloping. Then, one day, the KGB major summoned me to his office once again. He told me he had some good news:

all the statements I had made to him had been confirmed by correspondence with the Romanian State Security Service, and the KGB now accepted that I spoke the truth! 'That is good,' said the major, 'though it comes as no surprise to me.' But having confirmed my trustworthiness, the major got up from his desk and told me to follow. 'Come, I want to take you to meet my chief – the colonel,' he said.

We walked along the big corridor and entered a large office. I was possessed by a complete apathy. I am probably being taken to another, more senior interrogator, that is all. My young engineer friend had told me that our happiest moment would come when we finally left the Lubyanka *en route* for the camps. Prison destroys one, physically and morally. All willpower, all strength of spirit to resist, gradually vanishes, precisely as the KGB wanted it to.

The major introduced me, saying: 'This is the detainee I spoke to you about, sir.' An ominous introduction, but I hardly noticed; it was all the same to me. 'Sit down and we'll see what we can do for you,' said the colonel. The statement suddenly sparked a ray of hope. Perhaps my luck really had turned. Could this mean the end of my interrogation and, at last, being allowed to leave the notorious Lubyanka? But no, as I soon realized, this was the classic KGB way of saying they wanted you to do something for them.

The colonel continued: 'You now have several months of prison behind you, and I can see you have lost a lot of weight!' What a nerve to speak of my sufferings so, I thought, as he went on: 'Now we want to help you, to put you on a better diet and in better surroundings. In exchange, we ask you to do us a small service. Are you, in principle, in agreement with our proposition?' What could I say? It was out of the question, in the state I was in, for me to refuse or resist in any way. I must do everything to win the struggle to survive. But first I must find out what all this was about. 'What does it matter, after all? I will accept any change they propose for the sake of that extra bit of food, to help me survive a little longer. I don't care where the food comes from – from God or the devil. I will accept it because I do not want to disappear like so many other victims of this implacable regime.' So I told them as much, in a much more polite and diplomatic way of course and while my reply did not please them much, they decided to disregard it and outline the offer I could not refuse.

'If you are willing to co-operate this will not only entitle you to better conditions but will also favourably influence your final sentence. We know you speak good German. We have in prison here a German NCO, a Nazi and a war criminal. So far, he has totally refused to be interrogated. He refuses to confess or say anything at all. We thought that perhaps you could help us to achieve some results, help us to crack this hard case. You will be placed in the same cell with him, and since you, too, are a foreigner arrested by us, perhaps he will not be quite so unwilling to talk to you. Do you understand what I mean?' asked the colonel.

I understood only too well. The colonel wanted me to act as a stool-pigeon, to turn Queen's evidence, as the British say. I would have refused to co-operate in such a vile act against a Russian victim of the Communist regime, someone the KGB had designated as an 'enemy of the people'. But I had no scruples in helping to break a Nazi and a war criminal at that. It was they, the Nazis, who started the 'total war', who invaded Poland, massacring Polish units even after they surrendered. The poor surrounded Poles had accepted surrender, but still the German tanks and artillery mowed them down, annihilating all Polish youth in their path. And the persecutions and massacres begun in Poland continued in the Ukraine and in Russia itself, both against the civilian population and the unfortunate Soviet POWs who were allowed to die of hunger and thirst as they were marched to the camps in Germany. They destroyed city after city, first Warsaw, then London and Coventry, killing innocent civilians, these twentieth-century reincarnations of the hordes of Attila and Tamerlane. I thought of all the terrible suffering inflicted on the people of Poland, Czechoslovakia, Yugoslavia and France by the SS who systematically killed off all those listed as 'dangerous elements who resist the establishment of the hegemony of the German Reich'; of innocent hostages shot to combat the resistance of an occupied and defeated people, inhabitants of entire villages, including women and children, massacred in reprisals in France, Czechoslovakia, even Italy. At that time, Hitler's so-called 'Final Solution' for the Jews was still not generally known, but the horrors and crimes I knew about surpassed all imagination, and were a sufficient argument for me. Therefore I told the KGB officers that I had no scruples over helping to incriminate a Nazi war criminal. I had studied in Germany, I spoke German fluently, I knew the German people and did not hate them, but it was a different matter where the SS were concerned. They were murderers, savage ferocious beasts who should be punished for what they did. Even today, after so many years I still feel the same and have no feeling of remorse at having agreed to trap a Nazi war criminal.

When I returned with the major to his office, he told me that he would not summon me for the usual interrogation that night since he was going to a performance at the Bolshoi Opera. Taking advantage of his good mood, I asked to look out of his office window. After several months in Moscow as a guest of the KGB, I still had no idea what Moscow looked like today. The last time I saw it was in 1913 on the way back from summer holidays in the Urals. The major had no objection and took me to the big window facing on Dzerzhinsky Square. The square was quite unchanged. Everything looked exactly as it did in 1913: the same old houses, now in a lamentable state of repair. The new rulers had neither the time nor the means to maintain the city and its houses in a decent state of repair, or perhaps they did not care. I saw the same old electric trams, first introduced half a century before. The picture was sad and depressing, and it surprised me that this should be so in the very heart of the capital city. Thirty years after the days of the Great October Revolution there was nowhere any sign of the realization of the grandiose plans it promised.

That same evening, the guard came to escort me to my new abode. I bade farewell to my cellmates who accepted that I could not tell them anything. They put it down to just another routine prison transfer. So many came and went.

The guard took me to the seventh floor, a superstructure built on top of the old Lubyanka Hotel which originally had only six floors. It was a sort of modern open-plan apartment, with a guard at the reception desk in the middle and the usual register to log all movements of prisoners. All round the walls were doors of very small cells, for one or two people only. A gallery, built right round the room, was reached by an iron staircase, and on the gallery were more cells forming an additional eighth floor. Hence the guard at the desk could watch both floors at once. My arrival was recorded and another guard took me to the eighth floor.

The new cell was very small and narrow and lacked even a window. Two narrow bunk beds were separated by a folding table like those they have in railway carriages. And, of course, the small *parasha* bucket was in its usual place by the door. I settled down to wait. An elderly guard came in to meet the new occupant. A likeable Ukrainian, he asked where I came from and for what reason I was brought here, listening attentively to my story. 'I have seen many people brought here in the same way, people in a similar situation to yours. God alone knows why they do it,' he commented and left. I was impressed by his sincerity. He was probably an old soldier, finishing his years of service in a job he disliked. It was interesting that so many guards should have been chosen from among Ukrainians. Obviously the authorities considered them a well-disciplined people.

In the middle of the night, I was awakened by the arrival of the young German NCO, a Prussian whose name sounded like Reschke. As the door closed behind him we introduced ourselves. He was delighted that I could speak German, and as we chatted I soon realized that my new cellmate was not at all the dangerous war criminal the KGB officer described and therefore I decided to do everything possible to frustrate their plans.

A simple working man, he had been mobilized at the beginning of the war and automatically invited to join the National Socialist Party. Like most of his compatriots, he felt happy with the changes that had taken place after Hitler came to power. In place of unemployment and poverty, life had returned to normal. Assured of employment as a skilled artisan, he had earned a good salary. Then, when the war came, he was sent to the French front. Following that short campaign, he was promoted to NCO, and later, after Hitler attacked the USSR, was seconded as instructor for Soviet POWs of Central Asian origin: Turkmenis, Uzbeks and other Moslem nationals. These Hitler planned to form into an administration opposing the Soviets, once the victorious German armies had crossed the Urals and marched as far south as the Caspian Sea, into the regions populated by Moslem peoples under Soviet domination. The aim of the training was to prepare them to fight in Central Asia, and they went on exercises in the mountainous regions of the Black Forest in southern Germany. Well organized, methodical and far-seeing, the Germans were also training technical and administrative cadres to take over once the planned occupation of the Baku and Grozny oil fields in the Northern Caucasus and Transcaucasia had been achieved.

I may have been wrong, but I could see no reason for regarding Reschke as a war criminal. He was not a member of the SS, nor of any of the other special units of terror and execution who massacred even POWs, regardless of the Geneva Convention. I felt a sense of relief when Reschke said he had told his interrogator everything concerning his military service in France and his activities as instructor to the Turkmen POWs. Reschke's case was not as complicated as I had feared. When the food was brought in, I noted that we each received the same ration of buckwheat *kasha* – double my former portion. So I was already being 'paid' for acting as stool-pigeon. The German POWs in the Lubyanka were always better treated as a matter of course.

Yet if it was true that Reschke had already told his interrogator all, then why give me the impression he was a hard case who refused to say anything? Perhaps it was he, Reschke, who was the real stool-pigeon, placed in the cell to trap me. I thought about this for some time. But, even if it were true, what difference could it make to my fate? None whatsoever! And since I had promised to report my conversations with the 'war-criminal', I had to do something about it. What did it matter if Reschke was simultaneously reporting on me? To speed up our exchange of confidence and gather sufficient material, I therefore decided to tell him how I was accused of being involved in similar activities to his and of being friendly with an Armenian revolutionary who co-operated with the Germans in the formation and training of Armenian legions although I had played no part in any of it. In this way I hoped to prompt Reschke into further confidences and make it easier to ask him questions. As a result, he told me how, between his return from the French front and his appointment as instructor of the Turkmen units, he worked for a time in the Abwehr Intelligence Service, the equivalent of the French Deuxième Bureau or the British MI5, whose head was the famous Admiral Canaris. He told me details of the way the Abwehr was organized, and I tried to memorize it all, to pose different questions to increase the information which might prove to be of interest to the KGB.

Reschke was summoned for interrogation each day, morning and night, so I took the chance to rest and try to recover my strength. Suddenly one evening, after ten o'clock, when Reschke had already left for his nightly interrogation, I, too, was summoned but not for the usual interview. Instead the guard took me to a box-cell in which a small table had been placed. He gave me some pencils and paper and told me to write my report on 'the war-criminal Reschke'. I realized, of course, that I was expected to write my report in a certain way, confirming that he was indeed a war-criminal. I wrote several pages, describing his service in the Abwehr and how the

Abwehr was organized. Naturally I said that Reschke was nothing more than a junior clerk, with no real responsibility, who lacked the qualifications for an important position.

My physical exhaustion and lassitude made the task more difficult. I wrote very slowly and was relieved when, three hours later, at 1 a.m., the guard took me back to my cell. I felt certain that my KGB major already knew all the details of Reschke's story, but he must not realize I was aware of it. I felt equally certain that Reschke and I were being used by the KGB to spy on each other, this being their usual method.

Next day, when I was summoned to the major's office, he thanked me for my report but said it was insufficiently detailed. He needed to know more about Reschke's activities with the Turkmeni Legion (this probably being the main point of the accusation against him). And so, the day after that, I was returned to the box and told to describe in detail the composition, training and purpose of the Turkmen units. I tried to expand my report as far as I was able though I had little to go on. I was as certain that Reschke had already explained everything as I was that Reschke had told the major everything I had said about Dro.

The farce continued for almost ten days until one evening, Reschke was taken away and I was alone again. The KGB must have realized that our statements coincided and that there was nothing more to be got out of either of us. When I was summoned for another interview with the major and his colonel, they congratulated me on my report even though 'it is far from brilliant'. They told me: 'Now that you have become a specialist in questioning Germans, we have a much more important task for you, involving a far more important personage. We are very pleased with the way you accomplished your first mission and would like to see what results you achieve with the new one we now entrust you with ...'

My only hope was that my new assignment would help me pass several more days in better conditions than the usual ones for detainees. I had burnt my bridges. I had become an authorized stool-pigeon!

This time it was no humble NCO but a Dr Pilger who was brought to share my small cell. Dr Pilger was a career diplomat, getting on for fifty, who had served as Hitler's Ambassador in Kabul. After the German surrender in May 1945, the Embassy had no further reason to continue activities in Afghanistan and the Ambassador and his staff had to return home. When Dr Pilger approached the British Embassy in Kabul with a request for a free passage through India, the British replied that this would be very difficult and too complicated. They suggested instead that Dr Pilger return home via the USSR. Given no choice, and even though he had no confidence in the USSR, he approached the Soviet Embassy with a request to be allowed to return to Germany by way of Moscow. This was agreed, and on the Soviet-Afghan border, at the frontier post of Kuchka, they were expected and well-received. They and their voluminous baggage were then put on a train for Moscow, where they were taken straight to the Hotel

Lubyanka, the guard at the reception desk treating them exactly like all the other 'guests'.

Ambassador Pilger had prudently instructed his staff to fill several suitcases with tinned food, enough to last the two-to-three weeks' journey. At least this meant that he was not obliged to eat the *kasha*, but each week he was allowed to ask for some of the tinned food, and this helped him keep up his strength and morale. As for me, I felt stunned by his presence. I simply couldn't get over how a foreign Ambassador and his entire staff could be arrested and kept at the Lubyanka like any ordinary citizens accused of being enemies of the Soviet people. But the Soviet Union had won the war, and Stalin felt himself to be in a strong enough position to treat with disdain the clauses laid down by International Law. The war against Germany was won, and the KGB now wanted to know about the Ambassador's activities against the Soviet Union. They were determined to find out who were his secret agents amongst the Afghans, agents who, they were certain, he had passed on to the British, to work for them, and who were, therefore, 'against us', as the KGB saw it.

I listened with great interest to Dr Pilger's stories about life and customs in Afghanistan, but felt no enthusiasm for my special assignment of worming out of him the names of the secret agents left behind. But I also realized that, with a competent Ambassador, my task was well-nigh impossible, that Dr Pilger was not born yesterday and must be familiar with the methods used by the KGB, so similar to those used in Nazi Germany. It was only natural that he should suspect me of being a stool-pigeon, which gave me good reason not to hurry. In exchange for his stories about Afghanistan, I regaled him with tales of my life in Romania, and he expressed great interest in details of events in Europe that had never reached him in far-off Kabul.

He spoke much of Afghanistan. He told me that all power in the land rested in the hands of the reigning family, and that life there was very picturesque. All Ministers and high dignitaries formed the high ruling caste, every one of them related to the reigning family. What they feared most was the Soviet Union which, they felt, threatened their feudal structure. The Soviets had already penetrated deep into the economic life of the country, and the Ambassador confirmed what my young friend the mining engineer had also told me – that the Soviets sold their goods in Afghanistan at prices below the cost of manufacture, thus eliminating all competition from English merchandise coming in from India. All Soviet foreign trade is subsidized, they fix prices to defeat all competition, and they do it for propaganda reasons.

Then suddenly Dr Pilger's interrogations were suspended, I suspected to give him more opportunity to chat with me, everything we said being listened to through hidden microphones, as I realized.

Sure enough, I was soon summoned again by the major, who told me: 'I see you have established good relations with Dr Pilger, you chat freely together. What is important is to find out the details of the spy network which the Germans established in Afghanistan against us. Their agents are still at liberty and have been most probably handed over to the British. It is essential we have all the information on this subject.'

The major's words made me think. I told him that Pilger was not a child. If I started plying him with such questions he would suspect me at once. 'You cannot ask too obvious things about the spy network with that sort of person. The mission you have given me is impossible. Your interrogations have compromised my position.' Privately I was delighted that things were going wrong through no fault of mine but because of the major's clumsy blunders. My KGB 'boss' can no longer place great hopes in the results of my mission. He, too, must realize that Dr Pilger was no naive simpleton but a Nazi who knew all the tricks.

Back in the cell, I was determined not to broach the subject of the spy network. I continued to chat, telling Pilger about the good life I enjoyed during my twenty years in Romania, even after war broke out. He showed no sign that he distrusted me, and when his weekly consignment of tinned food was brought in, he offered me some. I was more than happy at this unexpected opportunity to supplement my meagre ration of *kasha*, and our relationship was excellent. I knew I must be very careful not to make a blunder, but at the same time realized that I must do something to feign fulfilling my task, otherwise the hidden microphones would betray me. I needed to find some way of making the Ambassador understand the role I was being forced to play. Perhaps I could do it with a gesture, or a discreet sign. The only visual surveillance was done by the guard peering through the Judas eye so I had to find the right moment. When I eventually asked my oblique apparently innocent question, I winked at the same time. Dr Pilger understood at once and did not reply, the subject was dropped and we talked of other things. I had done as instructed, put the question without bungling it. It was simply that Dr Pilger refused to discuss the matter.

Several days later, Dr Pilger was taken away and I never heard any more of him or his fate. Either the KGB realized that the stool-pigeon scheme was not producing the desired results or else they succeeded in getting the information they wanted from the other Embassy staff by using other more efficacious methods. If I had failed in my mission, I had not compromised myself in any way, and this was the most important thing for me. The authorities meanwhile promptly restored me to my old apartment on the fourth floor.

There had been some changes while I was gone. A new prisoner had arrived, a young Soviet soldier brought all the way from Belgium. As a POW in one of the camps in Germany, he was subsequently liberated by the advancing American armies. He had never been to Europe or seen any capitalist country before and it was interesting to learn how he took to the bourgeois way of life like a duck to water, despite all the Communist dogma drummed into him from an early age. He soon found his feet and embarked on a series of regular trips between Belgium and France after deciding to try his hand at some contraband. He bought cigarettes in Brussels to sell in Paris at a profit; in Paris he bought silks and perfume to sell in Brussels. He made a lot of money, lived a good life and even saved a little. He soon managed to build up a stock of merchandise and teamed up with some comrades, other freed Soviet POWs to help him run his successful business enterprise.

It is strange what a small place the world is. I was amazed to hear him say how, in Brussels, he met an Armenian family who emigrated from Russia. They were distant relatives of my family, established in the tobacco industry. Old Mkrtich was formerly a partner in a tobacco company in Tiflis, Georgia, and since there was no tobacco monopoly in Belgium, his business prospered. My new cellmate had met him through another Soviet POW, an Armenian who was the first to establish contact with the family of a fellow national. Mkrtich was prepared to offer them favourable terms for the sale of cigarettes, and so a business relationship was struck. He had treated them with sympathy. They were, after all, young Russian soldiers who had fought for the liberation of Europe. And so, through this extraordinary coincidence, I received news of my relatives, old Mkrtich being, in fact, the uncle of my cousin Ruben.

But despite its good beginnings, the life of the young entrepreneur soon took a tragic turn. His hopes were high, he had set up with his former comrades a small commune in one of the suburbs of Brussels from where he hoped to expand his business. But in their enthusiasm for their new life in the West, they had forgotten the long arm of the all-powerful KGB. The Soviet Government had declared a General Amnesty for all Soviet citizens who had been taken POW, even those who had collaborated with the enemy, if they returned to the Motherland. It was to be a general amnesty for everybody, and everybody was to be welcomed back with open arms. Even before the end of the war, Soviet planes were sent out to drop proclamations behind the German lines, promising a general pardon to the soldiers and officers who had served with General Vlasov in the so-called Russian Army of Liberation (ROA). But this promise of pardon, so solemnly given as proof of her honourable intentions, was not kept and I personally witnessed the punishment meted out to all those miserable people whom I met in the eight years. We lived and suffered side by side in prisons, forced labour camps and copper mines. And while the British, the French and the Americans were greeting the returning POWs with open arms, Stalin was making arrangements for their imprisonment and despatch to forced labour camps.

And so, a hunt was set afoot for all Soviet POWs in the West, organised by the Soviet Repatriation Commission with the co-operation of the French and Belgian authorities. Nobody must be allowed to escape, and the local Belgian authorities were helping in the hunt, having no reason to think that the 'amnesty' for Soviet POWs was anything other than it claimed to be. But our young Russian black-marketeers were unaware of this, they had no idea they were to be the prey of this hunt organised by the Belgian Police and Gendarmerie, and they went about their business. One day, they looked out of the window and saw that the house in which they lived was completely surrounded by police. They tried to escape through the garden at the back, but no luck. They were caught and taken to prison, where they were kept while the police awaited further orders from the Repatriation Commission.

The Soviet soldiers had thoroughly enjoyed their stay in the Belgian prison. They were put in comfortable cells, well treated and well fed. They were even given fresh apples for dessert! But from there, they were brought straight to the Lubyanka, our new cellmate clutching his two cases filled with silks, fabrics and cigarettes. He was accused of going into hiding instead of returning to his homeland. He was told he was a traitor for surrendering alive to the Fascist enemy, contrary to the oath given by every Red Army soldier, a traitor who had forgotten his oath. His punishment would be ten years in a camp for corrective labour and re-education, and only after completion of his sentence would he reclaim his suitcases which were kept for him in the Lubyanka depository. Alternatively, he could take his suitcases with him to the camp, if he so wished, but in that case he would soon be deprived of the contents by the *Blatnoj* - the camp Mafia, that is if they were not already stolen from him by the other prisoners on the train to the camp.

It must be repeated again and again that the USSR's treatment of returning POWs was not the same as that in the free world. The moment the train-loads of POWs arrived in the Soviet occupied zones of Germany, they were subjected to special interrogation sessions by the KGB, and all these miserable emaciated creatures who had miraculously survived famine and ill-treatment in Nazi camps, were now sentenced to ten years in camps for corrective labour and re-education. There were no exceptions. The order was applied to every single one of them. The minimum sentence was ten years, but it was far more severe for those who had accepted to work in the German factories or transport system, to avoid dying of hunger in camps; and it was worst of all for those who had agreed to enlist in the military units of General Vlasov's Russian Army of Liberation, who were all sentenced to fifteen to twenty years' hard labour.

How can one explain this cruel and inhuman policy towards these miserable victims of war, who had already suffered long years in POW camps where they were all exposed to hunger, disease and terrible suffering? It is an established fact that more than half of them died, some while being marched to camp without food or water, while others died during their detention. And whereas French, British and American POWs were allowed food parcels to help them better resist the cold and hunger, the Soviet POWs received nothing, because Stalin refused to recognize the existence of the Geneva Convention or Red Cross aid. He simply declared that there was no such thing as a Soviet POW, only traitors who had betrayed their oath and surrendered to the enemy and whom he, therefore, refused to help! The decision to send all returning POWs straight to camps, with massive sentences of ten – twenty – twenty-five years, was on Stalin's personal orders, and it was done for two reasons: first, because Stalin did not want the population to have any contact with the POWs returning from Western Europe where they had seen and learnt many things which did not correspond to the Communist dogma and structure of the country; and - secondly, because the massive losses suffered by the civilian population during the war as a result of enforced evacuation, sickness and so on, had so increased the figure of losses suffered by the Red Army in dead and crippled, that it now totalled over twenty million people aged between eighteen and forty. So, if European Russia and the Ukraine were to be rebuilt after being so utterly devastated by the plundering of Hitler's armies, vast reserves of manpower were needed, and Stalin's solution to the problem was to do it the Communist way: the shortage of manpower was to be overcome by sending millions to camps and then using them to work on the various reconstruction projects required by the State.

The preliminary interrogation process in Germany involved answering questions not only on the activities and behaviour of each POW in the German camp, but also on what the other POWs had done – whether they had collaborated with the enemy in any way. They were also required to indicate if they had worked outside the camp, and if so, to state exactly where. All POWs were expected to denounce all their comrades who had established links with the enemy. There were some fanatical Communists among the POWs who made a record of all collaborators, and this system of denunciation was applied 100%. The statements and denunciations were then checked and re-checked throughout the ensuing years.

There were several cases of POWs who had managed to escape from the German camps and joined either the French or Belgian Resistance movements, or formed their own independent partisan units. These brave patriots had risked their lives in continuing to fight against the enemy, but all the KGB officer said at the interrogation was: 'Thank you for your act of patriotism', and then proceeded to sentence them to ten years in a camp, for treason! It is the Communist way of saying 'Thank you, but rules are rules!' A soldier of the Red Army never surrenders, that is an integral part of the oath taken by every raw recruit, and the breaking of a soldier's oath means a sentence of ten years at least.

Time moves on relentlessly. It is already November 1945 when a day arrived when I was again summoned by the KGB major. The moment had come at last for the important act of signing the official document, confirming the interrogation was completed and 'the enemy of the people' in question notified of the accusation against him.

In the meantime, the major had been promoted to lieutenant-colonel and when I saw his new rank I congratulated him. He thanked me and proceeded to read out the text of my statement. I noticed several of the phrases I used had been altered, but I was not surprised, remembering the scene at the very beginning of my interrogation when the major explained to his assistant the manner in which the accused's statement should be phrased and the words used. Nevertheless I told him that the changes he had made gave an ambiguous sense to my statement. For example, when asked if I knew such and such a person as well as another, I had replied, 'Yes, I know the first person you mentioned, but not the second.' This had been recorded as reading 'as regards the second person, the accused *pretends* he never met him!' He insisted it was of no importance and that the text would remain as he wanted it. And I could see that, indeed, it was of no importance for the outcome of my case, since this had already been decided, formulated and recorded. So why waste time protesting?

There was another officer present at the ceremony. He was the representative of the Ministry of Justice, the Prosecutor. It was obvious that I had no option but sign the document. Why try to postpone what had to be? So I signed and that was it! As my cellmates had already explained to me, my dossier would now be forwarded to the OSSO Special Commission for its sanction, and in two to three months all the formalities would be complete. I would then leave the Lubyanka to start on the next stage of my journey to camp. And the sooner that happened, the better it would be for me.

Back in the cell I told my companions what had taken place in the office, how we had argued over the wording. They were all highly entertained, knowing the KGB's interrogation methods and how everything had been decided in advance. So what did it matter indeed? Nothing must delay the completion of formalities. From all sides of the cell came the same cry of encouragement: 'But of course you were quite right to sign.' 'To hell with the rest!' 'I would do the same.' 'I, too.' 'Me also, to finish with all this and be on the way to camp at last. Oh to have the chance to breathe again.'

My companions' calculations proved correct, and on 29 January 1946, after nine months of interrogation in the Lubyanka I was transferred to another prison, the equally infamous Butyrki. But as my friend the young mining engineer said to me: 'You're lucky, it's all over for you in this place. God alone knows how much longer I will have to suffer here.'

7. TRAVEL IN THE SOVIET UNION - WHY THE STATE COLLECTIVE FARMING SYSTEM DOESN'T WORK

It was already late in the evening of 29 January 1946 when I was summoned to collect my suitcase for departure. Even then I couldn't believe I was about to leave the Grand Hotel Lubyanka for ever. The guard escorted me downstairs and shut me in a box cell for about an hour until another guard escorted me to another box where I was given something to eat – the usual plate of *balanda* and oat porridge. A prisoner was never taken direct to his destination, but from one box to another to prevent him meeting anybody else along the corridor. When we finally arrived at the reception desk in the main entrance hall, I was handed back the small suitcase I brought from Bucharest and knew I was really leaving. I was led to the exit gate under the very same archway I was brought through in May 1945, outside which there waited a large Black Raven, a sort of windowless van, specially fitted out to transport detainees. Inside, a narrow corridor separated two rows of tiny cabin cells along each side, each one just big enough to take one person. The detainees were brought separately to the van and the cell door tightly shut before the next one arrived, to make sure none of them saw or recognised any of the others. It was forbidden to talk.

In one of the cabins I sat and waited, listening to the other passengers being brought in one by one, until, the full complement aboard, the van started off. The journey was long, and it was quite a while before the van stopped and we were brought out, one by one again. The van stood in a large garage, also fitted with cabin cells along the walls. As I would learn shortly, we were in the Butyrki – the old regimental barracks now converted to a prison. When I heard someone move in the adjoining cell through the thin partition wall, I knocked gently and asked his name. What joy! It was my cousin Ruben who answered.

After our interrogation, there was the obligatory visit to the bath-house. At the Lubyanka, we would be taken to the bath-house only once a month, one cell at a time, but here all of us went in together, and I saw that my friend Arthur was also here. We were told to undress and make parcels of our clothes and undergarments so these could be sterilized in special containers of steam under high pressure to get rid of any parasitic insects. We entered the immense and well-heated bath-house completely naked, each taking a bucket and a small piece of soap, just enough to wash oneself all over once. There was plenty of hot water – an exceptional circumstance indeed. The washing over, we were taken to another large hall, where all our parcels of clothing had been thrown together in a heap. The clothes were still warm and we had to rummage about to find our own. Next, we were taken to an even larger hall, fitted out as a dormitory. Planks on trestles were ranged along the walls in superimposed bunk beds, and there were also beds on a raised platform in the centre. About 250 detainees were already installed in these primitive bunks. When we tried to find a place near each other it was not easy, most of the detainees being asleep at that late hour. At last we succeeded. At last we were able to talk and relate our experiences over months of separation.

At least we were together again, the three of us, though we had no news of Michael's whereabouts. As we talked it became clear, from the questions put to each of us by our interrogators, that the reason for our arrest was a denunciation by an Armenian self-styled refugee from Russia, who arrived in Bucharest several years before the outbreak of war. He claimed to have fled the Soviet Union for his life, after being accused of being a member of the Armenian Hokist Nationalist Party. According to his account, the Hokists had, despite their nationalist tendencies, agreed to collaborate to a certain extent with the Armenian Communist Party. This made little sense, and we didn't believe him. Why should he have to flee the Soviet Union if his party accepted Communist rule, and how did he succeed in making his getaway? We had wondered a bit about all this but were not really concerned with such subtleties. On his arrival in Romania everybody had rushed to the aid of this penniless refugee, who was found a job and helped to earn a living. Nobody for a moment even suspected him of being a Soviet agent sent to watch and report on political activities in Armenian circles. And so he insinuated himself and quietly and for several years compiled lists of 'enemies of the Soviet state'. His KGB bosses expected him to submit impressive lists to prove his ability and justify his keep as a good secret agent. What did it matter if he included the names of innocent people? It was up to his Moscow bosses to research the information in depth, to sort the wheat from the chaff.

We felt certain it was this fellow who was responsible for our arrests and all the misfortunes that followed. During one of Dro's rare visits to Bucharest, I had been invited to a dinner-party, given in his honour by his brother-in-law, a highly educated man, a graduate of Zurich University, who was a teacher in the Armenian school in Bucharest. The dinner was modest since a school-master's salary was not big, and was supplemented by a monthly allowance I used to pay him on Dro's behalf. Suddenly the teacher had turned to Dro and asked how long he planned to remain in Bucharest this time, the implication being that he was worried about his allowance. Dro reassured him, saying that although he must leave Bucharest in two days' time, the allowance would be taken care of. Then, pointing to me, he added jokingly, 'There's my minister of finance. He will arrange that you continue to receive what I promised.' The Hokist was also present at the dinner, having particularly asked to meet Dro, and so, several years later, under interrogation in the Lubyanka, I was stunned to hear Colonel Guitzenko accuse me of having been earmarked for the post of the future Minister of Finance in the Independent National Republic of Armenia which the Germans had proposed setting up. I had completely forgotten Dro's jocular remark and had never been able to understand before where the KGB could have got such an absurd notion.

What was more, the Hokist was not the only one employed on such a task. To my utter amazement I learnt how, after the arrival of the Red Army in Romania, another Armenian whom Dro befriended, and whom he had personally recommended to me as 'a man of trust should the need arise to transfer money abroad', was in fact a Soviet 'resident' in Bucharest, carefully watching and recording all such activities. It emerged that even Dro himself, despite his past experience as a terrorist and resistance fighter, was far too naive to combat the cunning of the KGB.

There was a constant coming and going in the large dormitory. Each day, several new detainees arrived, while others left. As the old hands explained, detainees would be taken to another room where their sentences were read out. After that, they went to the old Regimental Church, now used as an embarkation point for the diverse concentration camps that formed the vast network of the Gulag.

Two days after our arrival at Butyrki, I had a conversation with my cousin Ruben on our daily half-hour morning walk, in one of the numerous inner courtyards of those vast barracks, about which I would often laugh. As a young man Ruben had studied law at the Law Faculty of St Petersburg, and now he began seriously trying to convince me of the feasibility of suing the Soviet government for damages for kidnapping and imprisoning us without a trial, as foreign nationals arrested on the territory of another state. I listened but made no reply. The harsh treatment he had received during his nine months' interrogation had clearly had a disorientating effect on his mental state. Of course, as a trained lawyer, it was natural that he should look at the question from the purely legal point of view, but to argue thus in our present circumstances was as if he had been born yesterday. He had lost all sense of reality. What Tribunal would be prepared to try such a case? What judge had the power to force the Soviet government to submit to any judgement when, for years, it had shown a complete disregard for international law? My poor cousin could not see the futility of his hopes.

As soon as we returned to the dormitory we were told to collect all our things ready for departure. At eleven o'clock in the morning there began the ritual transfer procedure which would last until late that evening. I waited in a box for two hours until another guard took me to another box. By then it was lunchtime: the usual thin gruel with several grains of millet floating in it, the gruel accompanied by a plate with 80 grams of porridge. As an old detainee song puts it: 'Krupinka za krupinkoj gonitsa s dubinkoj' ('One grain chasing another with a club, trying to catch it'). Three hours later, yet another guard escorted me to a third box, situated on another floor. What a vast organization: so many guards needed to effect these endless transfers from box to box, to serve the detainees their miserly rations of food brought up by the kitchen staff. Nobody was in any hurry. The important thing was not to mix the detainees or the boxes, or to muddle them up, mistaking one for another.

Finally, at eight o'clock in the evening, I was taken to another box for another hour before being escorted to an enormous hall, large enough to hold at least fifteen army trucks. There was certainly no lack of space at Butyrki. At one end stood a small table with two chairs, at which sat a man in civilian clothes. A representative of the KGB? Of the Ministry of the Interior? Of the Ministry of Justice? He asked me to sit opposite. On the table was a pile of fifteen or twenty dossiers, through which he rummaged to find mine. It had stamped on the cover the KGB classification 'Not to be destroyed' ('Khranit vechno'). From it he took a sheet and read out my sentence: 'Sentenced to eight years ITL for liaison with the Dashnaks.' At that time I was still unfamiliar with the various Soviet abbreviations, such as ITL, which, he told me, stood for 'Ispravitel'no-Trudovoj-Lager' – a corrective labour camp for the re-education of erring citizens.

The eight-year sentence was justified by my supposed liaison with the Dashnaks, even though I was never a member of this party nor acted on its behalf. My interrogator, Colonel Guitzenko, had reconciled the contradiction by using the formula 'liaison', for I had indeed known some of them. Otherwise the accusation and sentence would have been far more severe, for it was only the 'liaison' formula that justified the minimal eight-year sentence which, on the Soviet scale of justice, meant 'almost innocent'.

I was told to sign a piece of paper certifying I had taken note of the sentence passed before being escorted to another box for another two-hours' wait before finally being taken to the corridor where all the lavatories were. The corridor was already crammed full with about forty detainees eagerly awaiting their turn after the endless processes. I again met Ruben and Arthur, who told me they had each been given a five-year sentence, the minimum possible. In Soviet terms, these sentences were admissions of their complete innocence.

After another hour, we were at last conducted to the transit centre in the old regimental church. It was very large and fitted out with the usual beds on trestles, but so crowded we could hardly find any room to stay together. We were all political prisoners here, sentenced under Article 58 and coming from all classes and professions: military, civilians, priests – nobody spared. People in the neighbouring beds asked us avidly: 'How many years?' On being told it was five and eight years, they exclaimed: 'Oh, a child's sentence. You're lucky indeed. You'll soon be free. It's just a question of living through another winter, then a summer, another winter, another summer. You'll see how the time goes!' Months and years meant nothing to the long-suffering Russian people. Everyone meekly accepted the inevitable and submitted to his destiny. It is the old Slav fatalism.

The Soviet detainees, being more experienced in such matters than we foreigners, told us what to expect next. The same routine was repeated each day. In the evening, the guard called out the names of several detainees, but no longer to put them in separate boxes. Their sentences having been passed, there was no further need to conceal anything from them. First of all, we could expect to undergo a medical examination. The doctor was also a detainee. It was a pure formality.

When we three were called into the doctor's room he asked if anything ailed us or were we in pain? I decided to follow the advice of my friend the mining engineer and say or do nothing that might delay my departure so I told the doctor I was in good health and had no complaints. 'You can go, call the next one,' he said. My cousin said the same as me and he, too, was told he could leave. But Arthur was feeling unwell. He asked the doctor for some medicine with the result that he was told to return to the church hall, and his departure was delayed, probably for another week. We were never to see him again.

Ruben and I were then taken to the large departure hall where we were asked if we wished to take our luggage to camp or preferred to leave it in store here, to be collected on completion of sentence. I signed a form saying I preferred to leave it in the Butyrki, but nevertheless ten minutes later I was handed my small suitcase for nobody bothered to read the forms. And so my cousin Ruben and I left the Butyrki, that vast depot for the distribution of manpower throughout the various camps in accordance with the requirements of various industrial combines. With dozens of other detainees we were ushered into the fleet of Black Ravens for the next stage of our journey, squashed in like sardines, sitting or standing. Why bother over the comfort of enemies of the state? The forty-minute journey was made even more uncomfortable by our luggage being thrown in after us. Our destination this time was the Krasnaya Presnya (Red Presnya) prison in the Krasnaya Presnya district, so-called because this was where bloody battles took place at the time of the first Russian revolution in 1905.

This prison consisted of several highly primitive wooden barracks built alongside the railway tracks, it being the principal embarkation point for detainees leaving Moscow. There was no railway station as such, only platforms from which the trains were loaded with their human cargoes. We were herded into one of the barrack halls, built to take some fifty or so people but now crammed with up to 250 detainees. There was the usual scramble to find free beds, but there was none so we settled as best we could on the floor, between the rows of superimposed bunks or even underneath the bottom one. The atmosphere was suffocating. There was only one window, at the far end, and the detainees nearest to it had already smashed the glass to let in the freezing air, but still the temperature remained as high. The multitude packed together heated it better than could any central heating system. Those nearest the broken window could breathe fresh air, but those crammed at the other end, especially near the stinking *parasha*, found no relief. As soon as there was any movement as detainees were taken away for embarkation, those left rushed towards the window to secure a place nearer the fresh air. People fought for possession of the freed bunks.

On our second day, after almost half the detainees left, I was lucky enough to secure a place on one of the top bunks, quite close to the window. I felt happy with, at last, somewhere to lie down. Before long a new consignment arrived and the place was fuller than ever, people lying so close to each other that it became impossible to turn over without all the others changing position at the same time. My joy at getting some fresh air didn't last as the icy draught from the window brought on an inflammation in my left ear. Pus began to ooze, but fortunately the pain was bearable.

Each morning the barrack door was opened for a routine medical visit, a male nurse (also a detainee) asking if anybody was ill. Those who said they were were taken to the dispensary to be given an aspirin or some such elementary pill, which meant they returned to their bunk without any relief for the pain. Officially, medical services were provided in all Soviet prisons, but in fact medical care was practically non-existent. While I was in the Lubyanka, I developed scurvy from lack of proper nourishment. When I mentioned this to my interrogator, and asked for some medicine to alleviate my badly swollen gums, he at once phoned the dispensary with instructions to receive me. But the young woman doctor on duty could do nothing to help. She could provide neither the proper food, nor the required medicine. She could only advise me to brush my teeth and gums carefully every day, and when I pointed out that I did not even have a toothbrush, she could only suggest that I massage them with my finger dipped in cold water! When I reported sick at the Krasnaya Presnya dispensary, the doctor put a few drops of peroxide in my ear and told me to come back next day.

When I returned to the barrack hall I saw old Israelyan who had given himself up to the Soviet Kommendatura in Bucharest on hearing they had arrested his brother in his place. He was in a terrible state, ill and exhausted after many months of interrogation at the Lubyanka. His interrogator had been an Armenian lady comrade with the rank of captain in the KGB, and her treatment of a fellow Armenian was nowhere near as civilized as that which I experienced from my KGB colonel. She had not hesitated to slap the face of the old man, and shout obscenities at him, when his only 'crime' was to have escaped certain death with the help of Dro's commandos at the time when Van was under siege from the Turks. He did not survive all the privations, the suffering and the diseases of prison and camp life and died two years after being arrested, almost at the same time as my friend Michael.

After ten days my cousin and I were summoned to the departure point. We left the barrack hall at night to embark on the famous old rail coaches specially built for detainees, known as the 'Stolypinsky' after the Tsarist Minister Stolypin, under whose administration they were first introduced. Stolypin had calculated that this form of rail transport for detainees would meet the needs of the Tsarist regime, and they had been built like passenger compartments for eight to ten people, the difference being that the outside walls of the carriage were blind, the only windows being fitted in the inner wall of the compartment facing the corridor. Above the seats were two bunks, folded back during the day, and on top of the bunks a luggage rack. But by this stage the volume of detainees being transported between the various prisons and labour camps had increased so greatly that each compartment in a Stolypin car had to take up to twenty-eight detainees, pushed in by the guards with their rifle butts, shouting 'Move, move' ('Davaj, davaj'). My cousin and I tried to stay together, but the pushing and shoving was too great. While we were still in the corridor, my cousin was pushed into a compartment already crammed full and I was pushed into the neighbouring one. And so our initiation began into the *peresylka* – the enforced transportation of detainees.

Each coach was fitted with two lavatories: one for the MVD guards, the other for about 160 detainees. We were allowed to go to the lavatory only twice a day. Early in the morning the MVD guard on the train opened the grill door to the compartment and shouted: 'Prepare to go to the lavatory.' One guard stood at the door of the compartment, another at the lavatory door, both shouting 'Move, move, faster, faster' as a detainee ran along the corridor. The next detainee would be already waiting at the door once you were in; you couldn't linger. The guard kept shouting, telling you to hurry up and finish. And once the male detainees had completed this daily 'relay race', the women detainees were sent in to clean and wash the lavatories! One can imagine what faced these poor miserable creatures after 160 men had been chased and hurried to perform their natural functions in haste. The same performance was repeated each evening.

The food was always the same: black bread and salted fish (*kamsa*). As each detainee left the prison he was issued with the ration which was to last him for the duration of the journey: 600 grams of black bread and a piece of salted fish, and you needed to hold tight to it so as not to lose it! A bucket of water was passed from compartment to compartment twice a day, morning and evening. It had to be refilled whenever the train stopped at a station *en route*, but the guards disliked fetching water for the detainees so they only brought the minimum necessary, opening the grill door, pushing in the bucket with its attached mug and closing the grill as quickly as possible. Detainees were only allowed a mugful each – the minimum necessary. As soon as I realized this, I stopped eating the salted fish since it only made one more thirsty. The inhumanity of it all is indescribable. The detainees were squashed against each other, some sitting on the floor. There was no room to lie down, and the usual abominable filthy stench everywhere.

When the coaches had arrived at Krasnaya Presnya, they were already fully loaded with ordinary criminals – thieves, thugs and murderers. The MVD soldier-guards enjoyed excellent relations with these criminals, whom they regarded as 'kindred spirits from the social point of view'. That was to say, they were not enemies of the political structure of the Soviet state and had nothing in common with political detainees like us. There was even a sort of complicity of interests between the guards and the *bytoviki*, as the common law criminals were known. They placed several 'politicals' in each compartment full of criminals, and since the politicals were in a minority, they could put up no opposition to the *bytoviki* bullies, who proceeded to rob them as freely as if it was their privilege. The spoils were then handed over to the guards, who tried to sell them at the next stop *en route*, or to exchange them against food or vodka. The gains were then shared half-and-half between the guards and the criminals, who were happy to receive whatever share they were given.

The warmth generated by the mass of people crowded into each compartment was unbelievable. Everybody tried to shed as much clothing as they could. My small suitcase was pushed under the benches and I was forced by the heat to take off my overcoat and jacket. The only room for us, the new arrivals, to sit was on the floor between the benches. There were six of us on the floor, while the others huddled above us on the benches, the top bunks and the luggage racks. As the heat increased, the others offered to make things easier for us on the floor by taking our coats and jackets and stacking them in the top bunk, where, they said, they would be safe. After some hesitation (well-founded as it proved) I handed over my overcoat but not my jacket. By the time the train had arrived late in the afternoon at Yaroslavl on the Volga, my overcoat had mysteriously evaporated without trace.

At Yaroslavl our coach was uncoupled and shunted into the sidings where it remained several hours, the reason being that the next stage of our journey was on foot. We had to cross the town to reach the prison, and that could only be done in the early hours of the morning when the inhabitants were supposedly asleep.

Yaroslavl is an ancient city on the Volga. I knew it well for I had visited it on a school excursion before the First World War in the spring of 1912. The teacher in charge of our party took us round the old cathedrals and churches with their cloisters, icons and frescoes by the famous monk-painters of the thirteenth to fourteenth centuries. Now, marching through the empty streets of Yaroslavl in February 1946, I could hardly hold back my tears to see the churches abandoned, the windows smashed and boarded up. Only one church was still open, but not for the faithful. It had been transformed into a Club for Young Communists (*Komsomol*), as was indicated by the big notice board on the door. This was the only church building still in good condition. All the others had been allowed to fall into rack and ruin.

We marched through street after deserted street in the early-morning dark. It had been snowing but fortunately was not too cold, so I didn't suffer too badly without my overcoat. After an hour's march, escorted by MVD guards and their Alsatian dogs, we arrived at the prison on the escarpment on the right bank of the Volga, outside the city limits. The building, an ancient barracks with very thick walls, had been built in the eighteenth century. Our particular convoy had to wait in the great courtyard of the prison for an hour, in the bitter cold. The bureaucracy of the MVD prison system was never in a hurry. There were more than fifty detainees in our convoy, each with his individual dossier. The escorting guard must deliver his consignment of human goods; the prison authorities must complete all formalities according to the rules. It was a great responsibility, and it was necessary to ensure that nobody was missing!

When we were at last allowed to enter we were taken at once to the bath-house. This time the water was icy cold. Nobody complained. It would have been pointless to do so. At least the parcels with our sterilized clothing were still warm. There followed the body search, or *shmon* as it was known in prison jargon. Little by little I was learning the various slang expressions. The purpose of the *shmon* was to discover any concealed knives or other forbidden objects. The guard, noticing my amber rosary, confiscated it. I protested to no avail. He told me to apply in writing, asking that it be returned. Once installed in a cell I did so, and, miracle of miracles, my rosary was given back.

This cell was enormous, holding over 120 detainees and reached along endless corridors. All the top bunks near the windows were already taken by the *bytoviki*, the so-called prison aristocracy, those favoured by the authorities, who considered them 'sad victims of poverty'. A senior detainee was in charge, called the *Starosta* or Monitor. He addressed us, the newcomers, telling us he was responsible for keeping order and that any complaints had to be addressed to him. It was an excellent piece of theatre, all roles being perfectly acted by the *bytoviki*, the politicals, disdainfully known as the 'Fan Fanitch' (a parody of 'Ivan Ivanovich') being mixed up with the common law criminals. There were also many minors as no separate cells for youngsters existed. These youngsters were known as *India*, and their services were at the disposal of the *Starosta*. They carried out his orders to steal from detainees anything he fancied, or to beat them up.

The *Starosta* represented power, and everyone sought to ingratiate himself to gain his protection. Even the *blatnoj* Mafia respected his authority. When we arrived the *blatnoj* in our convoy approached him and exchanged several words in their special slang, so identifying themselves as 'friends'. Recognized as such by the *Starosta*, they could then join the others in the privileged bunks near the window, the more important ones taking possession of the top bunks, as was their right as members of the prison aristocracy. The other detainees – simple folk, peasants, workers or 'politicals' – were prey to be fleeced and robbed at will.

At night when everyone was lying down in their bunks and any new arrivals, exhausted by their long journey, were fast asleep, the *India* youths began their activities, ferreting around in the darkness, rummaging through the possessions of newcomers, stealing anything they could find and vanishing as fast as they appeared. All booty was deposited at the feet of the *Starosta*, and those who were robbed could complain to the *Starosta* as much as they liked. Naturally nobody would dare to search his holdall.

My own arrival provoked a sensation, my soft trilby hat at once attracting the attention of the *blatnoj*, who invited me to join them in their top bunks. They were keen to talk to me and were amazed and delighted that I could speak their language. They took turns to try on my hat, which even after all those months retained a slight aroma of hair-oil! The head *blatnoj* offered me a good Soviet cap in exchange for my hat and laughingly I accepted, so gaining their favour. I had not forgotten the advice of the mining engineer in the Lubyanka, when he told me it was always necessary to adapt oneself to circumstances and find the 'right approach'.

Our conversation soon became very animated. They wanted to know about life abroad and whether the *blatnoj* system existed in the West. They bombarded me with questions, which I tried to answer, explaining things in their own simple language. I told them I worked as an accountant, and then lied to impress them, saying I was also a lawyer, a profession highly respected by the *blatnoj*. At once several of them started to explain their case, seeking my advice and opinion from the legal point of view and asking whether they could appeal for a re-trial.

My sudden impulse to present myself as a lawyer proved to be inspired. The *blatnoj* took me under their wing and invited me to share their meal. Luck was on my side indeed, for they had plenty of food, forcibly 'donated' by the poor 'Fan Fanitch'. Another advantage of being favourably treated by the cell's Godfather was that I was no longer disturbed at night by the thieving youths and could sleep without anxiety.

The story of my being a lawyer soon spread to my other cellmates and one of them, a simple peasant, came to ask my help. He was an old man with a large family who had lived and worked on a *Kolkhoz* (collective farm). The poor old man had been sentenced to ten years in accordance with the notorious laws of the so-called 'Seventh of the Eighth' (7 August), the date on which the decree was issued. His sole crime was stealing a sack of potatoes to feed his large and hungry family.

Once a week prisoners had the right to ask the head guard, on his daily rounds of the cells, for some paper to write their petitions of appeal. I therefore agreed to help the old man, and wrote out the petition for him, pleading extenuating circumstances – his poverty, his large hungry family - and asking the tribunal for a reduction in the sentence. Imagine my astonishment when, two weeks later, my first 'client' received a letter from the Prosecutor's Office informing him that his sentence had been cut by half! Even considering that Yaroslavl was quite near Moscow, the quick reaction was dumbfounding. Everybody came to congratulate the old peasant and I found myself proclaimed the best lawyer in the Soviet Union. After such a spectacular success I was flooded with requests for help, each unfortunate hoping for a similar miracle.

I would like to mention here something about the savage law of 'the 7th of the 8th'. It was introduced because of the massive plundering of the property of the Socialist State. Squandering or embezzling State property is a criminal offence in the USSR. The authorities were determined to put an end to it, and the importance attached to its enforcement, without exception, needs some explanation in detail. The economic situation which was already catastrophic, was further aggravated by the agrarian reform, enforcing collectivisation of peasants' lands. Famine became widespread and everybody was forced to steal, so as not to die of hunger. So the law of the 7th of the 8th decreed that the penalty for stealing was death. Yet despite this threat, the thieving still continued everywhere, in collective farms (*Kolkhoz*), in factories big and small, and in offices and it gradually became obvious that practically the entire population would have to be shot as a punishment for 'stealing property of the State'. So it was decided that the death sentence could no longer be applied. The Government was forced to stop the executions and replace the death penalty with ten years in a Corrective Labour Camp.

But the new law did not frighten or deter anyone. Everybody was convinced that he wouldn't be caught. People had to go on stealing to stop their families from starving. The peasants had been forcibly made to work on State farms, so there was no other possibility of survival except by stealing the wheat and the potatoes produced, to feed themselves and their families. No law, no punishment, could deter these desperate, starving people. And so, the tractor driver in the collective farm, driving out to the fields at dawn, with his tractor loaded with seed grain, would drop off 2-3 sacks into a ditch. On return at night, he would pick them up again and hide them in his cottage. That way at least the family's food was assured until the next harvest.

Similarly, the women sent out to shear the sheep, would steal the wool, hide it under their voluminous skirts, and in their knickers. They left the shearing sheds at the end of the day much fatter than they went in. Everybody knew what they were up to but they were no longer being arrested because otherwise the authorities would have had to arrest everybody.

The collective farms created by the enforced collectivization of peasants' lands were obliged to deliver to the State granaries a fixed quantity of grain from each harvest, at a very cheap price, so that the State could ensure that the townspeople had an adequate supply of bread. It was essential that the factory workers and civil servants who were paid minimal wages could continue to buy their bread at low cost. Only after the obligatory quotas had been delivered to the State could the remainder of the harvest be distributed amongst the peasant-collective farmers. A record was kept of the 'working days' of each member of the collective farm, and each would receive his share of the remainder, accordingly. But it very often happened that what was left after the obligatory deliveries to the State Granary was not enough to feed the families on the collective farm until the next harvest. And because the farm also had to pay for the hiring of tractors and combined harvesters from the various 'machine stations' set up by the new regime, there was often nothing left of the year's crop for distribution amongst the peasant-farmers.

Quite apart from the fixed quota of grain deliveries, each family in a collective farm was obliged to deliver to the State each year a fixed quantity of milk, eggs and meat. They were allowed a small piece of land outside their cottage to cultivate for their own use. Its size varied according to the location of the farm in the various provinces of the USSR. Each family was allowed to own a cow, a pig, some chickens and geese; also to grow potatoes and vegetables on this small plot of land to feed its members, as their allocation from the harvest itself was often not sufficient to survive. Big animals like horses and bulls belonged to the *Kolkhoz* but the houses in which the peasant-farmers lived were their own property.

The incompetent administration, the overloaded bureaucracy, the general thieving, all contributed to the bad harvests which plagued the country year in, year out. Before the Great October Revolution, and despite the absence of mechanisation, the rich soil of the Ukraine and Siberia produced enormous surpluses of grain harvest and agricultural produce which was exported worldwide. The private co-operatives organized by peasant farms before the Revolution managed to export from Siberia enormous quantities of butter, eggs and so on to Western Europe, whilst the surplus grain produced by the Ukraine was shipped through the Black Sea to feed the world. Russia was the granary of Europe. But when the nationalized system of collective farms came into force, nobody any longer had either the incentive or the interest to increase productivity. Everybody stole as much as he could, whenever and wherever possible, working only the minimum necessary. The famous law of the '7th of the 8th' did nothing to stop it and the stealing continues to this day, everywhere across the land.

The result of the rigid collective farm system is well known: despite the introduction of modern mechanized techniques, despite a workforce five times greater than in the United States, the Soviet Union cannot even feed its own population. And instead of exporting grain worldwide the Soviet Union is now forced to buy grain everywhere – from the USA, from Canada, from the Argentine and from Australia. These are hard facts. It's up to the readers to reach their own conclusions.

During my time at Yaroslavl I made many friends among the *India* youngsters. I have always loved the young, and developed a particular affection for these miserable youths, who had among them many good and lovable lads. There was, for example, a sixteen-year-old who had been sent by his *Kolkhoz* to study at an agricultural college. When he could not adapt himself to the college regime he ran away and returned home, and was for this serious crime sentenced to ten years in a corrective labour camp. Such a rigid enforcement of the monstrous Soviet penal system must seem incomprehensible to anyone in the Western world, and many youngsters in Yaroslavl would have never been sentenced under the Western legal system. But Soviet justice is savage and implacable, and once these minors had been locked up together with hardened criminals their fate was sealed. They would inevitably become fully fledged criminals themselves.

The youngsters wanted to know what life was like in the West, what the schools were like, what sort of lives the peasantry and working classes lived. They wanted to know the truth since they did not believe what they had been told. Encountering someone like myself, who spoke frankly of the good and bad sides of life abroad, was a great event for them. I nevertheless cautiously refrained from openly criticizing the Communist system, knowing that even in prison I might be denounced for anti-Soviet activities and propaganda and my sentence increased for a further term.

When evening fell they formed a group to sing; singing being their favourite pastime. The Russians are deeply endowed with musical talent. It is enough for them to have heard a melody sung by their parents or friends, at home, in school or anywhere. The Russians do not sing like the Western Europeans, in unison harmony, but intertwine their voices – tenor, baritone and bass – each singing his own melody. And they do it instinctively, without having had any schooling and without a conductor to direct them. The lads in the Yaroslavl prison had a wide repertoire including popular folk tunes as well as songs written during the civil war which followed the 1917 Revolution and songs from the war against the Germans.

Meanwhile I was beginning to feel very ill and my left ear was extremely painful. In the prison dispensary the woman doctor (also a detainee) confirmed there was an inflammation of the ear but said that all she could do was prescribe drops of peroxide each morning, as the doctor at Krasnaya Presnya had done. More worryingly, she confirmed that I was suffering from something far more serious, for the black patches of scurvy were starting to appear all over my body. She must have reported my sickness, this explaining why I was detained so long at Yaroslavl. They now had to await further instructions to alter my destination from the originally designated labour camp for in my present weak state I could no longer go with the others.

After several weeks the entire *blatnoj* mafia ruling our cell was summoned to the departure point. We bade our farewells and they left with most affectionate assurances of friendship. The *Starosta* left with them and another inmate, a deserter called Alexis, pronounced himself the new *Starosta*. He had none of the authority of his predecessor but the 'politicals' in the cell were too weak and disorganized to put up any resistance and so he was accepted.

Alexis wasted no time and at once began grabbing anything he could, especially with the arrival of a new convoy. The nightly plunderings by the *India* youths resumed and I no longer had the protection of my departed *blatnoj* friends. Alexis, determined to exploit this advantage, suggested that I give him the shoes I had worn since leaving Bucharest in exchange for a pair of American army boots – part of the US supplies shipped to the Red Army under Lend-Lease. I raised no objections, thinking it might be practical to have the more solid footwear in a camp rather than my light fine old leather shoes. Alexis had set his heart on them because they were foreign shoes and he put them on at once. He then walked up and down the passage between the bunks to show off his new acquisition.

At night as I lay down to sleep, I put my American boots under my head to be sure they'd still be there in the morning. At dawn I could feel someone trying to pull them out gently. I opened my eyes to see an *India* lad trying to remove them and promptly grabbed him. I knew this was simply a manoeuvre on the part of Alexis, who wanted both sets of footwear. Sure enough, Alexis soon appeared and offered another exchange. This time he wanted to swap the boots for a pair of rubber galoshes. He tried to persuade me that galoshes would be far more useful in camp, but I refused to be intimidated, even though two youths suddenly appeared and started beating me about the head with the galoshes.

I refused to give in but swore and cursed them loudly. Alexis, certain of victory, bent over me threateningly with a cigarette hanging from his lips, and ordered me to hand over the American boots and take the galoshes. With a quick blow I succeeded in stuffing the burning cigarette into his mouth. The inside of his mouth was burned and he drew back, stunned. My blow was all the more effective, coming at a moment when he thought me incapable of further resistance. The two youths renewed their attacks from behind, but I couldn't have cared less. In my rage I hit back hard, defending myself as best I could and shouting curses at the top of my voice. Nobody came to my aid and I realized that my young friends would have liked to help me but didn't dare to intervene.

Seeing that I refused to give in, the two *India* lads ceased their blows and stood back to watch the outcome of the power-struggle between Alexis and me. Just at that moment there came the sound of the door being unlocked. The guard, attracted by my shouting and swearing, had decided to come in. The young lads promptly disappeared underneath the bunks. Nobody moved and there was a total silence. The guard came straight towards me, thus showing that he must have been watching everything through the judas spy-hole, and demanded to know the reason for all this disturbance. Alexis, standing nearby, looked at me. I fixed him with an icy stare and told the guard it was nothing serious, only an argument of no importance.

Since I did not wish to lodge a complaint, the guard left with the warning not to start again. He went out, locking the door behind him, but everybody knew he would continue to watch us. Alexis came towards me with an air of relief, having calmed down on seeing that I did not wish to denounce him. He was far from sure of himself. Being no *blatnoj*, he could not rely on any special relationship with the guards. Having lost all his bluster he told me I could keep my US boots.

Several of my young friends came up to me to congratulate me on the stand I took. But my success had mainly been because Alexis was in a weak position. He knew that I enjoyed great authority among the young, who had listened to my stories over several weeks and were on my side. The consequence was that he asked to be transferred to another cell. The moment Alexis left us and was in the corridor, all those he had robbed asked the guard to retrieve from Alexis the two big bundles he was taking away and return their contents to his former cellmates. The guard agreed and within minutes all of Alexis's loot was back with its rightful owners.

With Alexis out of the way another *Starosta* mounted the Godfather's throne. He was a young cossack from the Kuban region, north of the Caucasian mountains, and a likeable fellow. He chose me to be one of his two assistants, our task being the very important one of distributing food – the bread, the soup and the *kasha* porridge. The bread was brought to the cells already cut in portions, and the inviolability of the bread ration was an accepted rule. The soup was so watery that nobody wanted it anyway, but there was always some *kasha* left over, and this went towards an extra portion for the *Starosta* and his two assistants; and since it was almost a double portion it meant a lot.

Another important but rare event occurred when the detainees received their sugar ration. This was usually issued several days before the departure of the self-appointed Godfather, and the *blatnoj* simply grabbed it all, dividing it between themselves, the poor 'politicals' seeing none of it. On the other hand I received my sugar ration in view of my good relations with the Godfather. When I asked about sugar for the poor 'Fan Fanitch', I was told 'They don't need it'.

One day the cossack told me the fantastic story of his exploits. Mobilized at the beginning of the war against Hitler, he landed in the thick of the fighting. As more and more Soviet units were encircled, he was taken prisoner but he managed to escape and make his way south, across the Ukraine and the fighting zone. After several weeks of marching at night and hiding during the day, he finally reached his home province where people gave him food and hid him. He had no intention of revealing himself to the authorities, knowing well that he would be branded a deserter. Therefore he did not return to his own *stanitsa*, as cossack villages were called, but hid in a neighbouring one, not too far away so as to judge the situation in his own village. Thus he learnt that his wife, thinking he had been killed at the front, had lost no time in finding someone to console her. It being out of the question for him to go back to his own home, he found himself a woman living alone whose husband was away at the front, and settled in with her. She looked after him and fed him well to help him regain his health after all those weeks of living rough on the tough march home.

After regaining his strength he found a job as maintenance man on the telegraph lines. He always tried to avoid the more populated areas, but by sheer bad luck was seen one day by one of the neighbours of his former village who dashed back to tell his wife 'the good news'. The wife's reaction was to denounce him to the authorities. He was arrested and sent to serve the usual ten-year sentence in a forced labour camp in the Northern Caucasus, whose detainees were formed into labour gangs to build a strategic road across the mountains. The cossack did not relish the thought of spending the next ten years in such a camp so he teamed up with another detainee who felt the same and made a plan to escape. At the end of the day's work they hid behind some rocks, and although their absence was discovered, the guards decided to return to camp before raising the alarm and organizing a search party.

Seeing the convoy depart, the two fugitives took off in the opposite direction but his companion was not as strong as the cossack and soon tired and refused to continue, preferring to return and be rearrested. The cossack was determined to continue with his escape plans and kept running until the soldiers fired after him and a bullet hit him in the neck. He fell to the ground, fainting from loss of blood, and didn't move, pretending to be dead. One of the two soldiers who found him lying there kicked him, saying, 'He's dead'. The other one wanted to fire one more shot to make sure, but his companion thought this would be a waste of ammunition. Better to leave him lying there and hurry back to camp since it was getting late. A cart could be sent out next morning to collect the body. He managed somehow to bandage his wounds and continued his journey till he reached one of the mountain villages inhabited by the Cherkess tribes whom he knew would never betray a friend. His health restored, the cossack left the friendly Cherkess to continue his journey across the Kalmuk steppes, towards the Volga and beyond, until he finally arrived in the lands inhabited by the Ural Cossacks. He thought he would be safe among the Ural Cossacks but bad luck still dogged his footsteps. Several months later he was denounced as a deserter and sent to a camp in Siberia. The prolonged KGB interrogation revealed in due course that he was a fugitive from the Vladikavkaz camp in Northern Caucasus. It was decided to send him back to Vladikavkaz, where he would be tried for escaping.

But a free cossack cannot bear the thought of being shut in. Better to die on the run than be imprisoned for ten years. Again he found a prisoner willing to run away and together they worked out another plan. They packed their army greatcoats, knives and a few provisions, and, as soon as night fell, climbed over the wall, strangled the patrolling guard-dogs and made their getaway.

They travelled on foot along a railway from one station to the next but never actually boarded a train. When they reached the Volga a new misfortune struck. They were intercepted by a military patrol and found themselves back in prison, this time in Yaroslavl. And so, each week he was taken into town for his sessions with the interrogating officer, knowing what the inevitable decision would be: ten years in a camp. But, he said, he would never accept it. Never! He could not rot away in a forced labour camp. The indefatigable escapee was already making new plans for a getaway.

He used the half-hourly walks in the prison courtyard each day to do physical exercises and so improve his health. He ran around the courtyard to be in top form. He showed me a forged identity document he had made for himself and I marvelled at the ingenuity. The small piece of paper was printed as though it had been typed on a typewriter. Its forged official stamp was a perfect imitation of the real thing, all patiently done by hand. What a talent! He confided in me that he was being taken into town for interrogation in an open lorry, not in the usual Black Raven. It was too good a chance to miss. As the lorry was driving along one of the main streets one day soon, he would jump out and mingle with the crowds. He was certain that the KGB guards would not dare to shoot into the passers-by. Besides, he had already arranged a hiding place with a woman friend so all should go smoothly. But even if it didn't he would never give in. He was born a free cossack and without freedom he could not live. He showed me the scar on his neck and laughed.

My scurvy grew worse. All the camp doctor could do was promise to recommend that I be urgently transferred to the Shcherbakov camp for the sick. The food there was the same as everywhere else but at least I would not be forced to work. She kept her word and after several days I left Yaroslavl for Shcherbakov. To my great surprise I found my cousin travelling with me, but when we arrived at Shcherbakov we were separated, my cousin continuing his journey to an unknown destination.

The camp at Shcherbakov was surrounded by a high fence of wooden planks, blackened by the weather. There were several watch-towers manned by MVD guards with searchlights and machine-guns. Alongside the wall ran a strip of ploughed earth, edged with barbed wire fences and guarded day and night by big Alsatians attached by a chain to an overhead cable, thus allowing them freedom of movement within their limited sector. The half-savage animals were trained to attack anyone entering the zone, except their instructors, who came at regular intervals with another dog to relieve the one on duty.

As we entered the camp by a small postern gate, the first thing I noticed was a large banner declaring 'Those who do not work do not eat'. The camp was constructed of large wooden barrack huts, timber being plentiful in the thickly forested northern region of the USSR. Each barrack hut was designed to accommodate 500 people, and along each side of a central gangway were several rows of superimposed wooden bunks, two on the bottom, two on the top, each row being separated by a narrow passage. There was only one entrance door to the hut which had a small ante-room equipped with a double row of wash-basins, so that forty people could wash at a time. The water had to be brought in buckets by two detainees detailed from each barrack hut. In the ante-room there was also the inevitable *parasha* bucket for use at night when the hut was locked up, the camp latrines being in a separate hut. It was the duty of the two detainees on detail to empty the *parasha* each morning, to sweep the hut and bring coal for the iron stove in the centre. There was electricity but the light bulbs were so weak that the huts were in permanent semi-darkness.

There was the usual profusion of bed bugs and to get rid of them we were taken to the bath-house once every four or five weeks while our clothing was sterilized. We washed as best we could without hot water, and there was no soap either to speak of, detainees being given only a tiny piece. It was a sinister parody of a bath-house. When we left it we were given a pair of scissors to cut our nails, but this had to be done quickly because others were waiting their turn. Bath-day was also the day for shaving the head and all pubic hair for hygienic reasons – to prevent lice settling. The team of barbers was composed of men and women, themselves detainees, and the same team catered for both sexes.

Naturally there were no mattresses or blankets. Detainees had to lie on the bare boards of the bunk with nothing to cover them. Therefore they slept in their clothes, removing only their shoes and caps. In winter we were issued with felt-boots called *valenky*, and such things as socks simply did not exist. Instead, like peasants of old, people wrapped their feet in pieces of natural coloured cloth, called *portyanky*. At night, when these were removed with the boots and hung over the side of the bunk to dry, the stench may be imagined.

The Shcherbakov camp was classified as an invalid camp and the mixture of miserable specimens of humanity imprisoned there had to be seen to be believed – war invalids, cripples who lacked arms and legs, and no artificial limbs provided. One soldier had been shot in the arm. The bullet smashed the bone, but all the doctors had done was remove the splinters, promising to replace the missing bone later with a piece of metal. In the meantime, while awaiting the operation, he was arrested for some reason or other and sent to Shcherbakov. So there he was, the lower part of his arm hanging by the muscles. There was no medical care for enemies of the Soviet people, not even for a victim of the terrible recent war.

One may well ask why all these miserable war invalids had been sent to the camp. The answer was simple: on the personal orders of 'Old Moustachios' whom nobody disobeyed. As repatriated POWs they could not – as invalids – be employed on manual labour for the massive reconstruction work the country so desperately needed and there was no question of allowing freed POWs to come into contact with the rest of the population. The order was that they must all, without exception, be sent to the camps.

During the months I spent at the Shcherbakov camp I was sick and hungry all the time and absolutely exhausted. At least we were not forced to do hard labour, but we had to do light work all the same. For the first few days after arrival I was sent with five other detainees to hoe the ploughed strips of land between the fence and the two rows of barbed wire. There were two strips, each about three metres wide, one on the inside of the fence, the other on the outside. They were kept freshly hoed so that no one could pass without leaving an immediate visible trace. The work was not tiring, and it was pleasant to be in the open air. We could even see, in the distance, a small wood and a road skirting it – a symbol of the free world outside.

Later, when winter came and snow began to fall, this job stopped since the freshly fallen snow would have immediately shown up any footsteps.

The main work in the camp was making fishermen's nets of various mesh sizes. I managed to team up with an invalid preparing the string for him to make up into nets. It was a ruse to earn an extra privilege, involving a chance of extra food, my invalid 'boss' having a friend in the kitchen. This was very important because he sent me each afternoon to the kitchen to receive an additional portion of millet *kasha*, there being no buckwheat in this camp.

Remembering what Colonel Guitzenko told me in the course of my interrogation, that I would be allowed to write a letter a month so long as it was not destined for abroad, I sat down to write to a cousin still living in Baku, and to another in Moscow. My Moscow cousin, whom I last saw in St Petersburg in 1916 replied at once. He wrote to say that he was now a civil engineer in the Ministry of Transport, and told me he would never forget everything that my father did for him and his family, nor all the help given to his brothers and sisters to complete their university education. His sister, a great friend of my sister, had died shortly after the liberation of Leningrad, having survived the horrors of the blockade, the famine and all the privations. His brother, also a civil engineer, was now a professor at the Institute for Civil Engineering in Leningrad, but he begged me not to write to him, for reasons which anybody living in the USSR could easily understand. A climate of denunciation reigned supreme, and everyone was afraid.

Nevertheless my cousin in Moscow, and the one in Baku, both had the courage to reply to my letters with offers of help. My Moscow cousin unfortunately paid a price for defying the dangers, for probably because of that he, too, was arrested two years later and sentenced to five years in a corrective labour camp. In the meantime, he sent me each month a parcel with tins of sweetened condensed milk, bread and even some eau de cologne! As an experienced Soviet citizen he might have been expected to realize that such luxury articles were forbidden in the camps. The little bottle of eau de cologne was promptly confiscated by the guard who checked the contents of all the parcels. No doubt he kept it for his own use!

My cousin also sent a postal order in the hope that I might buy something in the camp canteen. In fact the canteen at Shcherbakov sold nothing but carrots! Naive as I was at the time, I queued up to pay in my money at the canteen office, but as soon as I approached the counter and was about to pass over the twenty-rouble order to the cashier, it was snatched out of my hand by one of the *blatnoj*. Within seconds it had been passed from hand to hand to his gangster pals who formed an impenetrable wall and stood there laughing.

The parcels my cousin sent were kept at the camp depot and I would go there each day to withdraw a little something, always accompanied by a friend. Otherwise, I would be sure to be attacked on the way back to the barrack-hut and robbed of anything I carried. On returning to the hut I would share the food with my friends, this being an accepted rule among detainees. I also received food parcels from my other cousin in Baku, and these usually contained rice, sugar or tinned food of some kind.

The iron stove, though quite big, was not designed for cooking, and the top surface was limited. Detainees therefore had to queue up to heat up their tins of food. The stove could take no more than eight or ten tins at a time, and these had to be watched with an eagle eye or else a tin could vanish in a flash, as if by magic. One day a group of us somehow managed to get hold of three kilos of potatoes with the help of 'the friend in the kitchen'! Each had contributed a small sum of money to obtain this luxury. The feast consisted of a purée of mashed potatoes, boiled with a little salt, and we took turns to have a spoonful. The pot was soon empty, for we were truly famished! Even though there was nothing to accompany the potatoes, I remembered it ever after for the magnificent meal it was.

Among the detainees with whom I had long chats at Shcherbakov was a young Russian Jewish bookbinder who had been taught his trade by his father, a famous craftsman in artistic book-binding. The father had worked for General Kuropatkin, the Minister of War who eventually took supreme command of the Russian armies during the disastrous Russo-Japanese War of 1904-5. Kuropatkin loved beautiful books and had an immense library.

When war was declared against Hitler in 1941, the boy was mobilized and attached to a regiment of reserves, from which he should, after a rapid training course, have been sent to the front. Instead he was arrested and accused of anti-Soviet propaganda on the basis of a denunciation by a fellow recruit. Not surprisingly he denied the accusation, telling the KGB interrogator: 'I am a Jew, and like all Jews, I longed for the Revolution to bring the freedom and rights denied to my people for generations. The Communist regime established my people's rights, so how can I possibly be accused of anti-Soviet activities?' The interrogator replied: 'Listen, you are not a child. You know what the KGB means and how it works. The fact that there has been a denunciation against you means you have probably said something to prompt it. Nothing can be done about it now, and you will be condemned according to the rules. It is useless to protest or deny anything.' He then went on to advise the young Jew: 'It is better for you to compromise. I believe what you say, for I, too, am a Jew. We must reach an agreement. You must make my task easier. You must sign this paper which states that what you said has been misunderstood by your comrades, who must have read into it an anti-Soviet slant not intended. You must confess it was your fault, and then I, for my part, will try to arrange for you to receive the shortest possible sentence. So make your choice: rather than being sent off to the front with the idiots who denounced you and where you risk being killed or wounded, you will spend several years in a camp and your life will be saved. Agreed?'

Naturally he agreed to sign the paper, and the interrogator arranged for him to receive the minimum sentence of five years. Now, with the war over, he awaited the day of his liberation and sat composing a poem dedicated to the 'Great Leader Stalin' and to the noble Soviet people! He planned to send the poem to the Kremlin, in the hope of softening the consequences of his sentence.

As I talked to him in my usual humorous way, making jokes and mocking the absurdities, he interrupted me to point out that denunciations had thrived with the Revolution and the terror which followed, and thrived to this day. The Russians had lost all sense of humour. Life had become too hard for anyone to want to make jokes or witticisms. Besides, he warned me in all seriousness, no one among the other inmates would understand what I was trying to say. Suppose someone became angry and denounced me, too, as 'an enemy of the Soviet people', even as he had been. He begged me not to forget what had happened to him and to try to understand the situation for what it was. I understood only too well.

8. SAVED FROM THE ARCTIC TRAIL

As time went by the food at Shcherbakov became worse and worse. We were told that the camp had been declared an 'autonomous economic unit' and therefore had to be self-sufficient and rely on its production and sale of fishing nets. A strange sort of prison! If the revenue from sales were delayed we just had to tighten our belts. Our already minute food rations were reduced even further. I was therefore only too pleased when, one day in the spring of 1947, I was summoned to the camp office and told I was being sent further along the line to a destination as yet unrevealed.

A few weeks earlier I had written to the Lubyanka Prison Governor, demanding the return of my wrist-watch, confiscated at the time of my arrest. I did this on the good advice of the book-binder, and sure enough, several days before my departure, the watch arrived. The guard in charge offered to buy it, an offer I accepted with alacrity. In exchange he gave me some bread and a litttle money. It was better than nothing and we were both pleased with the transaction.

I travelled with another detainee: just the two of us plus a guard as escort. Returning first to Yaroslavl, we were once again marched through the town to the transit prison. I could see barges and ships moving down the Volga, although the snow had not yet melted. At the prison there was no longer anyone I knew. I asked about the Kuban Cossack, but nobody could tell me what had become of him. Perhaps he succeeded in his escape plan at last.

I was not to remain long at Yaroslavl this time. Apparently my journey had been designated as 'urgent', and the prison authorities were in a hurry to send me to where I should have gone when my journey was interrupted by scurvy. The KGB Centre had not forgotten me and the time had come for me to travel to the destination originally allotted to me. Once again I found myself in a Stolypin rail waggon where the *blatnoj* told me we were travelling in the direction of the Urals, to Kirov (formerly Viatka). This ancient city lay on the other side of the Volga and, for the moment, it was still difficult to make any guess at our final destination. Despite this being their second or third time of travelling to Kirov as well as all their past experience, the *blatnoj* could not say whether we were destined for Siberia (considered a good direction) or for the camps at Vorkuta in the Northern Urals mountains, within the Arctic circle (which would be bad news indeed). There was a good reason for the sentiment in 'Tchupchik' ('The Forelock'), a well-known folk song sung by the detainees, when it said, 'I do not fear the Siberian wastes, for Siberia will always be good Russian land'.

We arrived at Kirov, near the Urals in the depths of thick forests, to find it still blanketed in snow. But it was not too cold, and by now I was better equipped to face the elements. On leaving Shcherbakov I had been issued with warm winter clothing consisting of quilted trousers and jacket and a pair of felt boots already so worn that no *blatnoj* had an interest in taking them from me.

From Kirov station we marched more than a mile through deep snow to the prison, situated on the outskirts of the small town. The prison's wooden huts huddled together, with nothing for miles around them but thick forest – a desolate sight. I had been warned by the *blatnoj* on the train to conceal carefully my wooden spoon, for the Kirov guards were known to confiscate even the most inoffensive thing out of sheer malice. This proved to be so and the guard confiscated my amber rosary, all my protestations being greeted with the usual response: make a written application to claim it back. This time, alas, my application failed and I never saw my rosary again. Doubtless the guard showed it to his wife who liked it and kept it. The one benefit of this mean act was that I succeeded in concealing my spoon as the guard was busy taking my rosary!

After the search or *shmon* came the bath-house where only a little tepid water in a bucket was provided for each person. The prison administration's sole concern was to fill in the regulation forms confirming that such and such a convoy had arrived, been bathed and disinfected! At least our clothing was returned still hot from the steam-cabinet.

In my hut were several Polish officers who had survived the partition of their country between the USSR and Nazi Germany in 1939. Arrested then, here they were in 1947 still moving from camp to camp eight years later. As I did not know Polish I spoke French to them. The *blatnoj* listened in amazement, never having heard French spoken before. The Poles were keen to arrange a party for bridge and invited me to join them. The only problem was they had no cards. I therefore volunteered to ask the *blatnoj*, who made them out of old newspapers, marking ink and glue being manufactured on the spot. Cards were an article of vital necessity, for the favourite pastime of the *blatnoj* was a game called *trynca*, something resembling baccarat. This they played with the same intensity and passion as any gambler in a luxurious casio, sometimes literally losing all they stood up in.

When I asked my friends among the *blatnoj* to make a pack of fifty-two cards they were mystified. What sort of game required fifty-two cards instead of thirty-six? Nevertheless they were happy to oblige and curious to see how we played this mysterious game. They had agreed to do it for me because I spoke their language, whereas the Poles were too proud to speak to the *blatnoj*, despising them and having hated the Russians for centuries in any case. As soon as the cards were ready the Poles and I settled down to a game of bridge, the *blatnoj* watching us attentively. In the event, they were not impressed! This quiet game, having nothing to do with chance or luck, seemed dull to their minds and soon they left us to return to their more animated game on the top bunks.

The barracks were very old and overcrowded, the stench terrible. Every day I became more tired and ill. I decided to ask to see the doctor, a Polish army doctor and, of course, a detainee. After a thorough examination he told me I had developed dropsy, as a result of several months of malnutrition. My stomach was badly swollen, I had a high temperature and felt very weak. He arranged for me to enter the dispensary sick-bay, which had twenty beds for the seriously ill. The sick-bay was staffed by the doctor, two nurses and two medical orderlies whose job was to empty the *parasha* twice a day. At night the orderlies returned to their huts but the doctor and nurses had to remain on duty round the clock.

They were kind and gentle and did their best, but could not prevent the dispensary seeming a sort of ante-chamber of the mortuary. Every day a patient died and if it happened at night he would be left there until, in the morning, the orderlies arrived to empty the *parasha*. Then they also removed the corpse, which was taken for a post-mortem examination. The doctor had to fill in the forms indicating the cause of death, which was invariably given as 'a weakening of the heart muscle' or something of the kind. The real cause, malnutrition, was never recorded.

I do not remember how many days I remained in the sick-bay, semi-conscious and dozing most of the time. But I do remember an argument I overheard between the doctor and one of the nurses. An order had come through that I be taken to the departure point to complete the formalities for joining the next convoy leaving Kirov for Sverdlovsk. I could hear the nurse pleading with the doctor to stop me leaving as I would never last the journey, but he insisted it was better if I went because then there was at least a chance that, if I survived the journey, I would get better treatment in the hospital at Sverdlovsk, whereas here in the dispensary I would be doomed to die like the others. I could hear every word, could grasp my terrible situation, yet somehow remained quite indifferent as though they were talking about the fate of a stranger.

Late the next evening I left the dispensary, taking with me the good wishes of the Polish doctor and his two nurses. The other patients also wished me well, envying my good fortune, for their own stay in the dispensary held out little hope for the future. Two more had just died, but their bodies could not be removed until the next morning, for all the barracks were locked up at night. The doctor himself escorted me to the communal barrack-hut where I spent my last night at Kirov and next morning we were marched on foot to the railway station. Spring had arrived and a general thaw had set in, bringing with it the famous Russian *rasputitsa* when the land was transformed into a vast lake. Since I had hardly any strength left, I was always lagging behind. Our group of prisoners kept having to stop and wait for me to catch up. Finally the guard commanding the escort ordered one of the young soldiers to stay with me to help me walk while the others continued their brisk march. As the roads were under water we had to climb the embankment, though I hardly had the strength to get to the top. The young soldier helped me as best he could, but we slid, climbed a bit, then slid again on the muddy slope until, at last, we made it to the top. It was easier walking on the firm wooden sleepers.

Our group now had to wait for the train a certain distance from the station, on one of the sidings reserved for the embarkation of detainees. The Soviet authorities being a model of discretion, did not like the general public to see the miserable detainees on their journeys to the various camps in the Gulag network. Besides, it was easier for the guards to control the convoys if they were kept isolated from the townspeople. When, at last, the train arrived I did not even have the strength to climb into it. The others had to help me and a guard pushed me into a compartment already crammed full. At that point someone snatched my bag of bread and salted fish, supposed to last the journey. Naturally the train was full of *blatnoj,* busy stocking up at the expense of their unfortunate fellow passengers.

It was useless to protest and my despair was complete. Here I was, fifty years old, sick, hungry and completely exhausted. Although there was space on the luggage racks, I hadn't the strength to clamber up. I just sat on the floor between the benches and stayed there for the whole three days and nights of the journey.

At Sverdlovsk (formerly Ekaterinburg, where the Tsar and his family were massacred in 1918), we were shunted into a siding where two Black Ravens awaited. Into these the guards squashed us like sardines in a tin, and half an hour later we arrived at Sverdlovsk prison to the routine reception: counted, searched and taken straight to the bath-house. For once the water was hot but I hadn't the strength left to wash myself. I just sat in the warm bath-house and waited for my clothes to be returned from the steam cabinet. When they arrived I started to dress with difficulty but suddenly hadn't the strength to lift my arms or move my legs, the heat increasing my feeling of faintness. After the other detainees had dressed I was left alone and when the old detainee who looked after the bath-house came in I could barely speak to tell him I was too weak to move. He helped me to dress, put on my quilted jacket and called the guard to explain my sad state. The guard stopped two detainees and ordered them to take me to a cell on the first floor. When they tried to help me walk my legs simply crumpled under me, so they dragged me along the corridor by my arms, like a sack of potatoes. On the staircase leading to the first floor they pulled me up several steps at a time so that I felt each step with my bottom. Then, on the landing halfway up, seeing no guards were about, they just dropped me and ran off. I lay, semi-conscious, dreamy thoughts of hot food and a soft bed flitting through my mind before I passed out completely. When I opened my eyes two guards were leaning over me and shouting: 'What's all this? Where are you from?' But I only lost consciousness again.

When I came to I was in the prison sick-bay, undressed and in a proper bed with sheets and a blanket. A nurse brought me some hot soup with rice, which I ate before falling into a deep, long sleep. When I awoke next day the nurse told me I would have to go to the prison hospital in the afternoon since they were not allowed to keep people in the sick bay for more than twenty-four hours, there not being enough beds. And so I had to get up and walk across several courtyards to the hospital, a large building of five or six floors, with high-ceilinged rooms but no lifts. An orderly helped me to climb the stairs all the way to the ward on the fourth floor, where I was expected.

It was a large ward with some thirty beds, most of the patients being ex-POWs from the German camps. Unlike those at Shcherbakov, however, there were no wounded, but only detainees like myself who had fallen ill from malnutrition in camp or while travelling. They were here to be fed to regain sufficient strength to resume their journey and made fit for work and, indeed, the food here was infinitely better than elsewhere. Each day we were given a cup of tea with sugar in the morning and had milk, rye bread (well baked for a change) and even meat. The portions were very small but nevertheless the good food helped to speed our convalescence and ensure we could be sent on our way as soon as possible.

One day a young twenty-three year old soldier was brought into the ward. He was seriously ill but happy to be so, having heard the constantly circulating rumours that a general amnesty was imminent and detainees who were seriously ill or maimed victims of the war would be the first to be pardoned. The psychosis was understandable and the young soldier was convinced of the rumour's truth. He could never accept the perfidy and cruelty of the 'great leader' Stalin, and to speed the happy day of his release did everything possible to aggravate his case. He exchanged his morning cup of tea with sugar for cigarettes. He managed to obtain some salt from a kitchen orderly and drank salted water. In no time he developed a serious dystrophy from which nothing could save him and on the morning they came to remove his corpse he was quite unrecognizable from the cheerful young soldier brought in a couple of weeks earlier, full of hope and faith in Stalin.

Three weeks after my arrival at the Sverdlovsk hospital I was told I was considered sufficiently strong to resume my interrupted journey. Besides, a new convoy had come in and my bed was needed. I was taken down to the first floor of the prison, to what detainees called the station waiting room, a large cell with a massive grill, where all detainees awaited embarkation for the next stage of the journey. About eighty of us waited all night, sitting on the ground. When morning came we were told our departure had been postponed. The detainees were sent back to their cells.

Three days later our journey was definitely on. We were driven to the Sverdlovsk railway station and once again pushed into a Stolypin rail-coach, already half-full. The train set off heading along the main great Siberian railway towards Kurgan, and then bound for Petropavlovsk, the capital city of North Kazakhstan, formerly Stopnoj Kraj (which meant the Province of the Steppes of Western Siberia). We were on our way to join a great convoy of detainees, bound for the Kar-Lag, as the extensive network of camps south of Petropavlovsk were known.

On leaving Sverdlovsk we had been given the usual meagre ration of black bread and salted fish, but I had not touched it after the experiences of previous journeys. When the train finally reached Petropavlovsk our carriage was once again shunted on to the depot sidings, where we stayed another two days. I felt very ill again, having left Sverdlovsk hospital far from recovered. The stifling heat in the carriage became unbearable. But even though I drank as little as possible, in my weakened state it required an enormous effort not to pass water more often than the twice daily trips to the lavatory allowed. This time I had managed to climb on to the luggage rack, and as we waited in the sidings after five days of that terrible journey, I was so worn out I could control myself no longer and urine started to drip on to those in the bunks below. They began shouting for the guard, pleading with him to let me go to the lavatory.

Meanwhile, a great convoy of goods waggons was assembled to take us first to Karabas, the sorting centre for detainees passing through Karaganda, the centre of the coal-mining industry. It was an irony of fate that I should be travelling over this particular route. In October 1915, as a student at the civil engineering faculty in St Petersburg, I had been offered my first job by my cousin Alexander Urbelyan, at the time prospecting for the construction of a new railway line to link the great Trans-Siberian line with Turkestan in the south. The job, in head office, involved examining and evaluating the prospecting done during the summer to fix the line's actual direction. I gladly accepted, especially since the job paid 25 roubles a month – a princely salary for a student in those days. And now, thirty-two years later, I found myself transported along that very same line in a prison train, a detainee on his way to the Siberian camps in the vast Kar-Lag territory, which stretched all the way down to the frontiers with Persia, Afghanistan and China.

There was no railway station but only a halting place at Karabas, in a region inhabited by Kazakh tribes. We arrived in the middle of the night, the train stopping on a high railway embankment completely surrounded by a cordon of troops. Powerful searchlights illuminated the train and the surrounding area and a command boomed over the loudspeakers, telling us to dismount and assemble at the foot of the embankment. Encouraged by the usual shouts of 'Move! Move!' ('Davaj! Davaj!'), we jumped from the carriage on to the narrow edge of the embankment and, unable to stop as we were pushed from behind by others, tumbled down the slope, blinded by the searchlights. Fortunately I reached the bottom without mishap, but there were many accidents – broken legs and so on.

At the prison barracks at least there was water to drink, and all those who had suffered agonies of thirst on the journey could drink their fill. I could not stop myself, swallowing five or six mugfuls one after another as my completely dehydrated body kept crying for more. Then I forced myself to stop, knowing how dangerous it was for me to drink in my state. We all lay down on the barrack floor, an ordinary floor of beaten earth, to await the usual formalities.

The next morning we were woken up very early and told we were to be separated into groups to be housed in the various barrack huts. A medical commission of detainees arrived to sort us out and there were many sick people among us, not surprisingly after the terrible conditions of the long journey. The medical examination was cursory, everybody being told to lower his trousers so the doctor could see if the skin of the detainee's bottom was black – a sign of advanced distrophy. When my turn came to drop my trousers, my poor state of health was obvious. The doctors agreed I must go at once to hospital.

Once there I slept round the clock for three days and nights. The nurses would wake me to give me injections and feed me from time to time, and then I fell back into a deep sleep. On the fourth day I felt better and could even get up a little. Only then did I meet the man who undoubtedly saved my life: Dr Sverdlik, a Jew from the province of Bessarabia, annexed by Romania in 1918 when Russia was in disarray after the Revolution. He was about thirty-five, born in Balti, a first cousin of Sverdlov, one of the founder members of the Bolshevik Party in whose honour the city of Ekaterinburg was renamed Sverdlovsk. Unable to study medicine in Romania, where anti-Semitism was rampant with the pogroms and persecution of Jews officially approved throughout the country, he was obliged to complete his university studies in Italy. Nevertheless he returned to Romania when he had his doctorate, though he still had to sit for a Romanian degree before he could practise medicine. The anti-Semitic excesses continued to grow in intensity, especially in the eastern provinces of Bessarabia and Moldavia. When Octavian Goga, the university professor and poet, became Prime Minister, attacks against Jews grew more and more frequent. Thus the Jews in Bessarabia were overjoyed when the province was annexed by the Soviet Union just before the beginning of the Second World War. It was the same sense of happy relief as had been experienced by the Armenians in Baku when the Soviet Union liquidated the Mussavat Government in Azerbaidjan, thus saving the remaining Armenians there from being massacred by the Tartars.

As soon as Besarabia became part of the Soviet Union, all inhabitants of the province became Soviet citizens. When war broke out, Dr Sverdlik too was mobilized and sent to work as a doctor in a military hospital. An intelligent, capable man, with initiative and a talent for organization, he soon moved up the ladder of the Soviet Medical Services. When the Red Army was retreating to Stalingrad, he was the chief medical officer of a big military hospital in the city itself. But his rapid promotion gave rise to much envy and the strict discipline he enforced turned some of his staff against him. The inevitable happened: someone denounced him for anti-Soviet propaganda. He was arrested and automatically sentenced to ten years in a corrective labour camp. But this was only to be expected – a 'normal' event in the Soviet Union, or *narmal* as the Soviet people themselves pronounce it. And so, after several years in various camps, he was once again appointed chief medical officer to a large hospital – this time in Karabas, the sorting camp for detainees on their way to the Kar-Lag.

Dr Sverdlik was interested to know what had been happening in Romania and, once I was stronger, was happy to have someone he could speak to in Romanian. Determined to help me regain my health and strength, he joked all the time, teasing me that I was costing the Soviet authorities a fortune because he was treating me with the best and most expensive medicines at the hospital's disposal. Every day he gave me injections bought in America at great expense, to rebuild my muscles. Each ampoule cost 100 roubles – rather expensive to waste on a British spy and an enemy of the Soviet people, he joked! I would just have to repay the state by working twice as hard when I was strong enough to resume my journey to the camps when he had declared me fit to do so! The laughter and joking restored my morale, my strength growing daily and my weight also improving. I could get up now and walk without fits of dizziness.

Gradually, as I regained my strength, he found tasks for me, letting me help the nurses. Twice a day I took patients' temperatures and entered them in the records and on the diagram sheets at the foot of every bed. I also handed out prescriptions and began to help with maintenance work on the wards. The doctor wanted the hospital to be always clean and cheerful, however sparse the resources. The ward floor of beaten earth was cleaned each day and a fresh layer of clay was spread and allowed to dry so the convalescing patients could paint a coloured border frieze along each side of the passage between the rows of beds. These had to be re-drawn each day, yet everyone did it with pleasure, each trying to show off his talent. It was an agreeable pastime for long monotonous days, and some patients certainly produced some very pretty borders.

There were all sorts in the hospital: bandits, murderers and petty thieves, as well as political detainees. One young fellow, aged about twenty-five, had been sentenced for banditry under Article 59 and told that he would be sent to the terrible camp at Vorkuta in the Arctic North. This he was determined to avoid for an extra special reason: his former partners in crime had already been sent to Vorkuta. The *blatnoj* had their reliable bush-telegraph, and through this he heard they were waiting for him there to settle old scores. It was a question of life or death for him, and his solution was a very simple one. On the eve of his desptach, he went to the carpenter's workshop, grabbed an axe and calmly chopped off the index and middle fingers of his right hand. Then he went to the hospital to report the accident. Obviously he could no longer go on the convoy to Vorkuta – an invalid was no good there. They would have to send him to some other camp. Thus was the whole matter settled in true Russian fashion, but retribution was bound to catch up with him sooner or later. The *blatnoj* had their own rules and an excellent network of informers. With his self-inflicted mutilation he had merely achieved a postponement of his execution. Once the *blatnoj* passed the death sentence on one of their own, it was inevitable that it would be carried out sooner or later. There was no escaping it, and he would be killed by someone unknown to him.

Arrangements to prevent my joining the trail to the Arctic Circle were made far more cleverly by Dr Sverdlik without any need for self-inflicted mutilation! When he learnt that I was to be included in the next convoy, he replied that I was not yet fit enough to go. In the meantime he explored the possibility of me being sent to a camp with better conditions and no hard labour. After two weeks he came to tell me that I was to be sent to a camp for agricultural research not far from Karabas. He had already spoken with the SHOS (Research Centre for Experimental Agriculture) doctor who assured him I would be placed in the most favourable conditions.

My eternal gratitude and affection go to the two men who undoubtedly saved my life: the Polish army doctor at Kirov, who risked sending me on the long journey to Sverdlovsk in the certain knowledge that, if I stayed I would die; and the Romanian Jewish Dr Sverdlik who looked after me like a brother. No only did he give me back my strength but he spared no effort to ensure my survival once I left his hospital.

On the day of departure from Karabas I bade an affectionate farewell to Dr Sverdlik, to the hospital staff, and several patients, all of whom wished me luck and health. We were a small group of travellers, bound for the SHOS, and had to go on foot all the 18 kilometres, although there was a cart for those who hadn't the strength to march the whole way. We arrived in the evening at a small encampment surrounded by barbed wire, but with no high fences or watch-towers manned by guards. I could just discern in the darkness a group waiting to receive us. The SHOS doctor came forward to speak to us. He told me that Dr Sverdlik had spoken about me and that I could always rely on his help in case of need.

Next, a sturdy young man came up to ask: 'Which one is the Armenian?' I identified myself. He told me that he, too, was Armenian, his name being Gasparyan. He was head cook in the camp, a most important post, and he invited me to join him in the kitchen, where he gave me a meal and told me to eat as much as I could of this special food, a special diet for the sick. He told me there was another Armenian in the camp who worked in the bakery. This lay outside the camp but you could go there at any time of the day since all detainees in the camp were allowed to come and go as they pleased in daylight. You just had to give your number to the guard when you went out and when you returned. There were no other formalities. No guards accompanied the detainees when they were out working in the fields.

The scientists and the assisting workers went out each day to the piece of land reserved for research experiments in cultivating various types of grain and other cereals. The detainees included men and women and 'politicals' as well as ordinary criminals. But life here was peaceful, with none of the excesses of the *blatnoj*. Everybody was on their best behaviour, anxious not to lose the advantage of being in this camp with its exceptional system of free movement. Truly Dr Sverdlik had been my saviour and benefactor.

My first work in the SHOS camp was in the fields, helping with the wheat harvesting. The people were all pleasant, including highly educated scientists, teachers and students. Amongst all these unfortunates was a woman aged about thirty-eight years with a small daughter. The widow of a former Minister – 'a Commissar of the People' as the Communists called them. Her husband was one of the victims of Stalin's many purges. All those accused or merely suspected of plotting against the regime were executed of course, but that was not enough for the blood-thirsty tyrant! The families of the accused had to be punished also! So whole families, widows and children were all sent to special colonies in Central Asia and Siberia – called the OLZHIR (the Russian abbreviation for Ossobyj Lager' Zhen Izmennikov Rodiny, which means the Special Camp for Wives of Traitors of the Motherland). They were sentenced to remain in these camps for ten years, after which they were transferred to the usual corrective labour camps for an indefinite term, extended automatically ten years at a time! So not only were the traitors executed but their families exiled as well. A highly educated woman, she had taught in a secondary school and was herself an old Communist like her husband. Her twelve-year-old daughter had already spent ten years in an OLZHIR and was now starting another ten years here in the SHOS.

At the first opportunity I visited the bakery to chat with an old Armenian. He was a former steel worker from Baku. As a youngster he had joined the Socialist Workers movement and, later, the Communist Party. But fifteen years before he had been denounced as a Trotskyite, an accusation probably as groundless as usual. After serving the standard sentence of ten years in various camps he had hoped for his release. Instead he was sentenced to another ten years without further interrogation or trial. It was an administrative decision taken by the infamous *Troika* on the basis of information in his old dossier. To be thought a Trotskyite was to be considered to be a very dangerous element, and several of his comrades also suffered the same fate, as did many foreigners, poor naive fellows who had fled from political persecution in Germany, Spain and other countries in the firm belief that – in the USSR – they would be received with open arms, and allowed to work alongside their Russian comrades to speed the arrival of the World Revolution. But Stalin did not trust foreigners so they were sent to corrective labour camps for re-education!

The old Armenian was delighted to have someone to talk to about old times in Baku and the Balahanny oil fields, the massacres of 1905, the Socialist Workers Movement, and so on. He spent his nights alone in the bakery. In the morning the bakery workers would arrive to bake fresh bread under his supervision: rye bread for the detainees, white bread for the camp administrators. Often he would pass me a small piece of white bread as we chatted.

I met several interesting people amongst the detainees at SHOS. I remember particularly a young Muscovite, the scion of a family of old Bolsheviks. His father had important connections in high places and through them the son was given the possibility to study at the College for Diplomats, a privileged school. During his first two years there he passed all his exams brilliantly in all subjects, whether history, foreign languages or the other arts and sciences deemed necessary to achieve the high standards required of men chosen to do honour to the Soviet Diplomatic Service abroad. In addition to the usual subjects, the students were taught Western manners: how to dance, play bridge and games of sport, so as to be accepted in the diplomatic circles of the capitalist world, without drawing attention to themselves through their uncouthness. The students were taken to receptions given by foreign Embassies in Moscow and were even given money to pay their debts, should they lose at bridge.

The young man was happy at the college. He was engrossed in his studies and eagerly looking forward to his future career in the Diplomatic Service. Then, suddenly, he was arrested and accused of indulging in anti-Soviet propaganda. Why?! How could this have happened?! Was it perhaps some misunderstood comment or just the envy of a colleague which had prompted the denunciation? Whatever it was, it was sufficient for him to be sentenced to the usual ten years in a corrective labour camp. Now, so as not to lose his ability to speak foreign languages, we conversed in English, French and German.

Another very intelligent and charming young man I met at the SHOS was a Soviet film actor. It was the same old story: he too had been condemned on the basis of a denunciation! After several years of camp life he was very ill. He had terminal tuberculosis and, three months after my arrival, he died. Burial of the dead in camp was very simple: no coffin or any such refinements. The only requirement was a wooden tag with the name and number of the dead detainee attached to his big toe, whilst the official autopsy report was filled in his dossier. But this time it was different. He had a close friend. She too was a film actress and anxious to avoid the usual degrading burial, she had succeeded in obtaining some wooden planks which were made into a coffin for him. Many came to the funeral, bringing wild flowers growing in the prairie. It was a sad and moving ceremony. Everybody in the SHOS loved him.

There were several Polish officers at SHOS, among them a Polish cavalry major called Yanushkevich, with whom I played dominoes during the daily lunch-hour break. Only when I returned to France several years later did I learn that he was related to my cousin by marriage, being a first cousin of her husband. Yanushkevich had been arrested as a POW when the Red Army marched into Poland after the partition between Hitler and Stalin, and like other Polish officers had been sentenced to ten years in a corrective labour camp. Luckily for him, he was not sent to the Katyn forest where so many Polish officers were brutally murdered by the Russians.

Yanushkevich told me how, at the height of the war, when the Allies reached an agreement with the Soviet Union to allow detained Polish officers to volunteer to serve in Egypt by joining special Polish units formed by General Anders, one of Yanushkevich's friends also volunteered. Freed for this purpose, he was sent to Moscow where he was told he would receive further instructions. On arrival in Moscow, and walking through Dzerzhinsky Square, he suddenly saw the Lubyanka and remembered his beautiful watch which had been taken from him when he was brought there in 1939. He had been promised, after all, that he could have it back when he was freed and so, naively, he took them at their word and went in to explain what he wanted! He was told to wait while enquiries were being made, and shortly afterwards a KGB officer arrived with a guard and told him he was under arrest. In reply to his protestations, the KGB officer merely said that he had been freed by mistake, and would be returned to camp again, under guard, as an example to others what not to do in similar circumstances!

Now, Yanushkevich's ten-year sentence was nearing its end, but he felt worried, and with good reason. A fellow officer had, on completion of sentence, been offered a Soviet passport and when he declined it, protesting that he was a Polish citizen who did not want to change his nationality, the answer came: 'Well, there must be some misunderstanding. We'll have to write to Moscow for further instructions.' Moscow's response arrived several weeks later: a further ten-year sentence for anti-Soviet propaganda!

This provided serious food for thought for all detainees, like myself, who had foreign passports. It seemed certain that a general directive had been issued concerning foreign detainees: that they were to be offered Soviet nationality. What was one to do in such an event? Accept Soviet nationality or be punished with a further term of imprisonment which might, according to the latest rules, be as long as twenty-five years? Yanushkevich and I discussed the matter but agreed that all we could do was wait and see what fate had in store. There was much talk of the repatriation of Polish nationals, the new Communist Government in Poland having reached an agreement with Moscow, and talk, too, of a similar agreement regarding the German POWs, for the German Democratic Republic, about to be consolidated, wanted her nationals back.

In all these cases matters moved very slowly. Months passed with nothing happening. Nobody hurried in the Soviet Union, except in a case when an arrest had been ordered, and then matters moved very fast indeed. The nightmare of waiting, not knowing what to expect at the end of your sentence was terrible. Would I be treated according to the Articles of the Soviet Penal Code (according to which all foreigners were, on completion of sentence, to be expelled from the Soviet Union), or on the basis of yet another more convenient directive thought up by the masters in Moscow?

During the winter of 1947-8 I had a bad attack of food-poisoning after we were given some fish which had gone bad. Although the taste was so unpleasant that I only ate a small piece, this was sufficient for the poison to spread through my greatly weakened constitution. Among my symptoms of acute diarrhoea and high fever the doctor also detected jaundice and ordered that I should be taken to the main Kar-Lag hospital at once. I did not want to go, afraid to leave the comforts of life at the SHOS and dreading not being allowed to return. Nevertheless the doctor insisted.

It was bitterly cold, forty degrees below freezing, when I was put into a sleigh to make the fifteen-mile journey flat on my back but well-covered with blankets. I arrived at evening to the usual reception procedure: bath-house and disinfection of clothing. At least the water was quite warm. Then I was given a thin hospital dressing-gown and a pair of slippers and told to cross the 100-metre barrack square to the ward at the far end. The square was covered with thick snow and I was almost naked, but I had no option. I ran through the snow and frosty air as quickly as possible, afraid of losing my slippers.

The barrack ward itself was barely heated. There was a shortage of coal, there having been no deliveries because of the heavy snow-falls. Heating was therefore cut to a minimum, here in the steppes of North Kazakhstan where blizzards would pile up the snow against the buildings until the barracks were almost completely buried. And, as soon as the snow stopped, the temperature dropped to produce intense frosts.

The ward was quite small and contained some twelve beds. I was given two blankets, but no more! Everybody was cold and there was nothing to be done about it. The young doctor who came to examine me, a charming Jew, knew Dr Sverdlik well and assured me that everything possible would be done to ensure I was well looked after. He spoke quite good French, and since he had never been outside the Soviet Union, he was interested to chat to me about life abroad. In return he brought me Soviet journals which the hospital administration received regularly, so I could keep abreast of events. On 30 December 1947 I heard on the news broadcast over the loud-speakers installed in every barrack-hut, that Romania, too, had been declared a People's Socialist Republic. King Michael had been forced to abdicate to please the infamous Vishinsky, whom Moscow sent as Soviet Ambassador Extraordinary and Plenipotentiary to keep the situation under the Kremlin's control.

The doctor prescribed a series of insulin injections for the jaundice, most probably having no other medicines at his disposal. After each injection I had to drink some water with sugar, to avoid a shock to the system. The trouble was that there was not always enough sugar for a daily dose, the heavy snows having interrupted deliveries. Thus my treatment was delayed and the hard winter prolonged my stay. It was amusing, however, to see the envy with which other patients watched the arrival of my sugared glass of water after each injection. They would gladly have had jaundice too, just to be given some sweetened water.

After five weeks I was told that my treatment was complete and that I should prepare to return to the SHOS. I had been so afraid that I would not be allowed to return there, but now my mind was at rest. I bade farewell to the doctor and patients but was not sorry to leave. The one diversion had been a soldier who achieved fame among the patients by his skills at reading palms. A good judge of character and a shrewd psychologist, he had exploited those wretched souls by always predicting a happy future and the realization of their dreams, which were not hard to guess at. Only too ready to believe him, they had flocked from all parts of the hospital, bringing whatever small gifts they could muster.

I joined a small group of convalescents to march back to the SHOS with an escort of two soldiers. It was a slow business, since we were all very weak. As night began to fall we arrived at one of the Kar-Lag's small agricultural stations, having marched about halfway. Arrangements had been made for us to spend the night there before continuing our journey in the morning. To my utter astonishment I saw several Armenians with whom I travelled to Moscow after being arrested in Bucharest. As they were all elderly, they had been classified as invalids and were not therefore required to work in the fields. We spent many hours exchanging news.

At dawn we resumed our journey and by midday, I was 'home'. My Polish friends had all been sent back to their own country during my absence. I resumed work in the laboratory. It was interesting and not tiring, and life continued unchanged – except for the rumours. The latest one was that detainees were to be separated into 'politicals' (those detained under Article 58) and 'others'. The 'politicals' were to be sent to special camps in accordance with a new directive issued by Stalin himself. I was told this by some 'politicals' who worked in the administration office, where they had been transferred because of their high qualifications.

Several months later the rumours became hard facts and it was confirmed that I, along with other 'politicals', was to be sent to a special camp in the steppes of Central Asia known as the Spetz-Lag.

9. THE BALLAD OF THE BLACK RAVEN

This time there were over 2,000 detainees in the convoy. Once again the MVD guards, with their Alsatian dogs, pushed everybody into the rail coaches with shouts of 'Move, move! Hurry, hurry!' Each night the guards checked the inner walls and underneath the coach floor to see if anybody was hiding there. After four days of travelling in a southerly direction we finally arrived at the rich copper mines of Djezkazgan in the middle of the desert that stretches between the Aral Sea and Lake Balhash. It was the end of the line in an utterly desolate area, completely surrounded by desert, a branch of the main railway ending at Baikanur, later to become the site for launching the sputnik space rockets, where total secrecy could be guaranteed.

We arrived in the middle of a sand-storm, the air so full of dust and grains of sand that one could hardly breathe, and were made to stand outside in the storm for several hours. It was late in the afternoon before we were at last taken to the bath-house for the usual wash, shave and disinfection of clothing. Then we had to queue for the medical examination, another wait of several hours, sitting on the floor or propped against the barrack walls. The convoy was very large and the doctors few. The doctors were mostly women, the wives of detainees, though the senior doctor was a pretty young woman who had volunteered as 'a free employee', as ordinary citizens working in camps were known.

The medical examination determined the category of work a detainee was fit for: 1st category – for working underground in the mines; 2nd category – for overground work only; 3rd category – invalids. When my turn came the senior doctor herself examined me and told her assistant to note down that I had emphysema and was fit for 2nd category only. I asked what emphysema meant but she merely said it was too complicated to explain. The important thing was that I couldn't breathe properly so couldn't work underground. I took note that my health must have improved since I was no longer classified as an invalid.

There were three sectors in all at the Step-Lag (Stepnoj-Lager, or 'Camp of the Steppes'), and I found myself attached to the 3rd Sector. The total number of detainees in the 3rd Sector was over 3,000 and it included no women. The other two sectors were slightly smaller. The camp was surrounded by a high stone wall built on the rocky ground, and the three sectors were separated from each other by stone walls, each wall having a small door guarded by a soldier.

In Sector 3 were six barrack-huts ranged along one side of a central pathway that led from the main entrance to the hospital-hut a bit further down. There was another hut close to the entrance and this one was surrounded by barbed wire: the camp prison for those sentenced to a 'Special Punishment Regime' (BUR).

On the other side of the central pathway was a large hut containing the dining hall and kitchens. Lower down was the guard house with its own small detention cell, and a fire station. At the end of the central pathway was the door to Sector 1. Sector 3 lay in the centre, with Sector 2 to the left, behind the barrack-huts, while along the dividing wall was the latrine hut. Each of the six barrack-huts housed about 500 detainees.

My working party consisted of forty men graded '2nd category'. We would be woken each morning at 5 a.m, and after washing as best we could in those primitive conditions, would await the call for our turn to go to the dining room. One of the kitchen staff was in charge of summoning each working party in turn for the half-hour allowed for breakfast, which consisted of a piece of black bread, a mug of hot water instead of tea and the usual ration of fish soup (*balanda*) and porridge oats (*kasha*). This was considered a normal ration for people detailed to do hard manual labour, and was supposed to last throughout the day.

The roll-call to start work came at 7 a.m. Each working party or *brigade* was commanded by a supervisor (*brigadir*); the departure of *brigades* from camp being controlled by a *naryadtchik* (chosen from among detainees) assisted by two aides who together with the duty guards monitored both sides of the exit control point. To facilitate their task the detainees were aligned in groups of five, holding each other by the elbow. The counting was then done line by line as each group of five detainees passed through the gate, the guards on each side then comparing figures to check that they tallied. Outside the gate the detainees then stood in formation, waiting to be counted yet again by a detachment of soldiers who reported to the guard-house to sign a receipt for the correct number of detainees. Only after all these formalities were completed could a working party march off to start its day's work.

On my first day we didn't have far to go to reach our place of work. We were led to a stone quarry nearby to dig out the ballast for building the foundations of a new building in the neighbouring town. Each detainee's norm was fixed at two cubic metres of stones (about two cubic yards) and we were issued with the three classic tools: pickaxe, crowbar and shovel. It was heavy labour and, having never worked in a quarry before, I was not very good at it. Soon enough, seeing how I handled the pickaxe, the *brigadir* came up to me, roaring with laughter and asking exactly what my profession had been. On hearing I was a chartered accountant the other detainees burst out laughing as well and said: 'You'd better give him a pencil, not a pickaxe to work with.' Solemnly they brought me a crowbar and told me to try that. I laughed with the others and carried on with the crowbar, which was easier to work with.

After a full day's hard work we returned to barracks for our evening meal: the standard fish soup and a little dish of porridge oats. Exhausted, I climbed into my bunk and fell asleep at once.

The mine was worked in two shifts – a day shift and a night shift, both lasting eleven hours. The day shift started at seven in the morning and returned to camp at six in the evening, while the night shift started at seven in the evening and ended at six the following morning. As each roll-call sounded the three *naryadtchiki* saw to it that the teams were properly aligned in groups along the central pathway, the underground workers' team in front, and behind them the groups of surface workers, each according to their work destinations: some for building work in the town of Djezkazgan, others for loading copper ore on to goods waggons and so on. The order of alignment was always to ensure that teams working on more distant projects were placed ahead, to march off first.

The counting formalities lasted about an hour and a half, until all the 1,500 detainees included in the work-parties were accounted for. This meant standing outside in the intense cold of winter or the stifling heat of summer, lashed by the desert winds of sand and dust, poorly clothed and weak and hungry. The counting took so long because the guards were not very good at sums, and the procedure was slow and rigorous, both for outgoing and returning teams, to check that no detainee had stayed behind in the mines or elsewhere, preparing to escape.

Although four years had gone by since the end of the war there was still a severe shortage of paper, so the daily control of shifts leaving or returning to camp was recorded on small boards of plywood. Each board was divided into vertical columns indicating the reference number of a working party, the number of detainees in it, how many of them were going out to work that day, as well as other details, such as how many detainees had been freed and how many were staying behind in camp that day, with comments. The horizontal lines indicated the projects detainees were to work on – the name of the mine or whatever – leaving a space at the end for the figure of total detainees going to each project. There was one plywood board for the morning shift and another one for the evening shift. After the shifts' return to camp, the entries had to be scratched out with a piece of glass to prepare the same board for next day's entries. There was also a shortage of plywood!

On return to camp all detainees were, moreover, subjected to a body-search for concealed knives or other weapons as well as for bottles of vodka, which could be obtained in town. Surprising as it may seem, not only those working on building sites in the town but also detainees working in the mines somehow always found ways of meeting women, especially those who worked in neighbouring mines. Detainees would tell me how the women came to them, crawling along underground passages, bringing food and bread saved from their own rations. The women sometimes managed to get hold of some vodka for their men-friends, or they brought delicacies sent to them in food parcels by their families. The guards knew perfectly well what was going on, hence the body-searches on return to camp.

When I arrived at Djezkazgan many of the detainees working in the mines had the initials KTR marked on their caps and tunics. This signified that they had been sentenced to 15-20 years hard labour (KTR in Russian). They were mostly old Red Army soldiers taken prisoner by the Germans and subsequently recruited by General Vlasov for his Russian Army of Liberation with the object of fighting alongside the Germans against the Soviet Union. Their sentences had therefore been heavy ones.

At the end of the war several units of General Vlasov's army surrendered to the British and Americans in the hope of escaping the tragic fate they knew awaited them in the USSR. Unfortunately they did not know about the secret agreement signed at Yalta, whereby the Allies agreed to repatriate to the USSR all Soviet POWs held in the German camps in their zones of occupation in exchange for all American and British POWs in camps liberated by the Red Army. Faced with this, many officers and soldiers preferred to commit suicide rather than surrender themselves to the Soviet authorities.

I met and spoke to some of the victims of Yalta at Djezkazgan. It was from a cavalry captain from the Kabarda region of Northern Caucasus that I first heard the story of General Vlasov's surrender and how, when the general arrived with his command in the Tyrol in the American Zone, the American commander refused to let him pass on the grounds that he did not have the necessary instructions. One of General Vlasov's officers was, in fact, a KGB agent, and he informed the Soviets of the Exact place where General Vlasov waited for permission to stay in the American Zone. And so, on Soviet insistence, he was arrested and handed over, to be tried together with other high-ranking officers under his command. All were sentenced to death, and the event was reported by Moscow Radio in a special communique. Everybody in the camps, including myself, had heard the announcement.

Then in 1946, Stalin decided that the ten-year sentence automatically given to all returning POWs was not enough, and he increased the basic sentence for all POWs to twenty-five years, exceeding even the twenty years meted out to the men in Vlasov's army. While still in the Kar-Lag, I had met a Red Army lieutenant, an Armenian called Avetissian, who told me the terrible misfortune which had befallen him. Taken prisoner by the Germans after the general debacle on the Russian front at the beginning of the war, he refused to work outside the camp. No way could he be made to collaborate with the enemy. He somehow survived the hunger and privations, and when liberated at the end of the war, he was cleared by the KGB commission set up to carry out preliminary interrogation of all returning POWs, who found absolutely nothing to reproach him with. He was allowed to return to his family in Armenia, whilst all his fellow POWs received the automatic ten-year sentence in a corrective labour camp. Two years later however, the KGB decided that no exceptions should be allowed to the ten-year sentence rule for all returning POWs. It was therefore decreed that a mistake was made in allowing Lieutenant Avetissian to return home. He was arrested, interrogated all over again and sentenced to twenty-five years, because in between Stalin had ordered the basic ten-year sentence to be increased. His only crime was to have allowed himself to be taken prisoner, whereas all Red Army officers take the oath never to be taken alive, and he was now paying the price of having enjoyed two years' freedom! He, the innocent one, received a much longer sentence even than Vlasov's volunteers, now dubbed as traitors for having fought so ferociously against their fellow-soldiers of the Red Army, knowing full well the value of Stalin's word of honour and promises of general amnesty.

And so now, following Stalin's latest decree, other detainees originally sentenced to ten years in a corrective labour camp were also being sent here to Djezkazgan to replace the detainees sentenced to hard labour who were now being moved elsewhere. Even the administrative office was being staffed by KTR detainees unfit for manual labour.

After a while, the working party I was in was transferred from the stone quarry to loading railway waggons at the mine-head. As we arrived each morning we saw large quantities of copper ore rocks piled up in heaps alongside the railway. with the waggons lined up, waiting to be loaded. There were no mechanical facilities whatsoever. We had ordinary barrows to carry the rocks from the heap to the truck, and then had to raise them on to the truck platform. We continued loading in gruelling heat or pouring rain, soaked through as the guards shouted, 'Get a move on! Faster, faster'.

When the rain stopped and the sun came out our clothes dried on our bodies, lashed by the hot wind. We worked in pairs, each holding one of the handles of the barrow, so a lot depended on whom you were paired with. One day I was so exhausted, and my hands were trembling so much, that I could no longer hold on to the barrow handles. I stopped, but my partner started cursing so loudly that the *brigadir* came along and started shouting too. But I simply didn't have the strength to go on. There was nothing to be done. I was allowed to rest a little and then paired with another partner, someone who worked at a slower pace.

That evening I returned to the camp with hardly the strength to move. I sat on the ground near one of the barrack-huts, awaiting for call to evening meal. Just then I saw an assistant *naryadtchik* walking by – a young ex-Red Army officer with KTR on his cap – and decided to ask him to help. I shall never know what divine inspiration prompted me to stop him in his tracks and explain that I was a weak old man who could no longer stand the hard manual labour. I had never done physical work in my life, and in my present state it was impossible for me. Could he not arrange for me to be transferred to other, lighter work?

Although obviously in a hurry and irritated at being stopped, he listened and asked what my profession had been before I was arrested. On hearing that I was a chartered accountant, he took me by the hand and led me to the administration offices where he showed me a small room with three tables and stools and two cupboards full of files. Then he turned to me and said: 'There you are, it's all yours!' He explained that he and the other KTR detainees were being moved elsewhere that very night, so I could take over his job and carry on with what he had been doing. 'But what was your job? At least show me, give me some idea,' I pleaded. But he was in a hurry. There was no time to go into detail. He simply told me: 'You'll see for yourself what's to be done. After all, you're an accountant. Goodbye and good luck'. There hadn't even been time to ask his name, so as to be able to explain to anybody wanting to know what I was doing there. I didn't know what to do. I sat down to think out my next move, took several files out of the cupboard and looked through them. There were endless reports submitted by the supervisors in charge of the various working parties, together with productivity graphs. It was all very clear and simple. I blessed this young officer who, even though in a great hurry, had taken pity on me and spared a moment of his time to help me. I would now have to use this opportunity given to me to try to get myself accepted in the camp administration office as one of the *pridurki* (half-wits).

I took advantage of the uncertainty reigning during the few days following the departure of the KTRs to get myself accepted by the new administration as the person appointed by their predecessors to be in charge of statistics. The new administration, formed from among the fresh intake of detainees sentenced to eight to ten years, consisted of a chief controller (also an ex-Red Army officer who had been a Mining Engineer) and two *naryadtchik* assistants. I found myself helping with the entries of reports in the register as well as doing the productivity graphs and statistics. They were delighted to let me do all the hard work, leaving them only the task of supervising the daily dispatch of the various working parties. My spontaneous decision to ask the departing KTR for help had completely transformed my situation, and since nobody else was appointed to do the statistical work, the new controller accepted that I was indeed appointed by his predecessor. I did nothing to enlighten him, and since it was I who was now responsible for recording the transfer of detainees from one working party to another, my own transfer to a desk job passed unnoticed and was duly signed by the new controller.

Like many other detainees, my new controller liked smoking cannabis cigarettes (extracted from hemp), which in Russia are called 'PLAN'. That was why he was always thirsty. There was no shortage of such cigarettes and all detainees, anxious to put themselves in the controller's good books, made sure that he was well supplied with them. It was also the accepted practice that, whenever detainees received a parcel from their families, the contents were distributed, first to the *brigadir* in charge of the working party, then to the controller and his assistants. Only what remained after that was shared out with one's pals.

My work in the statistics office was not too cumbersome and I had plenty of time to do what I liked. The camp had a group responsible for cultural activities, whose task was to organize shows and entertainment for the detainees. There was even a cinema that each week showed Soviet or foreign films – German and Austrian films captured by the Red Army forces in Germany and Austria. The cultural group was made up of former musicians and actors, headed by a former Red Army officer, Nicholas Krasnov, son of the famous General Krasnov who commanded the regiment of Don Cossacks that rushed to the aid of General Kornilov against the Bolsheviks in the battle of Petrograd in 1917. Young Nicholas Krasnov had graduated from the Moscow Academy of Dramatic Art, and was also a good musician. Taken prisoner by the Germans, he had managed to survive and was even granted permission to form, with other POWs, a jazz orchestra to give concerts in various camps. When the camps were liberated Krasnov was sentenced to the usual ten years in a corrective labour camp. Transferred to Djezkazgan, he began again to organize music and drama events, staging plays, concerts and film shows. He even managed to organize a library. During the day he continued to carry out his task as a *naryadchik* assistant controller and duty detail, while in the evenings he entertained us playing solo jazz trumpet.

There was another *naryadtchik* officer on duty detail, also a musician, called Bobrov, who played the accordion well. He and Krasnov would rehearse their shows in between the dispatch and return of the working party shifts. They were both great lovers of Western music, especially of American jazz, but I was able gradually to make myself invaluable to them by my willingness to prepare the plywood boards for marking all movements of detainees. This gave them much more free time, and thus helped them in their other activities.

Another task I had was of great importance for all detainees: supervising the distribution of mail. The most precious thing for a detainee was a letter, and they anxiously awaited news from home. When I arrived at Djezkazgan the distribution of letters was absolutely chaotic. After the censor's office had finished with them, they would be thrown into a large basket, which was then brought to the camp for each detainee to rummage through in the hope of finding his own mail. Letters were thrown about, many were lost, and people became increasingly desperate.

I spoke to the assistant controllers about the need for a more efficient mail distribution, and they were only too happy to entrust me with this. We needed a system for properly recording and documenting everything but paper was practically impossible to obtain. What could be done? The assistant controllers explained the problem to the *brigadirs* in charge of the various working parties and everybody readily agreed to help. They would steal paper wherever they could and bring it to me!

It took several weeks of patient diligence to complete the necessary records, listing alphabetically all detainees by sector, work-party number and barrack-hut, leaving space for daily transfers from one party to another, new arrivals and departures, and indicating dates of birth. There were many detainees with the same name, Ivanov, Petrov and what have you, distinguished only by their christian names and patronymics (Ivan Ivanovich,

Ivan Petrovich, Ivan Sergeevich and so on). It was a long and arduous task and one I could tackle only after completing my normal duties. Everybody came to congratulate me and I became known to all the inmates as 'the benefactor'. At last there was hope of all letters reaching their addressees.

In due course I had permission to move freely between sectors to deliver all letters to detainees personally. In other words, I was official camp postmaster. The duty guards on the gates allowed me to pass without trouble and often chatted to me on my rounds. They, too, approved of my new function, which they considered both useful and pleasing. Being detached from special units of the MVD, they were better educated than the ordinary soldier. Knowing I had lived abroad most of my life, they would ask endless questions, amazing me with their complete ignorance of how people lived beyond the frontiers of the Soviet Union. Naturally I was very careful in what I told them. There was always the danger of having my sentence extended for indulging in anti-Soviet propaganda!

By this time I often shared the work of the assistant controllers, replacing either Bobrov or Krasnov at the daily dispatch of working parties and so becoming a semi-official *naryadtchik*. I had now moved from the communal barrack-hut to sleep in the office on the table which served as my desk. It was just as comfortable as the wooden bunk in the hut and at least the air was fresh and there were no bugs! Early each morning I woke up at five to be ready at my desk as the *brigadirs* from the night-shifts arrived with their reports. By the time the controller arrived I would have prepared a brief summary of all work done during the night, by shift and location.

I became so used to the routine of work that filled my day from early morning till night, that my health greatly improved. When hungry I could go to the kitchen where I was now treated with respect as a member of the administration. Time no longer dragged, the weeks and months passed quickly and I began to think of when my eight-year sentence would come to an end. I became so used to the way of life that I ceased to notice or worry about the assassinations which occurred regularly in camp, especially after the arrival of new convoys of detainees.

Although the vast majority of detainees was made up of 'politicals' and former POWs liberated from German camps sentenced under Article 58, there were also some common thieves and bandits sentenced under Article 59, as well as murderers. Almost every week there would be a 'settlement of accounts' – an assassination of those who had infringed the *blatnoj* code. Those who knew themselves to be in danger tried to take all possible precautions, but the *blatnoj* network was well-organized and ubiquitous in the camps. As soon as a new convoy arrived the target victim's identity would be passed on to the local executioner with the order that he be eliminated. The executioner risked nothing. Already serving a twenty-five year sentence, even if he were caught he could only receive the same sentence again. Another assassination meant nothing, and anyway a *blatnoj* order was not to be refused. As soon as he had identified his victim he waited a few days for a suitable moment then walked up to him and killed him. Camp law was truly savage, and people were killed for the smallest thing, under any pretext. There was a young Romanian student in the camp, sent to work underground in the mines. On arrival at the mine, each miner was issued with a pneumatic drill, plus a reserve twist bit of the drill in case the other one broke. His place in the mine was next to a Ukrainian, and one day the Ukrainian broke both his twist bits. Afraid to stop work and thus lose his productivity bonus, the Ukrainian asked the Romanian to give him his reserve twist bit. The Romanian refused. Why should he give it away? What if his own twist bit broke? He would then have had no reserve twist bit and then *he* would have been left in the unfortunate position of losing his productivity bonus. There followed a heated discussion with the Ukrainian threatening the Romanian, and warning him that the time would come when he would bitterly regret his refusal!

The Working Party returned to camp and shortly afterwards everybody got into their bunks, including myself, for I was sleeping in the same barrack-hut with them. In the middle of the night we were all woken up by terrible screams and cries for help. Then the screaming stopped as suddenly as it had started. I asked my neighbour what was happening and he told me that as soon as everybody was asleep the Ukrainian went to the bunk where the Romanian was lying, sat astride him so that the poor fellow couldn't move, and then stabbed him in the chest until he died! He had prepared his vengeance well, he had a small knife with a very short blade, only seven centimetres long, which he could conceal on his person in such a way that it would be missed during the body-search on return to camp. The poor Romanian student didn't stand a chance, his cries for help went unheeded, nobody moved to come to his aid! For that was the law of the camp and nobody dared to challenge it.

When he was sure that his victim was dead, the Ukrainian walked calmly to the door of the barrack-hut and knocked on it. The guards were outside, waiting for him. They had come as soon as they heard the victim's cries, but would not open the door until it was all over and calm had returned. The Ukrainian gave himself up, confessed what he had done, and was taken to the BUR (the punishment cell) where he would await trial. He would be sentenced to a term of up to twenty-five years and sent to another camp but he had had his revenge. Those were the accepted customs. The cruelty of war and the harsh conditions of camp life had turned people into savages and a man's life counted for nothing.

In Djezkazgan I met a Spanish doctor, a surgeon who had fought on the Republican side during the Spanish Civil War. At the end of the war which resulted in Franco's victory, it was decided to send to the USSR a group of children from Republican families, and the doctor accompanied them to Moscow. He was given work in a Moscow hospital where he was much appreciated by his Russian colleagues. But gradually the restrictive atmosphere of the communist regime became intolerable to the Spaniard. It was not the utopian paradise he had hoped to find on leaving Western Europe. He became more and more determined to leave the Soviet Union by any means possible! He had some friends in a Latin American Embassy and they suggested he should try to leave by using a method which had already succeeded in the past; hidden in a crate marked 'Diplomatic Bag'. The doctor agreed to do it – anything to leave the stifling atmosphere in the USSR. And so, he was put into a wooden crate clearly marked in Russian and French 'Fragile', and 'This Side Up'. His misfortune was that the Russian airport staff loading the crate on to the plane paid not the slightest attention to the instruction labels and placed the crate upside down in the luggage bay! And as the plane took off the doctor fainted! When he regained consciousness he started to struggle, trying to move his body in an upright position but the noise of his movements attracted the attention of the airline staff and the pilot decided to fly back to Moscow to investigate what was happening in the plane's luggage compartment. The result was a diplomatic incident and an official Note of Protest to the Embassy in question, whilst the unfortunate doctor was sentenced to ten years in a corrective labour camp.

Another character I met in Djezkazgan was an old Armenian Communist, who had served as a colonel in the Red Army, called Petrosyan. Taken prisoner by the Germans, he was sent to a POW camp in Belgium. He concealed his party membership from his captors who, had they known about it, would have shot him on the spot! He managed to escape from the camp with the help of the Belgian resistance and joined other Soviet soldiers who were making their way to the south of France. There he organized a unit of professionals to continue the fight against the Germans, alongside the French Resistance, in the Nimes Region. Although there were also some Frenchmen in his unit, most of it was composed of Red Army soldiers, POWs who had managed to escape. They had machine guns and even some pieces of heavy artillery captured from the Germans, as well as army lorries. After the Allied invasion of France, the role of his unit became more and more important as they continued to attack the retreating German armies, thus clearing the way for the advancing Allied forces. And after the liberation, he received an official declaration of gratitude from the French Army command.

As a Party member and officer who had done everything in his power to combat the Nazi enemy, Petrosyan had no reason to suspect that he would be branded a traitor. He therefore requested the French authorities to repatriate him and his entire unit to the USSR. The French readily agreed and even allowed him to take all the military equipment they had captured from the Germans. They sailed from Marseilles through the Bosphorus to Odessa where they were greeted with a warm and joyous reception: military bands, flags flying, speeches – the lot! Happily, they got on the train which was to take them to an army camp in central Russia, together with all the equipment they had brought with them from France. But a nasty surprise awaited them on arrival at the camp; they were ordered to hand over their arms and warned that they were completely surrounded so there was no chance of escape. Petrosyan could not believe it, he refused to be numbered among the 'enemies of the people' but despite all his protestations, his entire unit, himself included, were sentenced to twenty years in a corrective labour camp. It was the old classic KGB formula all over again: 'Thank you for all you have done, comrades, the Motherland is grateful but by surrendering to the enemy you have betrayed her so you should be happy that we bear in mind what you did after being taken prisoners, and sentence you to twenty years only, instead of the usual twenty-five!' Still Petrosyan did not give up, he and his comrades wrote several letters pleading for their case to be reviewed but all to no avail. All appeals were refused, firstly because there had been no trial as such to be reviewed – their sentence being a simple directive from OSSO, and secondly because the KGB said 'no new circumstances had arisen to give grounds for a revision!'

Doubtless for the KGB the nationality of 'an enemy of the Soviet people' is a matter of no importance, and mere formalities such as nationality or country of residence of these enemies cannot and must not impede the task of the KGB or other security organs such as SMERSH. I encountered such an example of ruthless disregard for international law when one day one of the detainees asked me to come quickly to help a Frenchman, who had arrived in the latest transport and who didn't understand Russian. I hurried along to find the unfortunate fellow and hear the sad tale he had to relate. Aged about 35-40, he was serving as an Adjutant in the Commissariat of the French Sector of the Allied Forces of Occupation in Berlin in 1945. At that time the various allied zones did not yet have fixed boundaries indicated by barriers, and one could pass freely from one sector to another throughout the city. He had gone to the market to buy supplies for the French Commissariat when he was arrested by a Soviet patrol and deported to the USSR, ending up in the Kazakhstan desert, in a camp in Djezkazgan.

Before the arrival of a new convoy, tables would be placed outside the office hut and the administrative staff, including assistant controllers, stood by to fill in the forms for all the new detainees, attaching them to various working parties there and then, according to categories and functions. I had by this stage grown a small pointed beard, like my father before me. It was a constant source of amusement for the political officer, a jovial fellow who was always laughing and joking. He would often interrupt my work by shouting: 'You – the spy – Bukharin – come here, I want to speak to you'; Bukharin, an old Bolshevik liquidated by Stalin in one of his mad purges, in the 1930s, having sported a similar beard. By contrast, the MVD officer commanding Sector 3, a Red Army officer invalided out of the army with a broken leg, was a primitive brutal man. He refused to credit the fact that I had been sentenced to only eight years and kept asking questions about my life abroad and how I had earned my living. 'Did you own a shop?' he wished to know. One day, to cut the conversation short, I said, 'Yes, I was a shopkeeper.' But this only infuriated him the more and he insisted that, as a foreigner and shopkeeper, I should have been sentenced to twenty-five years rather than merely eight.

Days followed one another with the same wearisome monotony. We were now obliged to wear numbers on our clothing – just like the KTRs - with the letter 'S' for 'Step-Lag'. This didn't worry me. It made no difference. My position was now more bearable and I was no longer hungry. But my troubles were far from over. One day at the beginning of 1951, the jovial political officer summoned me in his usual way while we were all lined up for roll-call. 'Come here, Bukharin, I want to speak to you!' He explained there was a new rule attaching KGB interrogators to each camp sector and told me that this meant I had a new job: henceforth I would be an office boy serving the interrogator attached to the 3rd Sector. I at once tried to decline this unexpected 'honour', protesting that I had only two years to go and complete my sentence, and that, through taking on this job, I would at once be branded stool-pigeon and informer by my fellow inmates and executed by them as such. Someone was killed each week for the slightest infringement of camp law and I had no wish to suffer the same fate. I begged him to find someone else because I categorically refused to do the job. But he only laughed and said it was too late to protest. His decision was final and the KGB had accepted my nomination. I would continue to work as assistant controller but must, at the same time, carry out whatever tasks the KGB interrogator gave me. He felt sure that after everything I had done for my fellow inmates, organizing their mail deliveries and so on, they would accept my assurances that I was no stool-pigeon.

So I had no choice. Every evening I would be presented with a list of detainees whom the KGB officer wanted to see for further interrogation. I would therefore need to make sure that they did not go out with the working parties next day, but waited in barracks to be summoned. I would have to explain this to the *brigadir* in charge of their working party, and what was more, would be held responsible should any detainee not be available when required. It was bad news from every viewpoint. Not only would I have to tell detainees they were being summoned by a KGB interrogator, but since the camps were administered by the MVD I would also, as an office boy of the KGB, inevitably be dragged into the eternal conflict between the two government departments. While the KGB claimed to be the more important of the two, the MVD camp administration always dug in its heels over submitting to any orders from the rival service.

Several days later a KGB captain arrived, having charge of all three sectors of the camp. A well-educated man, he spoke English and German fluently, without the trace of an accent. Most polite, he always addressed me by my first name and patronymic in the courteous Russian manner. He was obviously a graduate of the same school as my Lubyanka interrogator, Colonel Guitzenko. Not for him the jovial coarseness of the political officer, always shouting, 'Hey you – the spy – Bukharin'. Although only a captain, he had under his command a major and two lieutenants who treated me with the same courtesy as their chief, so putting me in mind of the old Russian proverb: 'The softer the bed – the more difficult to get a good night's sleep!'

The captain would be at his desk at nine each morning and heaven help anyone late in answering his summons. My first day in my new job proved very tough going. Nobody had been told beforehand about the new KGB team and everyone was full of suspicions and foreboding. My explanations were received with mistrust, but I tried to put a good face on it, assuring the detainees that they would soon see for themselves that I told the truth, that they were being summoned to answer questions in connection with others and that it was in their own interests to co-operate.

After several days the tension disappeared as they realized I had told them the truth. They even joked with me, complaining that so and so was not on the list when he was tired and would like a day's rest from the backbreaking labour! I sighed with relief. They had not forgotten all I had done for them and accepted I was merely carrying out the orders of the controller. Once again they saluted me as they went off on their daily tasks and working parties.

The fact was that the KGB had embarked on a gigantic project: to double-check the dossiers of millions of ex-POWs. They had no computers to simplify the task, and all research and cross-referencing had to be done by tens of thousands of KGB officials, hoping to find new evidence, new facts that might have been concealed by those who kept their mouths shut during initial interrogations immediately after their release from German camps. As I brought detainees in for interrogation, I would see on the captain's desk a sheet of paper with three photographs on top. The detainee would be asked if he recognized any of them, and if so, what information he could give on their activities while in a POW camp in Germany. Once it was completed the sheet would be returned to the section in the KGB Centre investigating the matter. There were tens of millions of files in the KGB archives, all marked 'to be kept in perpetuity', even as mine had been!

By now everybody knew what these procedures involved, and since I was the officially designated method of transportation to the interrogator's office, I found myself in possession of the new nickname of 'Black Raven' after the Black Maria transport vans. I also found I had become very popular with both the detainees and the guards. Everywhere I went I would be hailed, 'Ah, here comes the Black Raven', and everyone knew what my errand was. The detainees believed my new function to be all-powerful, and would plead to be allowed a day off work like the ones on my list. I mentioned this once to the captain when I saw he was in a particularly good mood, arguing how it could improve my own security. But the captain only laughed. It was clear that he had no right to allow any irregularities and anything I did would be at my own risk. Nevertheless I had the example of my controller, who always gave special dispensations to his favourites, and so decided to do the same, but only in exceptional cases, say for a Working Party *brigadir* who could easily be replaced by his *naryadtchik* and who would never denounce me for what I had done for him.

Every afternoon the camp bell would be rung for the daily roll-call. All detainees not out on work details had to line up outside their barrack-hut, and one guard for each hut, including the hospital and kitchens, recorded on his little piece of hardboard the numbers of detainees present. Since most of the guards were not very good at arithmetic, the control-checks could last a long time and the counting often had to be done twice. This made the guards even more irritable, and woe betide any detainee who was late in attending. A search party would at once be organized and as soon as he was found he was taken to the punishment cell in the guard house - a small cell built to hold no more than five or six people. But however many laggards were found, they would all be pushed into the cell to teach them a lesson. There was one especially sadistic chief guard who sometimes kept as many as twenty people in there for hours. The poor fellows, squashed together, could hardly breathe, and the weaker ones fainted.

One day, sickened by this inhumane treatment, I summoned all my courage to complain to a visiting army doctor who happened to be in camp. I succeeded in persuading him to accompany me to the punishment cell to see for himself the poor wretches still locked up long after roll-call. The chief guard was severely reprimanded by the doctor and had to stand to attention throughout the reprimand, to the delight of the other guards, who were equally sickened by his sadistic behaviour. Some of the guards, with whom I had become quite friendly, would laugh about the event afterwards, saying, 'The Black Raven's a bold fellow. You have to watch what you're doing when he's about'.

Among the many interesting people I met while working as KGB office boy were Russians who had been brought all the way from China and Japan, thanks to the never-resting efforts of the KGB. One of these was a young Russian from Shanghai, whom I shall call Viktor. He had graduated from the American University in Shanghai, and spoke perfect English as well as several Chinese dialects. As the war ended, Viktor had been entranced by the massive Soviet propaganda campaign urging all Russian émigrés to return to a new free life in the USSR, where they could live and work happily ever after as they helped in the reconstruction of the New Russia! Unlike his American wife, Viktor believed everything the Soviet regime promised. He decided to leave Shanghai for the Soviet Union, despite the dire predictions of his wife, who refused to accompany him. And no sooner did he cross the frontier than he was sent straight to the Step-Lag to undergo the standard ten years of re-education and corrective labour before becoming a true Soviet citizen.

In a sense the regime kept its promise. He was given a job straight-away as a driller in the copper mines, where he could produce the metal so badly needed by the country, while all the time breathing in the deadly copper dust that would precipitate his death. A strong and vigorous young man on arrival, Viktor was soon an invalid, suffering from acute lung disease.

Another Russian from China was an older man, Konstantin Voloshin, the son of one of a team of Russian engineers sent to the Far East at the beginning of the century when the Russians were given concessionary rights over a large area of Manchuria to construct a rail link with the fortress of Port Arthur. Many Russians were sent to work on the project, not only engineers and management staff with their families, but also shopkeepers to cater for their needs. After the Revolution in 1917, the Soviet Government gave the Manchurian railway as a gift to the Chinese Government and the large Russian colony was dispersed all over China. The Voloshin family went to Dairen, where Konstantin was born and grew up, and he, too, married an American girl. He spoke excellent English and Chinese as well as Russian, and became a legal adviser to a Dairen bank.

Towards the end of the war, as the Red Army moved into Manchuria, it was accompanied as usual by the KGB, whose first move was to kidnap Russian émigrés and their descendants regardless of whether they held Chinese citizenship. Voloshin was brought to the Soviet Union and sentenced to ten years simply because his parents were White Russians. The story of the punishment meted out to young Krjijanowsky, enticed to the Soviet Union from Paris, was repeated with Voloshin, kidnapped in China to atone for his parents' opposition to the Bolsheviks.

Voloshin told how he had, as a small boy, watched the public executions of Chinese bandits. These took place in the main square in the days before Sun Yat-Sen's revolution when the Chinese still wore long pigtails. As the condemned man knelt, the executioner's assistant would lift the pigtail to leave the neck clear, and then the executioner took off the head with one blow of the sword.

Voloshin loved the Chinese, whom he described as gentle and kind people, unlike their aggressive Japanese neighbours. He had learnt how to be an excellent cook, for in China it was the husband who prepared the family meal on return from work. One evening Voloshin brought his wife a rare delicacy, much appreciated by the Chinese, but didn't reveal what it was. She enjoyed it very much, but when he told her she had just eaten a dish of serpent meat she replied laconically: 'Please, never do that to me again!'

Entering the KGB captain's office one evening I was amazed to see he was interrogating Voloshin, although his name had not been on my previous day's list. The obvious explanation was that, since Voloshin was an invalid, he wouldn't leave camp anyway, so it was not necessary to include him on the list. But it was late and Voloshin looked so ill and tired that I took pity on him and asked the captain if it was really necessary to detain him. The captain, instead of reprimanding me for my audacity, simply turned to Voloshin and said: 'You can go now. We've talked enough for today, and your friend begs me to let you go!' Voloshin left the room with me, thanking me profusely for my timely intervention. Perhaps the interrogation was not particularly important, but even so, the captain's behaviour convinced me that he was a human being, capable of treating people with some consideration. It also made me realize that the captain didn't really trust me. He had kept me under surveillance too, and knew whom I talked to and who my friends were. One could never relax one's guard.

I often stayed late in the office when the captain had to work late into the night. Sometimes he spoke to me of his service in Germany where he had been sent after the end of the war. One evening when I went to receive the list of detainees needed for interrogation the following day, I saw on his desk an excellent Anglo-Russian dictionary – a new Soviet edition. Intrigued, I asked him where it came from. 'Oh,' he said, 'I took it from one of the detainees, a young student who, the idiot, wanted to learn English while he was in the camp!' Without thinking I asked if I could take the dictionary as it might come in useful after I left myself. He agreed at once and gave an official authorization. Some months after I began working for him, the captain said that he and his subalterns were impressed with the efficient way I fulfilled my duties. He then gave me his word that I would continue to work in the KGB office until the end of my sentence in May 1953. I thanked him most sincerely, for this meant I would continue to be exempt from hard manual labour.

Now and again the administration would convoke a general meeting of all the 3,000 detainees in our sector. One of the detainees would preside in the presence of the military commander and the political officer, the purpose being to announce a competition for the highest productivity, with our sector, Sector 3, competing to outstrip our rivals in Sectors 1 and 2. Speeches would be made proposing various measures to improve productivity, each *brigadir* appealing to his particular group to make ever greater efforts. All the resolutions proposed would be passed with the unanimity expected from people condemned to hard labour! I found these performances absolutely ridiculous, but that was the way it was in the Soviet Union – endless rousing speeches and declarations, and only after you had voted were you allowed to leave the meeting. One had the impression of being present at a farce staged solely to enable the camp administration to assure their superiors in Moscow of the spontaneous and patriotic atmosphere reigning in their particular sector of the camp!

I often wondered what interest people sentenced to hard labour could possibly have in this fiction of excelling at such competitions. But when I spoke about it to various detainees, I was amazed to hear them say that they didn't consider it a farce at all. For them it was a real and sincere demonstration of how they felt! They had all become so accustomed to inflammatory speeches in the years following the October Revolution, always having to vote for the same resolutions, all worded in exactly the same way. Nobody dared to oppose, criticize or in any way express an opinion different from that of the leader of their enterprises, collective farm or camp commandant! They voted knowing that nothing would change.

Speeches, however, were not always enough. At the beginning of 1952, the administration at Djezkazgan decided to reintroduce the system that had been in force before the outbreak of war in 1939; namely, achieving effective increases in productivity by awarding bonuses for exceeding the specified norm. These took the form of 'better food rations' as well as cash. You could receive a bonus in sugar, or in sunflower oil for your porridge, but most importantly you could earn *money*. There was also the carrot that, by exceeding norms, the detainees could qualify for a reduction in sentence. This encouraged detainees to make superhuman efforts, and the miners doing the actual drilling began to earn large sums of money, some of them as much as 10,000 roubles a month. But the work was very dangerous and the miners had no protective masks and the dust from the copper ore penetrated deep into their lungs. Within two or three years their health would be ruined and they would have to be transferred to surface work. In their efforts to achieve an early release or earn money they were, in fact, precipitating their early deaths.

Detainees in my category, doing mere office work, were badly paid, and my monthly wage was 25 roubles. But there was little to spend it on and I tried to save as much as I could for the day when I would finally leave. There was a camp shop where one could buy sweets to replace the non-existent sugar, or tins of capers, of all things. The poor starving detainees thought the capers were peas and ate them with bread. When I explained that the capers were meant to be a garnish for meat dishes, they stopped buying them. The detainees cursed the administration, being perfectly aware that the administration officers and guards had their own shop well stocked with tinned food.

Of course, one must always remember that, after the war, the Soviet Union's economic situation was a total catastrophe. The 'Lend-Lease' supplies provided by America during the war were suddenly cut off. The country had lost twenty million people in the war and the land had been completely devastated, the Germans in their retreat having dynamited factories and whole cities. There were shortages everywhere and everybody suffered terrible privations. Detainees who worked in the town of Djezkazgan were told by 'freely employed' civilian construction workers how they envied them. At least, in camp, they were guaranteed their daily ration of bread and buckwheat porridge, whereas the townspeople often had no food or bread to eat at all.

One curious incident was to have serious repercussions for my own future. One night, after lights out, the captain summoned me to go to a barrack-hut in Sector 2 and bring back a detainee for interrogation. As usual I had to pass through the barriers separating the sectors and ask the duty guard to accompany me to the barrack in question, unlock the door, and summon the detainee. The guards already knew me as the 'Black Raven', and they would do this without hesitation. The detainee was duly brought out, but as we walked back to the KGB office, we were suddenly confronted by Lieutenant Golubev, the MVD officer in charge of Sector 3, just then on his nightly round. He stopped us and demanded to know why we were walking about the zone after lights out. I explained my mission, saying I had been ordered to take the detainee to the KGB office for further interrogation, but the explanation only irritated the MVD lieutenant even more. He started shouting at me: 'What do you mean? There are no interrogations at night! Take this detainee back at once to his barrack-hut and then return to your own.' He had no idea that in fact I slept in the office, and I was not going to enlighten him. What could I do? On the other hand, I had no option but to carry out the lieutenant's orders and escort the detainee back to his hut. He, poor fellow was none too pleased, having hoped that, after a night of interrogation, he would be excused work next day.

Now I faced the problem of explaining to the KGB captain why I had been so long and why there was no detainee with me. It was a cold night and the captain stood waiting for me, his overcoat flung across his shoulders. As soon as he heard about my encounter with Lieutenant Golubev he started to pace up and down the office in a mounting fury, waving his arms, calling Lieutenant Golubev obscenities and shouting at me to return at once to Sector 2 and bring the detainee as ordered. In his enraged state, pacing the room from end to end with his coat-tails flapping, the captain looked like a bird of prey about to swoop! I became more and more unhappy. What was I to do, a simple detainee quite unqualified to take part in a conflict between government departments? Because of the clash of ambition between the two men, I was now in serious danger of being locked up for several days in the punishment cell!

In the event, I confined myself to suggesting humbly that I was too insignificant a person to discuss this matter with Lieutenant Golubev. Perhaps it would be more suitable to send one of the guards on such a delicate mission. The captain stopped in his tracks and burst out laughing. As he calmed down he said, 'You're right. Find a guard and tell him to come to see me, and you go and get some sleep!' I ran off at once to look for a guard, happy to be out of it, but I was mistaken if I thought this was the last I would hear of the matter. The lieutenant now bore a grudge, and as the conflict between him and the captain deepened, I would become the innocent pawn in the middle.

Several days after that nocturnal encounter, the Sector 3 controller received an order from Lieutenant Golubev in his capacity as camp commandant, directing that I be sent to work underground in the mines, despite the fact that I was graded as fit for surface work only. Having been reprimanded for hindering a KGB officer, Golubev was determined on his revenge. Everybody in the camp, from the controller down to the detainees, began to take an avid interest in the conflict and its eventual outcome. Who would win – the MVD or the KGB?

Next day, as soon as the captain arrived in the office, I informed him that my duties as orderly and office boy were at an end and that I was being sent down the mines by order of Lieutenant Golubev. But the captain paid no attention. He told me to stop worrying and repeated that I would remain in his office until finishing my sentence. He spoke in calm tones, stressing every word. There was no doubt that the first round had gone to the KGB and that the lieutenant had made an ill-calculated move. The KGB captain held the trump cards, for had I not been officially transferred to his office by common agreement between the departments and was not my work as an orderly irreproachable? There was therefore no reason to punish me by transferring me elsewhere, especially since I had been graded unfit to work down the mines. Moreover, the MVD lieutenant was guilty of hindering the work of a KGB interrogator.

The three other KGB officers in the camp – the major and two lieutenants in charge of Sectors 2 and 3 – were also happy with this outcome and even came to congratulate me on my behaviour. One of the lieutenants was a Kazakh, with whom I got on well. An Oriental like myself, he was always reserved and courteous. Besides his office in the camp's central KGB office, he had another smaller office in Sector 3 where I worked. He would sometimes bring me white bread – a rare delicacy only on sale in the administration staff shop. Sometimes he would send me there to buy him fresh vegetables, and once he allowed me to buy some tomatoes for myself. He knew that I hadn't seen a tomato for six years since leaving Romania. What joy! How delicious they tasted!

We often chatted, whenever he had a free moment, and one day we discussed the deportation of Crimean Tartars. One of the detainees, a Crimean Tartar, had told me the familiar sad tale of his experience. During the war, having fought honourably, he was given leave of absence from the front. He went to see his family back home, only to discover they had all been deported. Granting him leave had been a serious blunder by his army superiors, who should have known that all the Crimean Tartars had been deported to distant Kazakhstan for collaborating with the Germans when they occupied their villages at the very start of the war when the German armies penetrated deep into Russian territory.

The young Tartar couldn't believe what had happened and thought there was some mistake. He applied to the authorities for his family to be freed, on the grounds that he was a hero and had been decorated for bravery in battle! The only reply he received was the usual ten-year sentence in a corrective labour camp. Why, I asked the Kazakh lieutenant, was this necessary? Surely the authorities could simply have refused his application. He was, after all, a war hero. The lieutenant insisted that the Crimean Tartar question was a very complex one. He told me how he had actually been one of the officers delegated to escort and oversee the deportation. It was an indisputable fact that the Tartars had received the invading German armies with open arms, and had collaborated closely with them. Therefore they had to be punished. Admittedly the young soldier and his family may have been innocent, but the order was a general one, applying to the entire Tartar population without exception. As soon as the Red Army liberated the Crimea, the entire population – women, children and old people – were bundled into railway trucks and transported across the Caucasus beyond the Caspian Sea and Turkestan to Kazakhstan in Central Asia. The operation was carried out in conditions so terrible that it was not surprising that half of them died on the way. But it had to be done. It was the order of Generalissimo Stalin himself.

Moreover, the law of deportation applied not only to those living in Russia who were guilty of being traitors, or a danger of becoming so. It applied also in Bessarabia – the Eastern province of Romania where, after its annexation by the Soviet Union, the new Communist authorities deported the populations of entire villages to Siberia. Both Romanians and Moldavians were forcibly enlisted as 'volunteers' in the so-called Labour Battalions (or 'Trud-Armya' as they were called in Russian), to replace the manpower lost during the war. Thus Stalin did exactly what Hitler had done! Able-bodied men were enlisted and their wives and families given 'the right' to follow them. And if anybody tried to abscond or in any way avoid this 'voluntary' enlistment, he was at once sentenced to 10 years in a corrective labour camp, for desertion from the Labour Front!

One day the captain called me to his office and I went in to find all the KGB officers already assembled. He told me that he had been promoted and would shortly be leaving Djezkazgan for Frunze, where he would be attached to the KGB HQ in the Republic of Kirghizia, bordering on the frontier with China. He was happy to be leaving the desert of Djezkazgan and looked forward to his new post. His wife, who had been working as an accountant in town, would be accompanying him in accordance with the Soviet system which encouraged husband and wife to work in the same locality. Before leaving he wished to thank me for the impeccable, organized way I had carried out my duties as his orderly. He had nothing but praise for how I had carried out his orders, and assured me that he had not forgotten his promise that I would continue in my present job until my release. He was being replaced by his No. 2, Major Orlov, who also assured me that I had no cause for worry. He would make sure I stayed on to work for him.

Deeply moved by these assurances, which guaranteed my continued survival, I thanked them for their confidence and protection. But now the MVD lieutenant was all the more determined to wreak his vengeance. Confident that Major Orlov would not carry the same weight as the captain, he ordered the controller once again to send me down the mine. When I informed Major Orlov he told me not to worry. To get round the problem without a direct confrontation he would transfer me to the KGB office in the 2nd Sector and this lay outside Lieutenant Golubev's control. There I would work with the Kazakh lieutenant.

Once again I had no option but to agree. I knew nobody in Sector 2, and continued to sleep on the table in the office. It was simpler that way. Happily the major's diversionary tactics were not required for long, and after several weeks the Kazakh lieutenant brought me good news. Lieutenant Golubev had been transferred elsewhere and I could return to my job in the 3rd Sector. I hurried back to find the detainees anxiously wondering about the reason for my absence. All at once they saw me at my usual place, standing with the assistant controllers to check the morning dispatch of working parties. They greeted me like an adored film-star and as they lined up in front of the exit gate, spontaneously burst into song, intoning the old nineteenth-century ballad 'The Black Raven':

Black Raven, Black Raven,
Do not fly round and round above my head,
You will not have your prey,
For I am not yours, no, I am not yours to catch...

The singing was in my honour and it was a truly exceptional and deeply moving occasion. For once the guards didn't hurry them along, but delayed the departure of the working parties until the sad ballad lamenting the fate of all political prisoners reached its close. The detainees repeated the chorus twice, and only then did the assistant controller give the signal to depart. I stood as the working parties marched by in front of me and out of the gate, as pleased with themselves as if they had been parading proudly before a famous colonel nick-named 'The Black Raven' because of his duties. They saluted and cried out as they marched past, these unfortunate victims of an inhuman regime, and to acknowledge their unexpectedly warm and spontaneous demonstration of friendship I raised and waved my joined hands like a victorious boxer.

My duties were resumed, and one day, as a new convoy was being checked in, I noticed among the others a group of deaf and dumb people, also condemned under that Paragraph 10 of Article 58 which dealt with anti-Soviet propaganda! But could such a thing be possible? There was also a group of gipsies who had objected to restrictions being imposed on their nomadic habits. And on another day I saw among the new arrivals a group of Orthodox Jews, with sideburns and dressed in their traditional clothes, like those worn by Polish Jews in the province of Galicia. Seeing that I sported a Bukharin style of beard, they assumed I was also of their faith. One of them approached me, speaking in Yiddish and begging me, from the few words I understood, to arrange for them to be detached to lighter work than the usual hard labour. I said that I didn't understand Yiddish, and anyway this was not my responsibility. The allocation of duties depended upon the decision of the controller. He began to curse me for 'betraying my people' and refusing to help. Just for good measure he threw in some obscenities in Russian, presumably learnt along the various stages of his imprisonment.

Most detainees in the camp, old Red Army soldiers and officers, would watch the faces of the new arrivals closely. If the chance came round, there would be the usual 'settlement of accounts'. It came naturally to them, after all they had been through. As for me, I would never forget the first savage execution I witnessed during the early stages of my imprisonment in the Soviet Union. It was in Yaroslavl prison, where we were first moved on the first stage of the long journey to the camps. The *blatnoj* had accused an old peasant of stealing a piece of precious butter from one of them and took the decision to punish him. They simply went up to him, one group grabbing his arms while another grabbed his legs, and then bounced him up and down, striking him against the stone floor of the cell until his pelvis was shattered. Three days later the old man died in the prison hospital. It was a warning from the camp mafia to all other detainees, and its impact was unmistakable. I had fallen among savages, brutish people to whom a human life meant nothing and where only the law of the jungle prevailed.

By a strange twist of fate, I had been transported to Djezkazgan which, many years ago, was run by a British company, given concessionary rights by the Soviet government to exploit it. The terms agreed were favourable to the British because the Soviet Union did not possess the means to do this. The British supplied all the equipment, the machinery, the lifts and pneumatic drills, in other words, all that was necessary to launch this great enterprise, whilst the Soviets supplied the work force. That is to say, they supplied detainees sentenced to hard-labour camps, as well as 'free employees' to staff the administration and the senior engineering staff, such as explosives experts required for tasks which the convicts could not be trusted with.

With their expert knowledge and organizational flair, the British quickly developed several deep-bore mines, to achieve a high productivity. The very names of these mines (the Peter mine, named after St Peter and the Paul mine named after St Paul) indicate their true origins and the fact that they were not developed by the Communists whatever they may now claim! But the Soviet Government, having observed how the mining operation was being successfully managed, decided to annul the concessionary rights and confiscate all the expensive equipment, without bothering to pay any compensation, of course! They arrested the British managment and technical experts and accused them of sabotage and economic espionage. And, in order to have the necessary docile witnesses at the trial that was to follow, they arrested also several Soviet engineers, who could be 'persuaded' to collaborate with the Public Prosecutor, and support the accusations in his indictment against the British, for the Soviet engineers knew only too well what to expect if they dared contradict him...

After several months of interrogation, the British engineers realized the uselessness of contesting or opposing the accusations levelled against them, however prefabricated they may have been. The company's Head Office in Britain decided to reach an amicable solution, realizing only too well the true import of the Soviet Government's action. They had to do something to save the British engineers who had already spent several months in a Soviet prison. And so, an enforced solution was reached: it was agreed that the British staff at the mine would be freed and allowed to leave the USSR, in exchange for all the expensive equipment brought in by the company. On his return to Britain, one of the young engineers who was personally involved in the whole affair (and who happened to be the nephew of my English Director in Ploesti) wrote a book about it, entitled *'Economic Spying and Sabotage'*.

10. EXILE ON A COLLECTIVE FARM AND THE TRUE STORY OF THE BAM RAILWAY

In March 1953, in the spring, we were told that Stalin was dead. Everybody's hopes began to rise. Perhaps we would at last see a radical change in the brutal system. But, for the moment, nothing seemed to have changed and life in camp went on as though nothing had happened. I asked Major Orlov what would happen to me when my sentence came to an end in May. He was evasive, but it was customary for freed detainees to leave on the exact date their sentence came to an end. According to the Soviet Penal Code, I should be deported from the Soviet Union like all other foreigners.

The long-awaited day, 8 May, when I must be freed, arrived; but still I was not summoned for any interview. The hours dragged interminably, and only two days later, on the 10th, was I told to get ready to depart. I bade farewell to my friends, some of whom had prepared little presents for me. Assistant Controller Bobrov had taken the trouble to prepare for my journey a small suitcase made of hardboard, about 10 x 16 inches square, and quite sufficient for the needs of any detainee. Only as I was about to depart was I informed that I was being deported for life to Kazakhstan, in Central Asia, and told to sign a declaration confirming I had been notified. The Republic of Kazakhstan had been designated as a final destination for the deportation of all Iranian subjects like myself, and that was why I was going there. And so, on the morning of 10 May, I finally shook the dust of the Step-Lag off my boots for good!

Together with three other freed detainees I marched through the streets to the railway station on a beautiful sunny morning. We filled our lungs with the fresh air of freedom, albeit that the MVD guards still marched alongside us, on our way to catch the train to Petropavlovsk, the capital of the province of North Kazakhstan, on the great Trans-Siberian Railway.

When we arrived we were again marched through the streets to the Militia HQ in the town centre, Petropavlovsk being a sprawling city on the River Ichim. Its tallest buildings were just a few old two-storey houses occupied by the authorities, the rest of the town being made up of wooden houses built before the Revolution. That night we slept on the floor of one of the militia offices, waiting for an official to arrive next morning to ask questions about our qualifications and comment on the jobs we could be offered. Our destination, we learnt, was a state farm in the steppes, some 120 miles to the south. We set off that same morning in an open lorry, travelling along the banks of the river. The road was no more than a beaten dirt-track across the steppes, and after a long, exhausting ride, we arrived at Marievka, the principal locality of the region, equivalent to a county town in Britain, but more like a large village. Marievka was not the end of our journey, but we stopped there to have a beer. For the first time for eight years I was actually able to sit at a table in a small cafe and drink as much beer as I wanted. We old detainees so rejoiced in our new-found freedom that we even paid for the drinks of our escort.

During the afternoon we finally arrived at Sovkhoz Stepnoj, which lay situated in the middle of large grassy plains with small woods here and there. A *sovkhoz* was a type of collective farm where the farmhands were paid in wages, in contrast to a *kolkhoz*, where the peasant farmers formed a co-operative and were allowed to divide any surpluses between themselves. The farmhands lived in small houses they had built themselves out of *saman*, large sun-dried bricks made from a mixture of clay and straw. The walls were thick and effective protection from the bitter Siberian cold, while in the summer they kept the rooms fresh and cool in the scorching heat. The houses were widely dispersed, and each farmhand had his allotment where he grew potatoes, tomatoes, cucumbers and other vegetables for his own consumption, these small vegetable plots playing an important part in keeping a family well fed. *Sovkhoz* farmers also had the right to own a cow, a pig and some chickens. Salaries were small, and varied according to hours worked, while bonuses also varied.

Sovkhoz Stepnoj was divided into three autonomous farm units besides the central farm itself, which housed the administration offices and the sheds for the tractors and other agricultural machinery, as well as the essential workshops. Tractors and machinery were all in a deplorable state. During the war, industry had been mobilized to meet military requirements and the production of agricultural machinery abandoned. One could only marvel at how the equipment worked at all, and there were breakdowns and punctures every other minute. The farmhands constantly had to improvise substitute spare parts, modifying pieces to keep the whole thing going.

I learnt I was to be attached to Farm No.3, about three miles from the central farm, as an assistant accountant whose task was to monitor the work in the fields and register each day's achievements. The chief accountant at Farm No.3, a Kazakh who spoke excellent Russian, was courteous and hospitable like a true Oriental. He had arranged for me to lodge with a war widow who had an eight-year-old daughter. Her husband, like so many, had been killed fighting Hitler's invading armies. It was noticeable how the country's population had been decimated by the war. Everywhere one went one saw only widows, children and old people.

I also met my predecessor, who had, like me, been deported to Kazakhstan after serving a term in corrective labour camps. A highly educated and charming woman, she was doubtless the wife of an important 'traitor of the Soviet people'. Even as in the so-called 'cursed days under the Tsars', when freed prisoners were allowed to settle in Siberia to populate its vast empty territories, so Russia's new masters continued the policy. She was most helpful in giving me practical advice concerning my work, and also with regard to interpersonal relationships. She was herself being transferred to the main office, and before she went she explained to me the rules regulating the lives of deportees. A militia control-check was carried out regularly, a piece of paper that served as an identity card being duly stamped by the militiaman, who also recorded in his register the time and date. It was forbidden to leave the *sovkhoz* without prior permission of the militia, and the identity card was not valid in the eyes of the local authorities.

The work done by each tractor team had to be checked daily, and the acreage of the land ploughed recorded in a log book. Each morning the daily log was presented to the chief accountant, who wrote it up in summary form for submission to the central farm by midday. I also inherited from her 'a highly advanced' Soviet instrument for measuring surfaces and distances: actually a primitive compass made up of two wooden poles which, placed in an open position on the ground, measured out two metres between the pole-ends. The fields could be measured by walking and turning the compass along two sides before calculating the square of the ploughed surface. it was simple and efficacious.

In this part of Siberia the winter lasted a long time and the work in the fields could only start after the end of the thaw, usually at the end of April or the beginning of May. My arrival therefore coincided with the beginning of the work in the fields, and I had to start work myself the very next morning. I had to walk long distances to some of the fields, but revelled in being alone and free at last – no more walls or guards and lots of fresh air. It was wonderful. True, I had been deported for life, but 'Moustachios' was no longer with us so anything might happen.

I soon made friends with the tractor drivers and farm workers, who couldn't have been friendlier and always did everything possible to make my task easier. Each of my days' work in the fields continued until quite late, when I would return to the farm office to write my report for the following morning. Every evening my landlady awaited me with a simple meal. The rent I paid her for the use of a bed in the single room of her tiny cottage also included food, which consisted mainly of bread and milk from her own cow, plus the usual buckwheat *kasha*. There was rarely any meat – only when some was delivered to the central farm.

The farming season is very short in Siberia, lasting from May to August, by which time all the crops must be gathered in. September brings torrential rains, which make harvesting impossible, besides creating great problems of transport and storage. Apart from the shortage of trucks and lorries, there are no roads, and the dirt tracks are transformed into a sea of mud. Lack of proper storage space and bad organization always meant that, as soon as the rains started, a considerable part of the crop was lost. The lack of silos or barns for storage explained much about the continually disastrous state of Soviet agriculture.

During my first year at the *sovkhoz* the weather was good, and all the harvest gathered in before the rains. November brought heavy snows, and for the first time I saw tractors building embankments of snow to stop the strong winds blowing all the precious snow away. As more snow fell, the walls grew higher and the fields became covered in deep snow which, melting in the spring sun, guaranteed their irrigation. Another simple method of farming was the way the hay was brought in. After being cut it would be left in enormous stacks in the fields, far from the farm and stables. As soon as winter came and snow settled, the tractor drivers could put a heavy chain around the base of a hay-stack and drive back to the farm, the hay-stack sliding easily on the snow. In this way, they lost not a single blade of hay and had no need to load and unload. One of my colleagues in the admin office of Farm No.3, was a former schoolmaster from Byelorussia – the province bordering Poland. He too was another victim of the perfidy which flourishes under the Soviet system. The only reason for his arrest – after a denunciation that he was involved in anti-Soviet propaganda – was envy and desire to acquire the little house where he lived. There was no doubt at all about that, for as soon as he was arrested, the people who had denounced him, moved into his house. Furthermore, the success of the operation was guaranteed by the fact that the new tenant was, in fact, a high-ranking officer in the KGB. The poor schoolmaster's wife was thrown out into the street. Fortunately, there were no children. Then, after ten years in a corrective labour camp, the schoolmaster was deported to Kazakhstan where his wife finally managed to join him, after all those years of enforced separation.

At Christmas 1953 I was transferred to the central office of Sovkhoz Stepnoj and given the job of assistant chief accountant for the supplies section. I had quickly learnt the peculiarities of the Soviet accounting system, which bore little resemblance to commercial accounting as practised in Western Europe. Everything was geared to the statistics so beloved of Russia's new masters. Always statistics and more statistics for submission to the Statistical Bureau of the Kazakhstan Republic which, in turn, sent them on to the Central Bureau of Statistics in Moscow, where all information was centralized and stored for future reference. All those five-year economic plans and projects, so beautifully set out and supported by statistics but so seldom realized! And the reason? Simply because the statistical information received did not correspond to the actual productivity. Everybody cheated on their statistical figures, and false information was submitted to obtain bonuses. Each day we worked in the accounting office from 8 a.m. till midnight, with an hour's break for lunch, but on days when the monthly statistics needed to be submitted we stayed later, often till 2 a.m. Statistics had to be submitted monthly by a certain date, and no delays were permitted.

There were five of us in the *sovkhoz* accounting office: the chief accountant and four assistants, all political deportees. We got on well, having been through the 'stages' of the Soviet penal system, and some of them had been subjected to terrible suffering. I became very friendly with one of them – an old Russian who had spent ten years in very hard conditions in the Siberian Taiga – the virgin forests of Eastern Siberia. He told me how tens of thousands of detainees had been sent there to work for years on the building of a new secret main railway line running parallel to, and to the north of the existing Great Trans-Siberian Railway. This so-called secret railway – known as the BAM (The Baikal-Amur Magistral) was considered to be of the utmost importance, and essential to ensure that transport was not limited only to the existing Trans-Siberian line. Conditions were terrifying, it was often impossible to survive, and many of the miserable detainees died there.

Years later, already free and living in the West, I learnt further details of this special 'secret' railway, from someone else who had himself personally witnessed the beginning of its construction – my cousin Alexander (Alik) Urbelyan, who, like me, was a graduate of the famous Civil Engineering Academy at the University of St Petersburg. He was subsequently employed by the Soviet Ministry of Communications, where he became one of the top management, but later, he too was arrested. I did not know the reason for his arrest at the time, and feared it may have been precipitated by his insistence on keeping in touch and helping me – a convicted 'enemy of the people'. Indeed, before leaving the Soviet Union, I wrote him a letter, saying that I would like to see him when passing through Moscow on my way to France, but he replied saying this was impossible as he would be away on an official trip to the Caucasus at the time. I was greatly saddened by his letter, for I understood only too well that he was afraid to see me, it was the terror felt by all Soviet citizens living for so long under a system of persecution and arbitrary arrests. I gave up all hope of seeing him but later, after I rejoined my family in the West, we invited him to Paris, and in 1968 he finally obtained a two-month passport with permission to visit France.

This is the real story of the BAM, as he told it to me, and the real reason for his arrest in 1947. The construction of BAM began shortly after the Second World War, nearly 40 years ago. The idea was to build a main railway line from Lake Baikal towards the Amur River, so as not to have to depend solely on the existing Trans-Siberian line which passes through Manchuria and borders Chinese territory. The BAM was declared to be of great strategic importance and the completion of its construction designated as *urgent*. Its construction was controlled by the KGB. Tens of thousands of detainees were used in its construction, but the Government was dissatisfied with the results. The work was progressing much too slowly. The terrain was very difficult mountainous country, covered with virgin forests – the Taiga, also known as the land of 'eternal frost'. The drilling of tunnels and building of bridges was not going well. The thaw of frozen ground when opened provoked caving-in and collapse of tunnels, which forced by-passes without tunnels to be built, changing completely the original project of the BAM railway. A new general was appointed to oversee the construction of the sector near the Baikal Sea. He found the existing administration there to be incompetent and unsatisfactory. Essential supplies were late in arriving or never arrived at all. So the General asked Moscow to send him urgently a capable engineer to help speed up construction. As usual, the KGB HQ in Moscow had a solution ready – the same solution used for other similar requests: since it was not easy to find someone to volunteer to work in these terrible conditions, they simply arrested the person with the necessary qualifications, and sent him to Siberia, to help the General with his urgent task.

This time, the KGB's choice fell upon my cousin Alexander, who had the reputation of a highly experienced engineer, specializing in the administration of railway construction projects. No sooner was the decision taken than things started moving. My cousin was arrested, condemned to eight years in a corrective labour camp – even though there were no grounds whatsoever for the indictment against him – and despatched urgently to help the General. Fortunately for the KGB, the Soviet Penal Code was very vague, it could be interpreted very loosely and one could always find a suitable paragraph to justify the necessary arrests!

The General was delighted to see Alexander, and received him with open arms. He explained the problem: the programme for the BAM's completion had been designated as an eight-year project (this was 1947), but if Alexander succeeded in speeding up the work sufficiently to enable it to be completed in five years, then the General would personally arrange for Alexander to be freed at the end of the five years! They discussed what had to be done to speed things up. In order to see the situation more clearly, Alexander asked the General to send him to the HQ in Irkutsk. There, to his amazement, he met some of his friends – all engineers who, like him, had graduated from the Civil Engineering Academy in St Petersburg, and also like him had been arrested for the sole purpose of being sent to work on the BAM Railway line.

Back in Baikal, Alexander discussed with the general the work to be done to accelerate the completion of the project. Again, the General told him: 'If you succeed in completing the programme in five years I will arrange that you should not serve your full eight years' sentence, but be freed after five!' Of course Alexander accepted the offer, he did his best to speed things up and, five years later, the General did indeed arrange for him to be freed. But still things didn't go according to plan, and now – 33 years later, the Politburo is still discussing the shortcomings and unresolved issues connected with the BAM project. Gaider Aliev – first Deputy Prime Minister in charge of Transportation – himself visited the project HQ at Tynda in June 1984, to check on complaints that essential equipment promised was never delivered. And the 1¼ mile tunnel bored through the Kodar mountains had caved in! What is more, TASS continues to issue official statements that the construction of the new BAM railway (officially opened on the 7th November 1984 – the 67th anniversary of the October Revolution) was begun only ten years ago, and that no political detainees were used in its construction – the usual sort of Soviet disinformation for propaganda purposes, sadly still believed by the Western Press which widely publicized it. The fact is that the Soviets could not admit that, even after 38 years, they still cannot complete the construction of this 2000-mile railway. To do so would be an open admission that, far from being 'the construction job of the century', it was, in fact, a record of the 'inefficiency of the century' coupled with the bestiality of using forced labour to clear the thick Taiga forests for this purpose.

By this stage I was lodged in the house of one of the farm's truck drivers. He was also a deportee, an Iranian living with a war widow and her two boys, aged thirteen and fifteen, who went to the *sovkhoz* school. He was away most of the time, driving the truck long distances along non-existent roads. It was a tough job.

My new lodgings were spotless and the atmosphere pleasant. My land-lady was delighted to have a lodger, the money helping considerably to make ends meet. We soon all became friends. My landlady's husband had also spent ten years in a corrective labour camp and been deported to Central Asia like the other Iranian nationals, but unlike me he had lost all hope. Whenever I assured him that there were bound to be changes now Stalin was dead, he merely laughed and laughed. 'There will be no change so far as we, the foreigners, are concerned,' he argued, and cited several cases of Iranian nationals who, after completing their sentences in a corrective labour camp, hastened to renew their Iranian passports. The result was that they were all, without exception, deported here. Undeterred, they applied for exit visas, but these were so long in coming that by the time they arrived the validity of their passports had expired. They then applied for the passports to be renewed again and by the time the new passports arrived the exit visas were no longer valid. And so, although there was no outright refusal of their request to leave the country, the bureaucratic machinery played the game in such a way as to leave no doubt in the minds of the applicants that they would never be allowed to go! Gradually they gave up the struggle, realizing there was no point in pressing their case. The Soviets were determined to populate Siberia with all the manpower available. They might as well adapt, work to earn a living and settle down for life. 'We must just do as the others have done,' the Iranian argued, but I refused to give up hope.

Indeed, I had been trying for a long while to get my Iranian passport renewed. I had written several times to the Iranian Embassy in Moscow, informing them that I, an Iranian national, had been arrested and sentenced to eight years in a Soviet camp. But none of my letters was ever responded to. This could be put down to 'normal' Soviet procedure: all correspondence was checked and undesirable letters were simply never delivered. Lacking any reply from the Embassy, I racked my brains to think of a means of letting my family know I was still alive. My brother would by now be almost seventy years old, so there was no time to lose. I had spoken in the camp to all German POW or Polish detainees about to be repatriated, begging them to contact my brother in Paris as soon as they returned to their own countries, and let him know of my plight. Many years later I discovered that one of the Germans did, in fact, keep his promise and write to my brother through the Iranian Embassy in Paris, telling him he had met me in one of the camps, and that I was in good health. But back on the *sovkhoz* I knew nothing of all this, nor that the Iranian Embassy had been making official inquiries as to my whereabouts, only invariably to receive a stereotyped Soviet response denying I was in the USSR, maintaining that the authorities knew nothing of me and demanding to know whatever made them think I could be in the country.

One day I received a postal order for 100 roubles from my cousin in Baku, and decided to try a different tactic. I sent the order to the Iranian Embassy in Moscow, without a covering letter to indicate its purpose but giving my name and address as sender on the accompanying form, as I was obliged to do anyway. Imagine my surprise and excitement when, a month later, I received a reply. At last I had succeeded in finding a loophole in the Soviet censorship system. The order had been automatically paid into the Embassy's current account at the State Bank, and the bank had, in turn, notified the Embassy of the payment order, indicating the name and address of the payer. It was a simple, routine banking operation, and as such had not fallen under the scrutiny of the KGB. The Embassy's letter to me merely confirmed receipt of the 100 roubles, and asked whether the purpose of the transfer was to pay to renew my passport. If so, could I please indicate my passport number and say where it had been issued? Wisely and cautiously they made no mention of the fact that they had been trying to find me.

Now I was in a real quandary. Should I reply to the Embassy's letter, and if so, what would be the consequence? Eventually I sat down and wrote that the transfer was indeed to renew my passport, impounded by the KGB authorities in Moscow, after my arrest in 1945. I wrote in fear and trepidation, hoping the the incidental mention of the KGB would not land me in even greater trouble. As an old Russian proverb put it: 'A frightened raven is scared of every bush.' In due course, a second letter came from the Embassy, saying that the Soviet authorities denied having my Iranian passport. Technically speaking they were right, for what the KGB impounded was not my passport as such, but the official certificate issued by the Police HQ in Bucharest, in exchange for the Iranian passport impounded on my arrest in Romania. I could not explain all of this to the Iranian Embassy, and I felt no surprise at the answers they had received from the Soviet authorities, who had constantly denied my presence in the USSR. Now, however, I was again faced with the problem of how to reply. But since the correspondence seemed to be developing normally, I took courage and wrote back that the passport had been issued by the Swedish Consulate in Bucharest, empowered to represent Iranian interests in Romania during the war.

My hopes rose again. The long-desired contact with the Embassy was established at last, and they now had my address. They had proof that I was in the Soviet Union, despite the authorities' denials. Perhaps things really were changing and the new government, headed by Bulganin and Khrushchev, was beginning to loosen the reins a little. But news travelled slowly to Central Asia. In Kazakhstan we were still busy attending mass meetings to pass resolutions prepared by the local party Committee condemning Comrades Beria and Malenkov as well as other principal actors on the Moscow stage at the time, and demanding the severest possible judgement for their misdemeanours. Only much later did we and the whole world learn that Comrade Beria, Stalin's KGB butcher, had already been executed without anybody bothering about a trial. Thus did we go through the farce of voting on an issue that was already resolved, simply to maintain the formalities. Then we returned to our respective tasks, for as everybody in the Soviet Union knows, it is 'dangerous for your health' to continue discussions after a party meeting has passed a resolution. One might easily let slip a comment that did not quite tally with the party line. So we carried on with our calculations and statistics, just like the slaves of old, too tired and busy to think.

The summer and the autumn months went by and another winter approached. Our tasks became less heavy as work in the fields ceased. Now everybody was busy repairing as best they could the tractors and other farm machinery, while we spent our time recording the changes in the classification of cattle and other livestock, according to age and categories, besides compiling other statistical data. There were always statistics and more statistics to be done, and we carried on regardless.

The latest letter from the Iranian Embassy informed me that the archives of the Iranian Consulate in Bucharest had been transferred to Belgrade, which made research into my case more difficult. But one sentence in the letter made my heart leap. The Embassy asked whether perhaps my brother could help them in the circumstances. This made it obvious that the Embassy was already in touch with him through the Iranian Consulate in Paris.

One evening, Marussya, the wife of the Iranian truck-driver, gave me a long lecture. She was worried that I was alone, friendless and exhausted by the late hours I had to work. The correspondence with the Iranian Embassy seemed to drag on without positive result, so why not arrange my life more comfortably? She had discussed it with her husband many times, and neither of them believed there was any hope of me ever being allowed to leave the USSR. So why not marry a good woman? It so happened that she and her husband knew just such a woman. On his daily travels to and from Petropavlovsk, he often saw a friend of hers called Katya, also a war widow – a Russian with three children, a son and two daughters, already grown up, married and living separately. Therefore she was free and independent. All people deported to Siberia ended up by marrying and starting a new life. Deportation for life was a lonely existence and hard to bear on one's own. Katya lived on a *kolkhoz* situated beyond Marievka, and anyway Marussya and her husband had decided to leave Sovkhoz Stepnoj and start working on the same *kolkhoz* as Katya, taking their children with them. For one thing, the *kolkhoz* was nearer Petropavlovsk, and her husband was certain that I, too, would be better off there. They were certain I could easily find work there as well. For example, I could take on the job of local schoolmaster. It would be more pleasant and less tiring than my present work. She suggested I go along with her husband and herself to meet Katya. If we liked each other, we could get married, and then decide if Katya would join me at the *sovkhoz* or whether I would move over to the *kolkhoz*.

At the weekend I obtained the director's permission to harness an old horse to the sleigh, and we left bright and early on the Saturday morning. It was snowing hard but not cold and was fairly smooth going when we left the *sovkhoz*, but as we crossed the steppes the wind became stronger. It was turning into a real *buran*, as blizzards were known thereabouts. After some seven or eight miles we entered a small wood that gave us some shelter, but as soon as we re-emerged on to the steppes, the wind picked up to gale force and all the tracks disappeared. Should we stop or continue the journey? Surely it would be more prudent to take shelter. But Marussya insisted that the horse would take us to our destination. He had done the journey so many times that he was bound to find his way. Therefore let us rest a little and then continue, for there was no other possibility, she declared with true Russian fatalism. The old horse advanced slowly. We could see nothing and had no idea of where we were as the blizzard continued unabated throughout the day. We got out of the sleigh and walked slowly behind it for several hours, so as not to over-tire the horse. As usual when there was a *buran*, it was not too cold.

The horse did indeed know his way and finally, as evening fell, we came to the outskirts of the village of Marievka. It was only by the grace of God that we had reached safety, for a *buran* could claim many victims and there was little chance of survival, the villages being dispersed over enormous distances across those vast steppes.

The *kolkhoz* itself was still some eighteen miles further on, but Marussya decreed that we should spend the night at Marievka. It would have been madness to continue the journey in such weather, having risked death already. By dawn next day the wind had dropped and the old horse was rested. We arrived at our destination without further complication. Marussya knew many people in the *kolkhoz*, which was why she was keen to settle there. We stopped at the house of some friends of hers, and a message was sent to my 'intended', to say we had arrived. Everything had already been discreetly arranged by my marriage broker, in accordance with local custom. As the first meeting was to take place in the house of a friend, both parties could make up their minds freely, without prior commitment.

Our first meeting passed very pleasantly and my first impression of Marussya's friend was very favourable. The next step was for the intended to invite Marussya and me to her house, to continue discussions there in private, to see what possibilities were open to us after marriage. She left it entirely to me to decide if we should settle in the *sovkhoz* or whether I should move to the *kolkhoz* where she already had a well-run house. Naturally she would prefer to stay on in her own home, as she could thus continue to be near her younger married daughter and little granddaughter. Her eldest daughter, also married, lived in Petropavlovsk, and her son had gone to work in the neighbouring Republic of Tadjikistan, where he was married and settled. There was now the question of my finding a job in the area, before deciding on any final move, and so it was arranged that I should go the following Monday to see the education authorities at Marievka and discuss the possibility of being appointed a language teacher at the *kolkhoz* school.

The regional school inspector received me very politely and explained that foreign languages were compulsory subjects in all schools, and pupils could choose between studying English, French or German as a principal language, plus one other. The *kolkhoz* primary school had four classes for children aged seven to eleven years, and languages were taught during the last two years. The inspector was only too delighted that I should be interested in taking the job of English teacher in the primary school, for there was a great shortage of foreign language teachers. He would have liked me to start at once, but there was one small problem: he needed my graduation diplomas, both the university degree and secondary school certificate. I explained that, alas, I had no papers to show him. A poor detainee possessed only the clothes he stood up in! I told him how I had completed the High School and Military Academy in St Peterburg, and how after the First World War I graduated from the Commercial Academy in Berlin, besides studying at the famous Pitman School in England in 1924-5. The inspector accepted everything I told him and, loth to lose the chance of a teacher, decided to pursue the matter through the Ministry of Education in Moscow. He proposed to ask for copies of my degree, which should still be in the Leningrad State Archives, and also to write to Berlin.

Sure enough, three months later, copies of all the relevant documents arrived at Marievka, still available from the archives despite the siege of Leningrad and the bombing of Berlin. This left only one more obstacle to be overcome: official agreement to a transfer from my job at the *sovkhoz*.

On returning to the *sovkhoz* I went straight to the director to request his authorization for my transfer to the *kolkhoz*. I felt optimistic about the outcome. Throughout my stay at the *sovkhoz* our relations had been excellent and he always said how satisfied he was with the way I carried out my duties. Our relations got off to a good start the very first moment we met in the fields of Farm No.3. In fact, so pleased was he with our first meeting, that he gave instructions there and then that I be promoted to the central accounting office. Now, however, he wouldn't hear of my leaving, and refused to accept my reasoning. Very well, he argued, I wished to get married. But why move? Far better to stay on at the *sovkhoz*, where he would be happy to promote me to chief accountant at Farm No.2. I could bring my wife to join me, and we could set up home together there.

But I had had enough of accounting and besides, Farm No.2 was far out in the steppes, which meant even more tiring work. I was already absolutely exhausted and it would be good for me to take up teaching instead. I therefore begged him to let me leave to take up the offer of the education authorities in Marievka. But, again and again, his answer was 'No'. He said I was too valuable to lose, and the *sovkhoz* was short of experienced cadres. And so all our discussions ended in total disagreement, both of us determined to have our own way.

After several days I was summoned to his office to find the chief of the Marievka militia there as well. He was a former schoolmaster who had found it convenient to change professions. The director, an important member of the local party committee, was now asking his support to force me to stay on and naturally the chief of militia did not want openly to oppose him. Nevertheless he was not as insistent as one might have expected and I gradually had the feeling that he was only there out of a sense of duty.

The director was very firm in his arguments, insinuating that, as a former detainee, I was not a suitable person to teach Soviet youth. I pointed out that the regional school inspector was perfectly aware of my past history and that this in no way affected his determination to have me as one of his foreign language teachers – a profession also desperately short of cadres. No final decision was taken, and as I left the director's office in the company of the militia chief, he assured me that the director's accusations concerning my 'unhealthy' political background were not to be taken seriously. Nonetheless, according to the law, I needed the director's permission to obtain a transfer, because otherwise I risked encountering all sorts of difficulties. He therefore advised me to give the matter serious thought before doing anything final.

But my mind was made up, and I decided to risk leaving the *sovkhoz* and go to live in the *kolkhoz* with my future wife Katya. As soon as I arrived there, she invited relatives and friends to meet me. They knew I was a foreigner but at once accepted me as the new teacher at the local school. I was especially anxious about my meeting Maria, for she valued her opinion whose husband worked in a metallurgical factory in Petropavlovsk. Katya was especially anxious about me meeting Maria, for she valued her opinion greatly. But she needn't have worried. Maria was delighted that her mother had decided to re-marry and settle down to a life with me. Each of Katya's children also had a child, so at a stroke I became grandfather to three children, who all called me *Deda* (the Russian for grandfather).

As the school year had already begun, I had to start my teaching activities at once. The *kolkhoz* consisted of three villages, situated around a small circular lake, less than a mile across, that had suddenly formed one spring in a large hollow filled with masses of melting snow after a very heavy winter. The lake was now stocked with carp and other fish that the peasant farmers caught to vary their menu. The school building was a large wooden house close to the lake and between the two principal villages. The third village, the smallest, lay on the other side of the lake, and a wide detour was needed to reach it – except in the winter, when you could walk across the ice.

The school had four classrooms and a small staff room, all leading off the large reception hall in the centre. There were some forty-five pupils, both girls and boys, and seven teachers – five women as well as myself and the director, who taught history. My duties included teaching English to the two senior forms – the third and fourth, as well as giving lessons in elementary physics and technical drawing. My basic salary was 500 roubles a month, the same sum I had been paid as a *sovkhoz* accountant. The other teachers earned more money, because they worked supplementary hours, but I felt very happy with the deal I had. I received the same amount of money as before, and the work was far less tiring. With Katya's already well-organized household as well as my salary, we were the second most prosperous couple in the *kolkhoz*: she owned a cow, a young calf and a pig as well as some geese, ducks and chickens. The only family to earn more was that of the *kolkhoz* president, a Communist party member, whose wife worked in the village shop where she had a good salary and percentages on all the sales besides the advantage of being in charge of the distribution of all sorts of goods, of which there was always a great shortage.

The Anglo-Russian dictionary that the KGB captain at Djezkazgan let me take with me proved invaluable in refreshing my memory and helping me to prepare lessons. The many years in prisons and camps had so exhausted my brain that my memory was not as reliable as I would have liked, no doubt as a result of all the hunger and illness suffered. Even during my first few months at Shcherbakov, after almost a year's interrogation in the Lubyanka, I had found great difficulty in remembering the words I wanted when giving French lessons to a cell-mate, the so of the Jewish bookbinder, even though I was bilingual. Now my task was even more important. Like the other teachers, I had to prepare the lessons in writing. Each lesson lasted an hour and was divided into three parts: the first twenty minutes to question pupils about the task given them in the previous lesson, the next twenty minutes to explain their new task and the final twenty minutes to discuss together what it involved, and the homework they would have to do in this connection.

The custom was that teachers used their free hour by attending a class taken by another teacher. Before the lesson there would be an exchange of views on the proposed task, and after the lesson a discussion on what was good or not quite up to standard in the pupils' performance. So there was always a colleague sitting in on my classes and I did the same for the others. The atmosphere was friendly and we all worked closely together. Discipline was good and the teachers very strict. If there was any problem with a pupil we would discuss it between ourselves and only, if all else failed, call in the parents. In one particular case, a young boy refused to continue his studies, insisting that all he wanted to be was a shepherd. What were we to do? He was only ten years old and secondary education was compulsory. The teachers spent long hours in trying to persuade him of the need to study at least some elementary subjects, his class-mates and his parents also joining in the discussion. It was to no avail. He was unshakable in his determination to leave school and spend his days roaming the fields. And so, in the end, he was allowed to leave.

The girls were far more docile than the boys. All schoolchildren automatically joined the Pioneers (the Communist equivalent of Boy Scouts and Girl Guides) and on completion of primary education would be asked to volunteer for the Komsomol (the Communist Youth Movement). The girls all volunteered without a second thought, but most of the boys didn't want to hear about it! They detested the endless political lectures and discussions, and in this were no doubt influenced to some extent by their parents. They were the sons of peasant-farmers who were thoroughly fed up with the ceaseless Communist propaganda thrown at them all those years. The first individual radio arrived in the small village shop only in 1956, three years after Stalin's death, but the *kolkhoz* had a central radio receiver connected by cable to speakers in every farm-house. People would listen with pleasure to music, but as soon as news bulletins or propaganda talks came on, the loudspeakers would be switched off at once.

On election days the polling station was located in the *kolkhoz* school. Voting was compulsory and those who could not get there because of sickness would be visited at home with the ballot box. It was considered essential to record as near a 100 per cent vote as possible, to allow the Soviet press to announce next day a participation of 98 or 99 per cent. The voting over, the *kolkhoz* director invited everybody to a party. There would be plenty to eat and drink and dancing to the music of an accordion – all at the expense of the *kolkhoz*. The same thing happened on each anniversary of the October Revolution. But the *kolkhoz* did not only indulge in official celebrations. There were also private parties for family and friends on special occasions, such as the house-warming party for Katya's youngest daughter and her husband when they decided to build their own house, as everyone had to do on a *kolkhoz*. You needed to be your own carpenter, locksmith and mechanic as well as bricklayer to get by. The first step was to make the bricks out of *saman*, the mixture of straw and clay dried in the sun, these being the only building materials available in the steppes. It took a family and willing neighbours several weeks to prepare the required amount before any building could begin. The big party came on the day when the shell of the building was finished, the home-made vodka, or *samogon*, having been prepared long before. The making of *samogon* in illicit stills was widespread throughout the Soviet Union, the operation being undertaken at night, with the curtains drawn, as in the black-out during the war so that no light showed from outside. Owners of clandestine stills, if caught, risked a 5-year sentence in a Corrective Labour Camp, but they were prepared to risk it, since they had no other means of getting it, peasant-farmers being paid in kind – in any wheat or grains left over after the compulsory quotas had been delivered to the State.

The amount of drink for a party would be calculated on the basis of a litre bottle of vodka for each man and half a bottle for each woman. Beer was also served, and to prepare this it was necessary to mount an expedition to a neighbouring valley to collect hops. The beer was then brewed in milk churns borrowed from the *kolkhoz*. Everyone knew that the churns were not going to be used for milk! As soon as everybody had sat down at table, the glasses were filled with vodka and passed round. It was customary politeness for a person to empty a glass at one go so it could be refilled and passed to the next person to him, so as not to keep the others waiting, there always being a shortage of glasses. Once everybody had their vodka the glasses would be filled with beer and passed round in the same way. Then came a second round of vodka, followed by another beer chaser and so forth. Between the vodka and the beer chasers we ate and talked. Nobody was in a hurry and the meal lasted a long time on account of the shortage of glasses. Afterwards the men continued to drink and talk, while the women began to sing old popular Russian folk-songs. The women had beautiful voices and the effect was deeply moving. First the one with the best voice sang a verse, then the others sang the refrain in various keys, like accomplished singers. The party, like all such parties, lasted far into the night, long after the food ran out.

Once the festivities were over, Katya's daughter and her husband had to get down to the hard work of finishing their new house, installing doors and windows, and building the famous Russian tiled oven stove which occupied almost half the living space. The timber for the woodwork and the heat-storage bricks for the stove had to be fetched from Marievka.

Because there was no timber in Kazakhstan the fuel used for heating was dried dung, called *kiziak*. This was taken from the vast stables where all the cows and sheep were kept through the long winter months. The dung, left to lie on the stable floor, became mixed with straw by the trampling of the animals. In the spring each farmer was allotted a section which he chopped up with a spade into small lumps before putting them out in the hot sun to dry. Sheep dung was best as it burnt slowly like peat and gave out a lot of heat. Preparing and building up fuel stocks for the long winter months was the most important task facing peasant farmers in the spring, and transporting the dried lumps of *kiziak* could be a problem. All methods of transportation, whether animal or mechanical, belonged to the *kolkhoz,* and while peasant-farmers were allowed to own cows, they could not keep horses or oxen. Katya's solution was to use one of the empty trucks that sometimes passed through the village. The truck drivers were always happy to earn something on the side, so we kept a watch out and, sure enough, succeeded in finding two who agreed to discreetly bring back two truck-loads of *kiziak* and unload them on our doorstep. In return we gave them something to eat and slipped them a bottle of vodka, and everybody was happy.

The *kiziak* was very bulky and took up a lot of room in the covered courtyard. All the courtyards were covered, to protect them from the heavy snow that almost completely submerged the village in winter. Often we had to cut a passage through walls of snow to leave the house or take the cow to the lake to drink twice a day. There was an old soldier, a veteran of the Russo-Japanese War, whose job it was to cut a hole in the ice of the lake to make sure there was always water to drink for the cattle brought twice a day from the three villages. He was a tough old man who, despite the bitter cold, with temperatures many degrees below freezing, never wore his old fur hat. He invariably put it down on the ice, next to the hole he was busy cutting with an axe.

In the spring of 1956, several months after leaving Sovkhoz Stepnoj, I received a summons from the court at Marievka to answer charges of desertion from my post, based on a complaint made by the director that I left without his permission – a grave offence!

The day before the case was due to be heard, I found a lawyer in Marievka to act in my defence. A young woman lawyer, she was willing to do it for a fee of 25 roubles, confident that my case would be dismissed. I was not so sure, and as we sat in the People's Tribunal waiting to be called I saw the *sovkhoz* director pass through the hall looking very sure of himself. As an important regional party member, he was shown at once into the judge's chambers, where he remained talking for a quarter of an hour before leaving with a satisfied look on his face. My heart sank. It was obvious that he had argued his case as a valid complaint against a former detainee, a deportee who had deserted his post, an offence to be regarded as an act of sabotage against the economy of the state.

Finally, the judge himself entered the small court-room, and soon after I was called to speak. Having heard my statement and my lawyer's defence plea, the judge calmly read out the sentence, condemning me to three months 'forced labour in the public interest'. I was to start serving my sentence in November, just as the school year began. I was in the depths of despair but my lawyer tried to calm me down, saying she would apply for an appeal to be heard in the Regional High Court in Petropavlovsk. In the meantime my sentence was suspended pending the outcome.

After everything I had been through I was not easily reassured and both Katya and I continued to worry. Where would I be sent in November? What sort of forced labour would I have to do? Would I even survive another stay in camp? Several weeks later, however, the lawyer brought us good news: the High Court in Petropavlovsk had quashed the sentence and that was the end of it. I subsequently learnt that a government decree was in process of being issued at the time to allow people to transfer from one job to another, prior permission from the director no longer being necessary when the purpose was to enable both husband and wife to work in the same locality. The object was to allow more flexibility while preventing too great a fluctuation in the work-force. Both judge and lawyer must have been aware that the decree was about to become law, and I could only assume that when the *sovkhoz* director swept into the judge's room, the judge thought it best not to contradict an influential party official and agreed to sentence me in the full knowledge that his judgement would later be overruled. Nevertheless the Petropavlovsk High Court decision was a great achievement by my lawyer, since Katya and I were not legally married. When we had gone to the local registry office in the neighbouring village to obtain a marriage licence and regularize our situation, we were told that it was forbidden for a Soviet subject to marry a foreigner so we must just continue living together. In the *kolkhoz* everybody was delighted that I could stay on and teach their children English.

11. THE RAVEN FLIES

Encouraged by my success in getting a letter through to the Iranian Embassy in Moscow, I decided to send a registered letter to the Iranian Embassy in Paris, for my brother Sarkis. I did not know the address he had moved to after the war, but I knew they were in touch with him and would probably pass it on. I worded it very carefully so as not to say anything offensive to the Soviet authorities, simply mentioning that I was in correspondence with the Iranian Embassy in Moscow and asking about family matters.

Once again I succeeded. The letter was passed by the censor and delivered to the Embassy, who immediately telephoned my brother to tell him the good news. Overjoyed, he ran all the way there to collect it. After ten years of silence, at last he had concrete proof of my whereabouts and proof that I was alive and well. Apart from the verbal message passed on by the repatriated German POW, the previous news he had of me was the letter taken from Bucharest by the French pilot six months before my arrest. My brother replied at once with a long letter addressed to the *kolkhoz,* but since this would take a long time to arrive, he sent me a telegram as well, confirming he had received my letter and announcing that a reply was on the way. The telegram arrived the very next day, having passed the censors in Moscow and Alma-Ata, who sent it to Marievka, from where it continued its journey by post as it was not customary to transmit telegrams by telephone to a *kolkhoz.* The letter itself came ten days later; a very quick delivery considering the vast distances and the delays caused by censorship.

I now started a regular correspondence, numbering each letter so he would know if any were missing. I asked for his help in getting my passport renewed, for a year after Stalin's death the new Soviet government had granted a general amnesty for all those sentenced to ten years' forced labour. Surely I, with my so-called 'child's sentence' of eight years, should be regarded as more than innocent. I had already seen several other deportees, living on the *kolkhoz,* being granted their freedom and the appropriate documents, having served ten years in the camps. But for my situation there was no change.

I sent off another registered letter, once again numbered, suggesting that my brother asked the International Red Cross to intervene for my release on the grounds that my health had seriously deteriorated as a result of the many illnesses suffered in prison and camps. The scurvy, distrophy, jaundice, dropsy and emphysema of the lungs had all been treated by the Soviet prison and camp doctors, but nevertheless had left me in a dangerously weak state. This time, however, my luck ran out and I have to admit I must have been naive indeed to imagine such a letter would be passed by the Soviet censors. When my brother wrote to say that Letter No. so-and-so was missing, I understood only too well that it was not just that an inefficient postal service had mislaid it. I was not beaten yet, however. The USSR is a member of the International Postal Union so I carefully studied the book of rules for correct procedure in cases of non-delivery of registered letters and submitted to the director of postal services in Kazakhstan a plea asking for an investigation into the cause of the letter's disappearance and also, should it be irretrievably lost, that I be paid the appropriate compensation in French gold sovereigns, as required by International Postal Code rules. The director soon grasped what had happened to my letter and three weeks later I received the impressive sum of 25 roubles in compensation. Obviously he had never even bothered to make inquiries abroad.

In the meantime another letter came from my brother, telling me that he was now trying to arrange for a new Iranian passport to be issued from Teheran. He had somehow managed to locate the former Swedish consul who issued me with my last Iranian passport but he couldn't help either, as all the consulate archives had been moved to Belgrade. So my brother got in touch with a cousin who emigrated to Iran after the Revolution, and with his help at last succeeded in having all the necessary formalities completed in Teheran. All the relevant documents were now with the Embassy in Moscow. The formalities would all take several more months, of course, but at least things were starting to move.

There were other obstacles to overcome, however. One day I was summoned by the Chief of Militia at Marievka, who had given me moral support in the confrontation with the *sovkhoz* director. He told me there was a new decree, and every foreign national must now be issued with an identity card, a sort of residence permit to replace the sheet of paper on which the militia recorded their periodic checks. The new rule would be to my advantage but I had to pay a fee of 25 roubles a year for the privilege. He also said it would be to my advantage to apply for a Soviet passport, since this would give me the right to vote and to choose my place of residence in the USSR. I explained that I would like to rejoin my family in France, that I have been corresponding with my brother and the Iranian Embassy to this end. The Militia Chief agreed that this was only natural and asked what their letters said. 'But my dear friend, you know perfectly well, since you read all my letters,' I replied ingeniously. 'Yes, yes,' he said, 'of course, but you misunderstood my question. What I am interested in is to know about life abroad in general. I would like to hear from you, for I, too, would like to go abroad one day.' I could only express the hope that he would one day have the chance.

Time dragged on and I wrote several letters to the KGB asking that the amnesty decree be implemented in my case and the order for my deportation for life annulled. All I received in reply was a printed circular stating that there were '*no* grounds for the revision of your trial or the Court's decision in your case'. The nerve of it! There had never been any trial. I wrote another letter saying that I was not asking for a review but demanding the implementation of the general amnesty decree. Several weeks later I received the same old printed circular.

In the end an accountant in the *sovkhoz* who had helped me from the start of the correspondence, gave me some good advice: 'You will never solve the problem by writing to the KGB. You should write to the Party Secretariat in Moscow. The Party is the conscience of the state, so you must write to the Party Secretary, Khrushchev himself, for it is his duty to defend and protect the innocent!' I had nothing to lose and, who could tell, it might work this time. I addressed the letter simply to the Secretary-General of the Communist Party, Nikita Sergeevich Khrushchev, Moscow, and dated it 29 March 1956. I set out the facts of my case and explained how, for two years, the Iranian Embassy had been unsuccessfully trying to obtain my release; that I had written to the Prosecutor-General, to the Ministry of the Interior, and twice to the KGB, but all I had in reply was the circular, a copy of which I attached. I pleaded that, in accordance with the Act of General Amnesty, I should be declared completely innocent, stating that I had been sentenced to eight years for nothing, for during the war I had worked for the Allied cause by serving the British Embassy in Romania.

The reaction came like a thunderclap two weeks later. Summoned urgently to the office of the *kolkhoz* president, I found the chief prosecutor for North Kazakhstan waiting to speak to me. It was still the height of winter with the roads covered in deep snow, yet he, an important functionary of the Ministry of Justice, had travelled over ninety miles from Petropavlovsk in a four-wheeled jeep to see me. A telegram from Moscow had ordered him to do so! A highly cultivated Kazakh, speaking excellent Russian, he invited me to sit down and asked what I was complaining about: was there something wrong with my position in the *kolkhoz*, or with my financial situation perhaps? I replied cautiously that I was very contented with my position, my salary was quite sufficient and my relations with my colleagues and pupils were excellent. No, it was simply that I was still waiting for the implementation of the General Amnesty in my case, since this seemed to be delayed for inexplicable reasons, especially since several other deportees had already received their papers and were free to leave. Why, then, was an exception being made in my case? I wanted my freedom, I continued, I wanted to finish with this miserable life of a deportee, to leave the *kolkhoz* and live in whichever town I chose. Perhaps I could move to Petropavlovsk and get a job as a teacher in the High School? Everybody in the *kolkhoz* knew I was a deportee, a former camp detainee. I was in constant danger of denunciation. Anybody might, for envy or personal reasons, accuse me of anti-Soviet activities and have me returned to a corrective labour camp. Such things happened all the time. Moreover, my health wouldn't stand another spell in camp. At this the prosecutor interrupted, protesting: 'But you are mistaken. Such things are no longer possible. Times have changed!' I retorted at once: 'Mr Prosecutor, you are imprudent to say this. How can you explain your statement in the light of what I have just told you, and what if the authorities come to hear of this strange view you have of the regime?'

I saw from the expression on his face that my bolt had struck home. He quickly changed the subject and assured me most amiably that he had taken note of my wishes. Shortly afterwards I received an official letter from the Prosecutor-General for the Province of Kazakhstan, dated Petropavlovsk, 23 April 1956, confirming that I was now freed from the sentence of deportation, following my conviction based on the decision taken on 19 January 1946. Meanwhile I continued my correspondence with my brother, who was full of hope that the documents for issuing me with a new Iranian passport would be finalized and dispatched to the Embassy in Moscow. Aware that the Iranian authorities were not over-enthusiastic about issuing passports to Iranian Christian nationals, my brother found a way of speeding things up at the Moscow end. By happy coincidence his sister-in-law, a Frenchwoman born in Moscow (one of the large colony of French industrialists' families who had to leave Moscow after the 1917 Revolution) had a cousin who worked at the French Embassy there. An entry visa into France had already been granted for me and was awaiting collection at the French Embassy in Moscow, as was the money for a plane ticket to Paris. This distant cousin then personally undertook the harassment of the Iranian Embassy to pressurize them into speeding up the issue of my passport and obtaining the necessary documents from Teheran. And sure enough, within a few weeks, I received a letter from the Iranian Embassy in Moscow, asking me to send some passport photographs.

In the meantime complications had arisen on Katya's family front, her son having suddenly arrived from Tadjikistan. He turned out to be an aggressive and disagreeable young man, not very intelligent, unskilled and quite illiterate – a product of the hard years of the war. After spending several years in Tadjikistan trying unsuccessfully to find work, he married a local girl and soon a son was born. He treated his wife abominably, having soon learnt from the Tadjiks not to regard women as human beings. Despite many years of Russian influence, the habits of the tribes of Genghis Khan had changed little. The years of living in misery with no prospect of a job eventually made him even more restless and he decided to return to the family home in the *kolkhoz*.

He was received with open arms, but poor Katya now had three more mouths to feed and look after, for the young couple did nothing to help with housework. The son was, moreover, determined to force her out of the house so he could take over. Katya replied that he was not the sole heir to the house she and her husband had toiled to build with their bare hands when he was only three years old, for there were also his two sisters. But he was deaf to reasoned argument. He started to threaten both his mother and myself. He would come home totally drunk practically every day, quarrelling with his wife and mother and claiming he had found good friends in the village, who advised him to apply to the *kolkhoz* president to support his claim.

Trying to cope with this irresponsible and dangerous drunkard, subject to bouts of violent hysteria, we decided to speak to the *kolkhoz* president, to get our word in first. He promised to summon the son, but we realized he had no intention of helping. He needed every single labourer he could get hold of, for far too many young people had already left the *kolkhoz* to find less strenuous work in town. Katya was thoroughly frightened of her son and feared especially that he would denounce me for anti-Soviet statements. Therefore she decided to give in. We two could move in with her youngest daughter, in the *kolkhoz* itself, until such time as I received official authorization to move to Petropavlovsk. We could then both go to live there, close to her favourite daughter Mary.

Accordingly we moved to the *kolkhoz*, taking with us the basic pieces of furniture, as well as the cow, the pig, the chickens and the geese. Katya's daughter was delighted. She had never liked her brother, and the cow's milk would be a welcome addition for feeding Ludmilla, her little girl.

For me it meant another trip to Petropavlovsk to apply for a job as language teacher at the High School and seek the authorization of the Petropavlovsk Militia to reside in the town. When I called at the Militia HQ I found myself faced with a severe lady commissar, aged about forty, who told me that it was obligatory, first, to obtain an identity card, and this required 25 roubles' worth of stamps. Alas, even ten years of Soviet prisons and camps had left me as incorrigible as ever. I teasingly expressed the hope that I did not have the same experience as the poor deportee in the *kolkhoz* who paid his 25 roubles long ago but was still awaiting his card. Visibly offended, she took the remark as a serious personal accusation and ordered me to go at once to the State Bank, buy 25 roubles' worth of stamps and bring them back to her. She would then issue my identity card on the spot! I hastened to obey, remembering too late the wise advice of my fellow inmate at Shcherbakov, who warned me time and again never to tease the Soviets, for they took everything seriously and as a personal affront.

When I returned the lady commissar completed the formalities and handed me my identity card. Then, duty done, she suddenly relaxed and told me: 'I have good news for you. Your application for an exit visa has been approved. It arrived at my office this week.' What a surprise, and what an astonishing change of atmosphere. She seemed truly pleased to be able to give me the news. The stern look with which she greeted me an hour before had completely vanished.

But now my own passport had almost expired after months of waiting for the exit visa. I confided my anxieties to the lady commissar, assuring her that it was no sarcastic joke when I told her of the cruel bureaucratic delays that other Iranian deportees had suffered. Once again, I was amazed at her reaction and sympathy now that she knew I was completely rehabilitated. Like the Prosecutor before her, she assured me that things had changed in the USSR. I could set my mind at rest and she would keep my exit visa valid until my passport was renewed. I should send it off at once, and as soon as I got it back return to her office with it and there would be no problem.

Back at the *kolkhoz*, Katya was greatly upset by the news. She burst into tears as she saw our plans to go and live together in Petropavlovsk dashed. Yet this simple woman, who could not read or write, showed her truly noble and generous spirit as she at once urged me to think only of myself: I must go and rejoin my family in France now that, at last, I had the chance to do so. She did not want to expose me to the dangers threatening us because of her son. She knew that no normal life could ever be possible for me in the USSR and that I was in constant danger of re-arrest. She had no illusions or hopes about the present changes or promises of future freedom. I should escape while this was still possible.

I said that she must come with me but she was sure that the authorities would never allow it. We were not even married, and had already been warned that marriage with foreigners was forbidden. Moreover, it would be difficult for her to adapt to life in the West, and she had her own family to think of - her daughters and grandchildren. She could not desert them. So her answer must be 'No,' 'No,' and again, 'No'! She would stay but I must go, and as soon as possible.

The daughters supported her decision. Once I was gone it would be easier for Katya to cope with the problem of her son. Of course, it was a tragic blow for her to lose me, but then she was used to tragedy, that had been her fate! She was brave indeed, my true, loyal friend who could only think of my well-being. Here was the classic spirit of fatalism and self-sacrifice of the poor Russian peasant who, having suffered so many misfortunes, accepted having to face up to yet another disaster. I insisted that she accompanied me to Petropavlovsk, at least to try and get her a passport and exit visa. She agreed, but only to humour me, for she knew full well that nothing could ever come of it.

I sent my passport to the Iranian Embassy in Moscow by air mail, with the request that it be extended. But now there was an inexplicable delay of a whole month before the new passport reached me. As soon as it came I notified the director of the *kolkhoz* village school of my intention to leave the USSR, to give him time to find another English teacher. It was by now August 1956, and so my teaching activities had lasted exactly two years. All my colleagues expressed their sincere regrets at my departure. We had worked well together and had helped each other in our tasks in a most friendly way. But I was most touched by the distress and affection shown by my little pupils. They did not want me to leave, and when the new teacher arrived they made her life very difficult. The unfortunate young woman had just graduated from the English language course at Petropavlovsk, but the children criticized her accent and competence and compared her way of teaching with mine all the time, which naturally infuriated her.

Almost two and a half years had passed since, in March 1954, I received the first letter from the Iranian Embassy in Moscow, confirming receipt of the 100-rouble postal order. Now it was October 1956, and the day of my departure was approaching. Katya had decided to move to Petropavlovsk, to live with her elder daughter Mary, and had given the cow, the pig, the poultry and all our other possessions to the youngest daughter in the *kolkhoz*. Now her ginger-haired granddaughter, little Lyudka, would have her own cow to guarantee her a daily supply of milk. The young couple did not have the means to buy a cow of their own, for they were very poor , like all peasant farmers on a *kolkhoz*.

The young couple gave us a farewell family party, and everybody on the *kolkhoz* wished me a happy journey home to rejoin my family in the West. Those simple, honest, warm-hearted Russian peasant farmers had accepted my straightforward ways and now congratulated me on succeeding in reversing the order for my deportation. The president of the *kolkhoz* gave us permission to travel on the lorry taking the produce to Petropavlovsk. He was glad to see the back of us at last. For him, our departure meant a satisfactory solution to the confrontation between Katya and her son, with no inconvenient complications. Although there was no snow as yet, the wind was absolutely icy. By the time we reached Petropavlovsk I was, after spending ninety miles sitting in an open lorry on sacks of vegetables, frozen through and through.

At the house of Katya's elder daughter Mary, Katya explained the wretched distressing time she had had because of her son. Mary was disgusted and only too happy that her mother wanted to move in. It would be a great help for them, and good for their little son to have a loving granny around.

Next day Katya and I went to the Militia HQ for another meeting with the lady commissar whom I felt I knew quite well by now. But when I asked her what the chances were for Katya to be granted a passport, the answer was the classic impersonal response of a government official. Namely, that every Soviet citizen had the right to demand such a passport and that applications should be submitted in writing to the Moscow authorities who alone were entitled to grant the necessary permission. Katya was not in the least surprised, being under no illusions about the Soviet system, and I had to admit that I, too, had not really expected any other answer.

As regards my own papers, everything was in order, as promised. The exit visa was entered on my renewed Iranian passport, but the exit point had been changed to indicate departure 'by rail' whereas I had asked to leave by air. I protested but the lady commissar could not alter anything. This was Moscow's decision. She assured me, however, that it could be changed once I arrived in Moscow. All I needed to do was go, on arrival, to the Office for Exit Visas and Passport Registration (OVIR) and ask them to alter it.

On 21 October 1956 I was at the Petropavlovsk railway station bright and early with all the family to see me off – Katya, Mary, her husband and little son. I left all my money with Katya, except for a small amount I might need for the journey. During our two years together I had given her most of my salary, and now I gave her the rest, for I had spent hardly any. The train arrived on time and stopped for ten minutes – just long enough to embrace and bid a tender farewell. From the carriage window I looked out at the little group on the platform. They had become so dear to me, but now I had to leave them and this sad country, so full of kind-hearted people who had suffered under such a cruel regime.

Luckily I found a seat in the so-called 'hard-seat' carriage. The benches were made of plastic, but it was clean and comfortable. My only luggage was the hard-board case presented to me as a farewell gift by Assistant Controller Bobrov at the Step-Lag. It was small and light enough not to exceed the regulation air-luggage limit. All it contained were two shirts, some black bread, a piece of bacon and, the heaviest and the bulkiest item, my Anglo-Russian dictionary.

The train journey itself was pleasant and uneventful, and two days and nights after leaving Petropavlovsk the train pulled into the pretty Ryazan station in Moscow. With my little case I walked out of the station into the street to the taxi rank. I got into the first cab and asked the driver to take me to the French Embassy on Great Yakimenka Street. He agreed but the taxi didn't move. When I demanded to know why, he explained that the only way he could make ends meet was by taking as many passengers as possible on each trip. One always had to earn something on the side to survive in the Soviet Union, he said. Only after he had filled the cab with several others did he switch on the engine.

I was the first to be dropped at my destination, but when I came to look for the building housing the French Embassy, I couldn't find it. There was the number preceding it and the number following it, but the number itself wasn't there. Just as I was wondering what to do next a well-dressed man approached and offered to help. He had seen me looking lost, an elderly, bewildered man in a quilted jacket and trousers, big boots and a peaked cap - an obvious visitor to the capital from some far-flung *kolkhoz*. When I told him I was looking for the French Embassy, he said, 'But of course, come with me, I'll take you there.' He led me to a militia guard on duty nearby, said a few words to him and bade me farewell.

I should have realized that the Embassy would be well-guarded and under constant surveillance! I went up to the guard, who similarly saw before him a simple *kolkhoznik* who had ventured far from his familiar territory. 'Where are you from?' he asked, not unkindly. 'From Petropavlovsk,' I replied. 'And what do you want at the Embassy?' 'I am an Iranian subject, travelling to France, and I have come here to obtain the necessary French visa.' 'Show me your documents,' he said. Once he was satisfied with my proofs of identity, he took me along a narrow alleyway to the Embassy garden, where there were more guards at the gate. The Head Guard telephoned someone inside the Embassy and was told to let me in, and as I walked alone through the gate into the garden itself, I saw a lady running to greet me, crying, 'Come quickly, this way!' It was our French cousin who had been waiting impatiently for me to arrive ever since receiving my letter several weeks before, containing the good news that my exit visa had at last been granted.

In the Chancery she introduced me to everybody as 'my detainee'. I was received with acclamations, then taken to the office of the French consul, who stamped the visa on to my passport there and then. We talked a little about my enforced travels, and then he asked my cousin to take me to the military attaché, who also wanted to ask some questions. But as a mere deportee from a Siberian *kolkhoz* there was little of interest that I could tell him and soon my cousin took me to her small apartment, situated within the Embassy. She gave me a drink and we sat down to make a list of all the things I had to do. First, I must go to OVIR to ask them to change my point of exit so that I could leave from the airport instead of the railway station. Then I must go to the Iranian Embassy to ask them to give me a bed for the night or until I could catch a plane to Paris. Not being a French national I could not stay at the French Embassy.

My cousin handed me the 800 roubles sent by my two nephews to pay the air fare to Paris. Then she showed me a plan of Moscow and told me how to find my way around by Metro. But it all seemed too complicated, and so she arranged for a taxi to take me to the OVIR office. There, to my amazement, the lady at the desk assured me that changing the relevant entry in the exit visa wouldn't take long. Sure enough, half an hour later, I was handed my passport, stamped for exit via Moscow airport. I couldn't believe it was really happening. Out on the street, I decided to take the famous Metro to the Pokrovsky Boulevard where the Iranian Embassy was located.

The Iranian Embassy entrance had no guards, I walked in unchallenged and found the commissionaire – an elderly Iranian who spoke a little Russian. He told me that the offices were already closed. I explained my situation but he said he could not help. It was out of the question for me to spend the night at the Embassy. Tomorrow was the Shah's birthday and the Embassy was giving a grand reception with Soviet Ministers, foreign ambassadors and other dignitaries attending. 'So what am I to do with you?' he asked. In the end he took pity on me and my impossible situation and offered me his own bed. He himself would be working right through, preparing for the reception. But, he warned me, I must be out of the building first thing in the morning. He also made it a condition that I helped him to move the heavy furniture around, change the pictures, and so on. I readily accepted, and by 11 o'clock all the furniture had been pushed into place and the Embassy was ready to receive its grand visitors. Then we went to the kitchen where he offered me some of the food and titbits prepared for the Shah's guests. After a while I went to lie down to try and get some sleep. At 6 a.m., ready to leave, I thanked the old man from the bottom of my heart and asked him to grant me one final request. Might I leave my small hardboard case with him while I went to get my ticket? He didn't see why not and told me to put it under the stairs in the corridor. In those days nobody worried about terrorist bombs in suitcases.

It was a beautiful October morning and I breathed in the crisp air as I strolled along the Moscow streets. When the Aeroflot office opened I managed to get a flight for the very next day, leaving at 7 a.m. from Vnukovo Airport. They then told me that, having bought my ticket, I could reserve a room for the night at a transit hotel through the department for foreign passengers located in the Hotel Metropole in the centre of the town. I went there and was allocated a room without difficulty, in one of the big hotels serving the Agricultural Fair that took place in Moscow.

My cousin had already arranged that I should lunch with her at the Embassy, so I spent the rest of the morning like an ordinary tourist, seeing the sights – Red Square, St Basil's Cathedral, the Kremlin, then crossing the river to visit the Tretyakov Picture Gallery, which was not far from the French Embassy.

My cousin had prepared a truly sumptuous meal, in accordance with the rules of the French culinary art, with choice wines, brandy and coffee – somewhat different from the staple diet I had been fed by the KGB. After lunch we composed a telegram to my family in Paris, announcing my arrival on the 26th on an Air France flight from Prague. She advised me not to book into the hotel indicated by the Metropole Agency, since it was far away from the airport, in the north of the city, whereas the airport lay in the south-east. I would only waste a lot of time getting there and back. Far better to go tonight to the airport itself and try to book in at the special hotel they had there for transit passengers. Then there would be no problem about arriving in time to catch the plane the following morning.

By the time I hurried to the Iranian Embassy to collect my suitcase it was already after six o'clock. There was a flurry of cars and a small crowd of onlookers, but as soon as I tried to walk in through the main door, one of the 'onlookers' stopped me with a brusque: 'Where are you going, comrade?' 'I am going to the Embassy.' 'Just one moment. Please come with us further along the street so as not to disturb anyone, and tell us exactly why you want to go to the Embassy,' he said. The two policemen in civilian clothes, for that is what they were, looked me up and down, in my shabby peasant suit, and asked to see my documents. I explained that I had come to pick up my suitcase, that I was an Iranian citizen, and showed them my passport. Then they apologized for preventing me from entering the Embassy, but said that since there was an important reception, it would be far simpler if I told them exactly where I had left it. They would then bring it to me! I agreed, of course, not wishing to complicate matters now that freedom was so near.

The reception desk at the airport hotel said they had no free rooms and could do nothing to help me. There was nothing for it except to sit up for the night in the large departure lounge. Towards midnight, weary of waiting and unable to sleep, I decided to go to the restaurant on the first floor, to have something to eat and shorten the waiting. But the place was absolutely packed with other pasengers whiling away the night by eating and drinking. Finally, I spotted a fairly large table occupied by only one person – an Uzbek with a beautiful black skull-cap heavily embroidered in silver. I approached the table to ask whether I might join him, and at once he invited me to sit down, rising to his feet to greet me in the courteous Oriental manner.

There was a small carafe of vodka on the table, and he offered me a drink while I waited to place my order. I thanked him, and we drank together until the waitress finally arrived. I ordered an escalope of veal, and another carafe of vodka, so that I could offer him a drink in return. He readily accepted, although by now it was clear tht he was very drunk indeed. Just as I was tucking into my veal he suddenly launched into a political peroration. Speaking in a very loud voice and addressing the room at large, he declared: 'Vladimir Ilyich Lenin was a truly great man, but the people ruling us today are worthless! I refuse to work with them! They have asked me, but I will never agree to it. Never! Vladimir Ilyich was a truly great man, but his successors are rubbish...', and so on and so forth. Those sitting at neighbouring tables stopped eating to stare as the Uzbek's loud voice boomed across the room to the accompaniment of forceful thumps on the table.

I was gripped by a feeling of terror. Somehow I managed to attract the waitress's attention and paid for the meal I had barely touched. I walked as calmly as I could towards the stairs, trying to control my feelings and not show any fear. I dashed downstairs and disappeared amid the vast throng of people milling about in the departure lounge. I found a seat from where I could see the staircase and watched nervously for any movement indicating danger, wondering what I would do if they really arrived to arrest me. But there would be nothing I could do. It would really be the end of me. And all because of a drunken 'friendly' Uzbek on the very eve of my departure. What would I say when they demanded to know why I sat drinking with the Uzbek if, as I claim, I had never met him before this evening. 'Whom he *pretends* not to know,' Colonel Guitzenko had put in the official report, disregarding all statements to the contrary. For the KGB my links with the Uzbek would be proven by the mere fact that I had shared a table with him – obviously a prearranged rendezvous. All explanations and denials would be worthless. Did they not have a big dossier on me already?

When I noticed an empty seat further away, I hastened to change places. The waiting became intolerable, the minutes seeming like hours. The fear that gripped me became stronger and stronger, despite all my efforts to reason myself into a calmer frame of mind. At last dawn broke and the morning light flooded in through the windows. But it brought no relief. There was still no announcement to summon passengers to board the flight to Prague. Seven o'clock, the scheduled take-off time, was long gone, yet there was no news of the plane's departure. Only at two in the afternoon was the delayed take-off finally announced. The reason for the delay: bad weather which also meant a change of route. Instead of flying via Vilnius (capital of Lithuania in the Baltic States), the plane would now take the more southerly route through Minsk in Byelorussia.

I boarded the plane with the other passengers. It was a small twin-engined propeller aircraft, built to take some fifty passengers but there were fewer than twenty on board. I settled down in my seat, and as the plane finally took off breathed a sigh of relief. I had escaped the dreaded consequences of my ill-fated encounter with the 'friendly' Uzbek. At last I began to calm down.

Most of my fellow passengers were Soviet officials travelling on missions abroad. The rest were journalists, travelling to Western Europe, France and Germany, through Prague. I was the only private passenger and, as such, an object of immediate interest. My quilted attire of a *kolkhoz* peasant made me instantly noticeable in contrast with their Western-European suits (albeit all too visibly tailored in the USSR). Soviet officials were instructed to dress in the Western style, so as not to attract attention when travelling abroad. My attire, on the other hand, was an open gesture of defiance to the Soviet authorities – a bad advertisement abroad. They looked at me suspiciously and whispered among themselves. Then one of them came to sit in the empty seat beside me. He started chatting, trying to find out how I came to be on this plane at all. I explained that I was an Iranian subject, travelling to Paris to rejoin my family, and that I had spent some time teaching in a school attached to a Siberian *kolkhoz*. 'But why are you leaving?' he inquired anxiously. 'Surely as a schoolmaster you were sufficiently well paid? And why are you dressed like that?' he added crossly. I side-stepped all these hints and insinuations, preferring to play the idiot and protesting: 'Why, don't you like my suit? I consider myself very well-dressed. These are the best clothes one can get on the *kolkhoz* farm I come from. All I have on me is brand new. I bought my quilted jacket and boots just before leaving.'

My replies did not please him but there was nothing he could reproach me with. So he returned to his seat and continued his whispered conversation with his lady companion, a journalist being sent abroad as a foreign correspondent for several Soviet newspapers. She, obviously considering herself more intelligent than her companion, and certain of success where he had failed, now came to continue questioning me in a more delicate and indirect manner. She was vivacious and nonchalant, speaking with a sing-song lilt to her voice, and told me how she, too, spoke several languages. Since I was an English teacher, she would like to pass the time chatting to me. She said a few words in atrocious English, probably to see if I really knew the language, but I replied in Russian in the usual teasing manner I kept for pompous bullies, hinting that her accent was not very good and so hoping to put her off. But although she was obviously displeased, she would not let matters rest and continued to pester me with questions, determined to get to the bottom of why I was dressed as I was. But, equally determined, I continued to play the naive Iranian fool. Eventually she retreated. I heaved a sigh of relief, for I was still in danger, so long as I remained on Soviet territory, and had to watch carefully every word.

The plane landed at Minsk, the last stop before Prague. We had to get off the plane to have our documents checked again, and then went to the restaurant where we were served the regulation meal: borsch soup, rissoles and a dish of kisel (a sort of jelly made from wild bilberries with cornflour). When we were warned that it was forbidden to take roubles out of the Soviet Union, I tried to change my 25 roubles for Czech money, only to be told this was impossible, the Currency Exchange Bureau was already closed (probably because the plane was so late). 'So what am I to do with this money?' I asked. I was told to buy some sweets, but instead bought a postal order to send to Katya. Not only did every rouble help, but she would then know that I had sent the money on the point of successfully crossing the frontier. I had learnt that the only guarantee of messages being delivered in the Soviet Union was by postal order – first to the Iranian Embassy and now to Katya.

The formalities for the postal order took time. We were supposed to stay in Minsk less than an hour, so the departure of the plane was further delayed, but at least I had got a message through to her. And so, finally, I crossed the frontier without a kopeck. The plane arrived in Prague late that night – far too late to catch the Air France connection to Paris. I spent the night in a small hotel, halfway between Prague airport and the city itself, where the hotel restaurant produced the same sort of food as at Minsk, the only difference being that a small bottle of beer was put on the table. When I asked the porter if I could ring Paris to warn my family that I would be twenty-four hours late, I addressed him in German, telling him that as I had no Czech money to pay for a call I would like to book it on reverse charges. The porter's reply, also in German, was curt: 'Impossible! One could do that in the good old days but not now!' All I could do was go to my room to try and get some sleep. The room itself was comfortable and like the hotel itself, a reminder of the Europe I had been forced to leave eleven and a half years before.

At midday next day we left for the airport in a special bus. Once again we had to go through passport control before boarding the little Air France plane to take us on to Paris. Most of the passengers on the plane from Moscow had already gone their separate ways, but the lady correspondent was still there. This time, however, she made no effort to speak to me. We were, after all, already on foreign territory, on a foreign plane.

As soon as the plane was in the air the steward came round with a batch of that morning's newspapers from Paris and asked which one I would like. I asked for two or three, explaining that I hadn't seen a French paper for eleven years! He looked at me in astonishment and gave me a whole bunch. The first thing I saw were front-page headlines announcing the entry of Soviet troops into Budapest following the outbreak of the Hungarian revolution. What a contrast with the report in *Pravda*, which merely said there had been some disturbances in Budapest but that order was restored. I realized how lucky I was to have obtained an air ticket to Paris when I did, and allowed to leave Moscow on the next flight. Indeed, as I subsequently heard from my cousin in the French Embassy, three days later a case similar to mine was prevented from leaving. As I saw the newspaper headlines, all I could think of was to pray to God that the plane wasn't forced to return to Prague. As soon as the pilot announced that the plane had crossed into West German air space I made the sign of the cross, thanking God for bringing me safely home at last.

It was already dusk as we approached Orly airport and as I looked out of the window I could see the twinkling lights of the roads leading to Paris as they teemed with cars. As we got off the plane, I took my little case and walked towards passport control where the officer examined my passport, then he looked at me closely, with great interest. So much so that he recognized me at once six months later when I flew to London and had to pass through the same passport control. But there were still the customs to get through, and as I walked towards them I cast anxious glances at the people massed behind the barrier, waiting to greet arriving friends and relatives, to see if anybody was there to meet me. Suddenly I saw my brother standing with his brother-in-law, waving his arms and calling my name. He was the first to recognize me in my heavy *kolkhoz* outfit. My nephew was there, too, waving and shouting. But I was at a loss for words, overcome by this unforgettable and long-dreamed-of moment. I tried to hide my emotion and to show a calm I did not feel. The customs officer, realizing what was happening, waived all formalities, saying: 'Go on, I see they're waiting for you.' All I could do was make a small sign with my hand, totally speechless. At last I could embrace my brother, who had expended so much time and effort on saving me.

My brother had received the telegram, saying I was arriving the previous day. The whole family went to Orly, but the plane from Prague arrived empty! They did not know what to think. The Hungarian Revolution had just been crushed and they feared the worst. Nevertheless my brother decided to go to Orly once again the following day just in case, and this time the joy was boundless as I appeared among the other passengers. Twenty years had passed since we were last together in Paris before the war. He had, in the meantime, lost his wife, and all his children were grown up and married. We embraced and clung to each other after all those years of war and terrible anguish.

Back at my brother's home the whole family waited to greet me. I met for the first time my nephew's wife and my niece's children, recognizing them at once from photographs my brother sent me in Siberia. Now, at last, I could embrace them all. My niece's French husband produced some champagne to celebrate, but I declined, explaining that I was more used to a 'short' drink, such as a small glass of vodka or brandy. A bottle of 3-star cognac was produced and I downed my measure in one go, in the traditional Russian manner! The French family members were thoroughly shocked to see a good *fine* being drunk this way. It was unthinkable not to sip brandy slowly, savouring every drop. But I had acquired different habits in the past years and I knocked it back, drinking the health of my beloved brother and my dear family.

Formalities over, we settled to exchanging news of all the events of the intervening years, my life in Soviet prisons and camps and the suffering and privation endured by the family in France during the Nazi occupation. At midnight I telephoned my younger brother in New York, but he mistook my exuberances for inebriation and asked if I was drunk! But alcohol had no influence at all on my state of sheer joy and excitement and as the younger generation departed to go home to bed, my brother and I talked late into the night.

The next morning my niece came to take me shopping to get proper Western clothing so that I should not attract the attention and curious stares of passers-by. After eleven and a half years in a Communist paradise, I felt completely lost in the West, a stranger in the streets of Paris. Listening to the small talk of family and friends, I found their preoccupation with trivia truly bizarre. I especially remember feeling utter astonishment on hearing two old friends of the family gravely discuss the serious problem of finding the right colour and shape of buttons. For me, after all those years, such a preoccupation was inconceivable, indeed a comical waste of time. In the Soviet Union, where even essential things were lacking, you concentrated on basic things, such as thick winter clothing, and especially felt boots, of which there was always such a shortage. You had to wait months before a new consignment came in and even then only had the chance of obtaining a pair if you had a good contact in the shop, someone willing to notify you the moment they arrived. People often bought items in the wrong size, in the hope of later exchanging them for the right one. They were certainly not bothered about any particular shape or colour.

I also listened with interest and amazement to news of recent world events, about which the USSR had maintained a total silence. The Korean War was one example, probably because its outcome was unfavourable to the Communist Republic of North Korea. Then there was the Suez crisis in which the US joined the USSR to defeat the united campaign of British and French forces, thus giving rise to a situation which later precipitated many still unresolved problems in the Middle East. And there were the bewildering changes of government in France, as well as her internal policies – all very difficult to follow.

I continued to worry about Katya, and arranged to send her some parcels through our cousin at the French Embassy in Moscow. I knew only too well how useless it would be to send anything through the Soviet postal service, which imposed prohibitive customs duties. I remembered how, one day, I accompanied Katya to the Marievka post office to collect a parcel that had arrived from Israel. It came from a Jewish family, deported to Kazakhstan during the war and billetted in her house. Good, kindly people, they had been very nice to Katya and her fatherless children and after the war, having managed to emigrate to Israel, they wrote to her regularly. The parcel contained some used clothing, but on arrival at the post office we were told that the parcel had been opened in accordance with Soviet postal regulations to value the contents and fix the customs duty payable. This was so high – far above the value of the contents – that Katya could not pay it. We had been advised back at the *kolkhoz* that the usual way round this was to sell part of the contents to the post office official and pay the duty with the money received. But this time there were no buyers, the clothing in the parcel being old and worn. Hence the parcel had to be returned to the sender, with the comment that it had been refused.

EPILOGUE

Three months after my return to Paris I had the good fortune to find a job with a French firm, despite my advanced age of almost sixty. Surrounded by loving family and friends, and good colleagues at work, I was helped to resume a normal lifestyle and to forget, bit by bit, the sad years spent in the USSR. Gradually, even the terrible nightmares in which I saw myself back there, struggling to find means of escape, became rare occurrences.

As for my other companions in misfortune, I subsequently learnt that my cousin Ruben, who had suffered with me the rigorous prison conditions in the Lubyanka and Butyrki, had also succeeded in obtaining freedom on the grounds of his Iranian nationality. He was freed three months before me, and before leaving the USSR managed to meet Alik, our other Moscow cousin – the engineeer who had done so much to help me with parcels and money before himself ending up in Central Asia. But Ruben was most careful not to see him in his flat. He went first to his niece, the daughter of another cousin, and she rang Alik to ask him to come round to her place. Only thus had the two cousins managed to meet without compromising each other. People in the West cannot, and will never, understand this terrible fear implanted for ever in the hearts and minds of every single inhabitant of the Soviet Union, even after surviving the awful years of terror.

I also learnt that my other companion, Arthur, had been sent from Butyrki to a camp beyond the Arctic Circle, situated at the mouth of the Yennissey River in Northern Siberia, where there were some nickel mines. It was a severe punishment indeed for someone sentenced to only five years, a sentence usually deemed to indicate that no proof was available to substantiate the accusations. They could not force him into heavy manual labour because of his poor health, so he was given the job of camp librarian. On completing his five years he was deported to Narylsk, the neighbouring town. But since he did not have a work permit, the only way he could survive was fishing out of the river the odd log that became detached from the bundles towed down the Yennissey in the summer months, then selling it to the city dwellers who needed timber to build themselves houses and so on. He did not live in Narylsk itself, but in a tiny log cabin on the outskirts on the river bank, which he shared with another unfortunate deportee. In the Arctic regions there is constant daylight through the three months of summer, the other nine months of the year being shrouded in darkness. We had corresponded regularly after leaving the Lubyanka, and he wrote to say that life in camp had been paradise compared to what he had to endure as a deportee. Sixty years old and a sick man, he only survived with the help of money sent from time to time by his mother's cousin who still lived in Soviet Armenia.

He spent four whole years in Narylsk, and after being freed under the terms of the General Amnesty in 1954, was allowed to rejoin his mother's family in the small city of Kafan on the Iranian border. Things improved after that and he got a job in the local metallurgical (copper) factory. After all the hell he had been through even the minimum seemed paradise! He lived like that for another two years but two months after my return to Paris his elder sister received a letter saying he had died suddenly from a heart attack. The nine years in prisons, camps and as a miserable starving deportee had finally taken their toll, and even the two years of comparatively peaceful life in Kafan could not undo the damage. His already frail health had been ruined.

In contrasting my fate with Arthur's and wondering how I survived to tell the tale when he did not, I often found myself thinking about the difference between the KGB's treatment of us. According to the denunciations made by the Armenian émigré in Bucharest, I was the more suspect of the two because of my personal relationship with the Dashnak Dro. I had been an employee of the company of which he was a leading shareholder, and my interrogator made it clear from the start that my fate was sealed. The sentence the KGB were going to impose was the 'holy truth', as an old Russian expression puts it. The individual was powerless in the face of the all-powerful KGB, and any opposition would be instantly crushed. I realized this, but also knew I had to do something to ensure I would not perish like so many million others. My intuition told me that the only way to soften the impact of the blow was to try to establish some sort of human contact with my interrogator, so instead of maintaining the rebellious attitude of an unjustly accused innocent, I joked with him, talked of frivolous subjects, regaled him with stories of the pleasures of Bucharest night life. I even accepted his offer to collaborate with trapping Nazi war criminals, at the same time taking care not to hurt anyone else. And all this was probably why I received the relatively lenient sentence of eight years, with subsequent deportation to Kazakhstan, rather than being sent to a camp in the terrible conditions of the far northern regions.

Arthur, on the other hand, chose to adopt an exactly opposite attitude. True, his protestations of innocence resulted in the minimum sentence of five years, but his relations with his interrogator were very bad. When he was reduced to a state of total exhaustion, and offered some food – the usual KGB trick to get one to lower one's defences – his curt reply, 'The only thing I can accept from an enemy is a glass of water', did nothing to improve the atmosphere. It was, of course, a magnificent act of defiance, but not appreciated by the KGB, and it only served to irritate them, thus prolonging the interrogation and further delaying the closing of the dossier for which they hoped to gain the regulation bonus payment. The inevitable outcome was the interrogator's recommendation that he be sent to a camp in the most savage climatic conditions, and his dossier followed him to Narylsk, where he was deprived of any possibility of getting a job when finally released, thus further reducing his life expectancy.

It was only much later, after my return to France in 1956, that I was told that Michael had died in 1947. The cause of his death will never be known. Camp doctors are obliged to carry out an autopsy on every detainee who dies, but the doctors who staff the camp hospitals are themselves chosen from amongst the camp detainees, and can only fill in the post-mortem forms with the stereotype formulae allowed by the camp authorities – cardiac arrest, cancer, tuberculosis, etc. Never dystrophy (weakness through defective nutrition) or cachexy (chronic debility of body and mind) which are often the real cause of death through hunger. To indicate this or other similar diseases might make people think, and the poor doctor-detainee's main concern was, after all, to hang on to his privileged position in the camp hospital. Unless he carried out all the orders given to him, he could be sent to do heavy manual labour along with the other detainees, as punishment for insubordination. And, after all, since the detainee was dead, what did it really matter what he had died of?

In Romania too, all those against the present regime – whether Conservative, Liberal or Republican Socialist – did not stand a chance. The fate of the great democratic ministers and politicians of the past is well known – Bratianu, Maniu and many others died of sickness and hunger in a Communist prison. So, although not actually sentenced to death, death inevitably followed soon after, and the enemies of the Romanian people, just like the enemies of other so-called democratic republics, were quickly liquidated without any complications.

It took the KGB five years to find a suitable paragraph to justify my internment in various prisons and camps. When I was finally informed that I had been sentenced under paragraph 4 of Article 58 for political crimes, even the camp controller did not know what it meant. It was only when I finally arrived in Paris, that my brother showed me a small booklet he had obtained on the Soviet Penal Code. Article 58, paragraph 4, was framed in very general terms: *"Anyone giving support, by any means, to those elements of the international bourgeoisie which refuse to accept the equal rights of the Communist system to be a replacement for the Capitalist system and aim to overthrow it, whether influenced or directly controlled by this bourgeoisie or its organisations, is engaged in acts hostile to the USSR. This carries the following penalty: loss of liberty for a period of not less than three years with confiscation of all or some of his property, with the sentence being increased – in the most serious circumstances – to that of death or of being declared an enemy of the working class...."* Thus, this very useful little paragraph allowed the Soviet authorities to condemn anybody they wished, no matter whom, for any activity whatsoever, if he or she did not accept the Communist doctrine.

On my return to Europe I was also given a copy of the first book written on the Gulag system by Alexander Solzhenitsyn, the novel approved by Nikita Khrushchev himself and called *One Day in the Life of Ivan Denisovich*. I found it a true masterpiece, with its vivid descriptions of terrible sufferings. The picture it drew was instantly recognizable by anybody lucky enough to have survived a term in the Gulag, not only by the Russians who were subjected to that calvary, but also by the innumerable foreign nationals who found themselves inexorably drawn into its coils, including the French priest, Father Nicholas S.A.

I would like to end by quoting his words in the preface to his own book: 'All facts and events described herein are the absolute truth.'

INDEX